D0571574

The Flavors of MODERNITY

The Flavors of

MODERNITY

Food and the Novel

Gian-Paolo Biasin

PRINCETON UNIVERSITY PRESS

PRINCETON, NEW JERSEY

Published by Princeton University Press, 41 William Street,
Princeton, New Jersey 08540
In the United Kingdom: Princeton University Press,
Chichester, West Sussex

Library of Congress Cataloging-in-Publication Data
Biasin, Gian-Paolo.
[*Sapori della modernità*. English]
The flavors of modernity : food and the novel / Gian-Paolo Biasin.
    p.   cm.
Includes bibliographical references (p.) and index.
ISBN 0-691-03275-0
1. Italian fiction—19th century—History and criticism.   2. Italian
fiction—20th century—History and criticism.   3. Food in litera-
ture.   I. Title.
PQ4181.F64B5313   1993
853.009'355—dc20   93-16289

This book has been composed in Janson Typeface

Princeton University Press books are printed on acid-free paper
and meet the guidelines for permanence and durability of the
Committee on Production Guidelines for Book Longevity
of the Council on Library Resources

Printed in the United States of America

10 9 8 7 6 5 4 3 2 1

Il n'y a rien dans l'intellect si le corps n'a roulé sa bosse, si le nez n'a jamais frémi sur la route aux épices.

(There is nothing in the intellect if the body has not knocked about the world, if the nose has never been thrilled along the road of spices.)

—MICHEL SERRES, *Les cinq sens*

CONTENTS

A CKNOWLEDGMENTS

THIS BOOK is my translation of the original Italian *I sapori della modernità: Cibo e romanzo* (Bologna: Il Mulino, 1991), but parts of it have also appeared in English: an early version of chapter 1, "The Juice of the Story," in *Forum Italicum*, 21, 2, Fall 1987, pp. 320–34; chapter 7, with the same title, in *Primo Levi as Witness: Proceedings of a Symposium Held at Princeton University, April 30–May 2, 1989*, ed. by Pietro Frassica (Fiesole: Casalini, 1990), pp. 1–20. I am grateful to the respective editors for permission to reprint my contributions here. Part of chapter 6 was published as "Italo Calvino in Mexico: Food and Lovers, Tourists and Cannibals" in *PMLA*, January 1993, and is reprinted by permission of the copyright owner, the Modern Language Association of America.

All translations from Italian and French sources are mine, unless otherwise indicated in the corresponding notes.

Many friends have read or listened to various parts of my text: Antonio Alessio, Nino Borsellino, Margaret Brose, Enzo Coniglio, Alessandro Falassi, Alessandra and Domenico Ferrari, Pietro Frassica, Gina Lagorio, Nicolas J. Perella, Mirto Stone. I thank them, as well as Robert Brown, Ginny Vander Jagt, and the two readers of Princeton University Press, for their useful comments and the moral support they have provided. My warmest thanks go to Ezio Raimondi, who, with his wisdom and generosity, read and glossed the whole manuscript, making it more appetizing and flavorful with his suggestions; and to my wife, Maria Rita Francia, who patiently shared readings and recipes with me.

The Flavors of

MODERNITY

The Flavors of Modernity

PREMISES AND BOUNDARIES

If it is true that at the foundation of an entire trend of the novel, intended as the bourgeois and modern literary genre, there is the fiction of the representation of reality, it is equally true that a fundamental part of this reality is made up of food, nutrition, meals, the various rituals that surround and accompany the fulfillment of an elementary, biological need like hunger. Since its very origins the novel has had to concern itself with such reality, as the name itself of a famous character, Sancho *Panza*, emblematically points out: the anthropology of nourishment, the sociology of classes, the politics of power, and the culture of values interact from the beginning with the literary dimension.

There is no doubt that at the base of such a system of relationships there is the fundamental fact that the human mouth is the ambiguous locus of two oralities: one articulates the voice, language; the other satisfies a need, the ingestion of food for survival first of all, but also for a pleasure that becomes juxtaposed with the value of nourishment. The richness of the culinary sign stems from this fundamental fact. Indeed, the culinary sign is the process transforming a food (an edible thing) into a dish to be consumed, and at the same time it is the result of this process; and "exactly like the elements belonging to the other systems of signification," says Louis Marin, "the culinary sign will, in its own way, represent the economic transformation of a thing into a good, the erotic transformation of an object into a body, and the linguistic transformation of an entity into a sign."[1]

When the novel deals with food, a culinary sign, it adds richness to richness, it superimposes its own system of signs and meanings onto the signifying system, variously codified, of cooking. The most immediate and effective way the novel has in dealing with culinary signs is the mimetic one. In fact the mimesis of reality was, and still is, an extremely important and rich trend and a conception of literature. Suffice it to recall that Erich Auerbach's study *Mimesis* spans from Homer to Virginia Woolf, and that the novel—especially the French and the English novel of the nineteenth century—has contributed to the critical idea of realism predominant in the whole genre, to the point of making readers almost forget the other, metanarrative, tendency which however does not give up realism, of a Diderot or a Sterne, for example, who have been revalued only recently.[2]

Therefore in the novel the representation of reality plays an important role, and in particular the representation of food (a metonymy of the real) occupies a well-defined, albeit little-explored, literary space: it is worth examining such a representation because it carries meanings that have to do with human experience. These meanings and this experience point necessarily to a context (which is anthropological, sociological, political, and cultural, beside being literary) to read and interpret by means of the various disciplines involved in a precisely interdisciplinary and intertextual discourse that promises to be fascinating.

Already at the linguistic level, whether codified or not in literature, food is an incredibly rich area that harks back to the ancient Greek "symposium" and to the Latin "convivium"—in both words the prefixes underscore the social, communal nature of the acts of drinking and eating and transpose them into the philosophical realm. Let us consider the adjective "macaronic," which characterizes a whole trend in Italian literature and seems to be the concentrated expression of a certain mentality, possibly of an entire people. In the oral tradition of Italian folklore there is a song that states in rhyme: "If you want to win the war (guerra) / both by sea and on land (terra) / make it so that the guns (cannoni) / are filled with macaroni." And a popular saying from the region of Romagna, "la mnestra l'è la biêva dl'óman," soup is man's fodder, indicates not a rough animality but a solid physicality, the naturalness of our being. While this saying illuminates the naturalistic-positivistic conception of man the beast, it expresses an ancient wisdom that recognizes the primary and, above all, biological value of nourishment.[3] In any case, there is no doubt that all languages retain numerous traces in their lexicons of the history of food, with its discoveries, inventions, and transfers from one continent to another, from one country to another, over the centuries.[4]

Some contributions in the disciplines mentioned above should be considered classic by now. There are, for example, the trajectory outlined by Claude Lévi-Strauss from the raw to the cooked (and from honey to ashes) and his inquiry into the origin of table manners,[5] manners that have been examined in greater detail by Norbert Elias in their historical development from the Middle Ages onward as a typical civilization process.[6] Pierre Bourdieu has studied the formation of taste and "distinction" as models and values functioning powerfully on social classes.[7] And Mary Douglas should be remembered for her "deciphering" of a meal by involving religion, sociology, and culture: Jewish dietetic prescriptions derive from the world view elaborated by sacred texts, but also reflect economic reasons of exchanges and prohibitions.[8]

It is then necessary to reflect upon the fact that culinary referents (the material ingredients of cooking, rituals, gestures) are real as well as cultural signs that are transformed into verbal signs in the the various treatises on gastronomy and alimentary hygiene that, from antiquity to today, have accompanied and systematized human experiences and discoveries in nutrition. To read the history of gastronomic sensibility proposed by Jean-François Revel,[9] Emilio Faccioli's history of Italian cuisine,[10] or Folco Portinari's novel of gastronomy,[11] gives a historical and cultural framework necessary to understand that the discourse of cooking, in becoming discourse *on* cooking, increasingly unites gastronomy and literature. After all, if Revel is right that gastronomy is characterized by a series of contrasting dichotomies, such as the opposing values of tradition and innovation,[12] the same can be asserted for literature. In fact, T. S. Eliot deals with the relationship that is necessarily established between tradition and the individual talent of a particular writer; and for Harold Bloom the interpretive-critical act must explore the influence exerted by old authors on new ones, with all the connected anxiety, which becomes an innovative agon of the latter in their creations.[13] In *La terra e la luna* Piero Camporesi rightly emphasizes that

> while the cookbook used in bourgeois houses innovates and upturns, mixes, experiments, and invents, on the contrary, the oral tradition of the popular classes is led, by economic necessity and because of the law inherent in its very system, to keep and reproduce fixed and stereotyped forms. It may seem a paradox, but in the kitchen, only the bourgeoisie was and is revolutionary, while popular classes have always sided with conservatism.

As a consequence, while written literature can effect revivals of obsolete genres (as, for instance, the contemporary experimental novel does with the "manner" of the baroque treatise), "the bringing back of folkloric poetic forms is unlikely or even impossible once the representatives of a certain [oral] tradition are extinct"; analogously, "authentic alimentary folklore cannot be reborn once it is extinct," while bourgeois cuisine "can have more or less temporary renaissances, even if they are substantially different from the original models." Camporesi also asserts that "just as peasant cuisine gave the urban one its own archaic models, its own simple but fundamental archetypes," so, too, "the dialects and their innumerable village varieties antecede city language and national language."[14]

In Italy, since the Nineteenth Century

There is no doubt, however, that beside the articulate relationship between tradition and innovation, other historical-anthropological factors powerfully influence both gastronomy and literature.

At the beginning of the nineteenth century, Italy, which was characterized by a laborious process of national unification and by a still agricultural economy, was late in Europe, where nation-states like England and France and an already developed industrialization dominated the political scene—and the mental one as well.[15] The geographic, institutional, and economic fragmentation of the Italian peninsula was felt long after the unification and into the twentieth century, with serious social unbalances, and with entire groups, such as hired hands and peasants, reduced to hunger or to mere survival, throughout the territory from the Veneto to Sicily. There are eloquent documents on the subject, like the Jacini parliamentary inquiry begun in 1877, and in particular, the study by Giuseppe Cocchiara in his classic *Il paese di Cuccagna*,[16] which was taken up antinomically and paradigmatically by Piero Camporesi in *Il paese della fame*[17]—fundamentally, the problem of the south in Italy can be seen as the continuation and the concentration in one specific area of such unbalances.[18] In any case, the fundamental historical-sociological datum is that in Italy, as in the rest of Europe, the bourgeoisie slowly asserts and consolidates itself, and along with it a certain type of gastronomy (for instance, restaurants are now an option together with the traditional trattorie and inns) and a certain literary practice (specifically, the growth of the novel as a genre) have also spread throughout the territory.

During the period that is most interesting for my initial analysis, at least two works, one in the middle and the other at the end of the nineteenth century, unite gastronomy and literature in different but equally important ways. The first is *L'arte di convitare spiegata al popolo* by the Milanese physician and writer Giovanni Rajberti,[19] an elegant book of etiquette on alimentary and convivial matters addressed specifically to "the middle class" (that is, the bourgeoisie), but also a literary divertissement, an antibook in which the declared topic is only and exclusively a pretext for writing, and in which the writing itself is its own subject, in a continuous self-reflective or metanarrative gesture. It is worth quoting a page that refers to the publication date of the "operetta," or small work, one volume of which appeared in 1850 and another in 1851:

> In a few weeks the first half of the century is over, and soon afterwards, without a moment's interruption, the second one begins ["a chance that occurs only once in a writer's lifetime, and not for all of them"]. And I, with the first half of my work, I am still in time to say goodbye to the half-century that is about to fall in the abyss of the past, and with the second part I shall salute the other half-century as soon as it is activated. . . . The greatest man of our epoch sat as an arbiter between two centuries (as the greatest lyrical poet of all ages wrote) and made them silent: *ei fe' silenzio* . . . and I am satisfied to sit just between two half-centuries, and I even let them chat. The juice of these images is this: my intention is that my work belong equally to the two halves of the century: therefore I publish the first small volume with the last turnips of 1850 and shall publish the second with the first radishes of 1851. (468–69)

It is not really necessary to underscore the delightful intertextual play achieved by Rajberti through his recalling of the Napoleonic celebration of the poem "Il Cinque Maggio" by the *other* great Milanese writer, Alessandro Manzoni, whose "juice of the whole story" concluding *I promessi sposi* is also quoted. Rajberti's wholly literary irony is then displayed in the choice of a date that perhaps could be found "meaningful" by Italo Svevo's Zeno in the implicit comparison between a Napoleon who silences two centuries and the writer who lets two half-centuries chat, and in the "diminutio antiaulica" of a half-century juxtaposed with a whole one and of the literary work considered, as if it were any other produce, along with turnips and radishes (which, incidentally, were dear to Giulio Cesare Croce's Bertoldo and will also be popular with a third Milanese writer, Carlo Emilio Gadda, in some of his "drawings.") In any case, in his work Rajberti manages not only to give a complete phenomenology of dinner invitations (from the selection of guests to the form of the invitation cards, from the number and quality of dishes to the wines to be served and the type of conversation to be held, from "illustrious" dinners to casual ones, from soup to coffee), but also to survey numerous figures of Italian (and non-Italian) literature while linking them to foods or convivial situations. For instance, forgetting beef in a good dinner "would be similar for me to forgetting Dante Alighieri in writing the history of Italian literature. Yes indeed, beef is the Dante of meals, just as a succulent pâté of truffles and wild game would be Ariosto" (525).

The second work is *La scienza in cucina e l'arte di mangiar bene* by Pellegrino Artusi, the amiable *letterato* from Forlimpopoli who had written, with little success, about Ugo Foscolo and Giuseppe Giusti.[20] This work is the indispensable yardstick for understanding not only gastronomic but also political, historical, and cultural developments of Italy in the nineteenth century. It is the cookbook that marks the definitive, hegemonic affirmation of the bourgeoisie, to the detriment of the popular classes during years in which, Camporesi reminds us, Giovanni Pascoli publicly advocated the establishment of "bread houses" for the "disinherited classes":

> Pascoli's and Artusi's are two different voices, two distant languages without a meeting point, which reflect not only a fracture between proletarian and bourgeois Italy, but also two different alimentary languages, two different cuisines, two cultures and two histories juxtaposed and marked by a dialectic without mediations and meeting points, the history of emptiness and that of fullness, the culture of the cooked and that of the ill-cooked.[21]

At the level of alimentary history, then, there is again a confirmation of what was well known and well documented in political historiography. This confirmation does not diminish the singular importance of Artusi, beginning with the connection in his title between art and science, that is, between fin de siècle positivism and aestheticism, and ending with the linguistic contribution of a national cooking terminology and of a simple, clear style understandable to a great number of male and female bourgeois readers (from the same "middle class" addressed by Rajberti). As Artusi states: "After the unity of our fatherland it seemed to me a logical consequence to think of the unity of the spoken language, which few care about and many oppose, perhaps because of false pride and even a long and uninterrupted habit to one's own dialect" (384).

In this connection it should suffice to recall here that in his fundamental introduction to the cookbook Camporesi traces a well-documented picture of the economic and social conditions of nineteenth-century Italy, and rightly remarks that "in a discreet, underground, and almost impalpable way," Artusi "also performed the highly civilized task of uniting and amalgamating—first in the kitchen and then, at the level of the collective unconscious, in the unprobed folds of popular conscience—the heterogeneous medley of peoples who only formally declared themselves to be Italian." In order to illustrate even more clearly the unifying function the book had in times when there were not yet any mass media ("only Gabriele D'Annunzio was practicing the techniques of mass manipulation"), Camporesi insists: "the witty booklet . . . worked its way into many houses in all the regions of the country," by discarding both the too poor and the too sumptuous recipes and by leveling the hottest tastes and the heaviest ingredients to an acceptable average (xii–xiii). The conclusion is undoubtedly exaggerated, even considering it as a desecrating *boutade*, consonant with an "eccentric" critic like Camporesi: "We must acknowledge that *La scienza in cucina* did for national unification more than *I promessi sposi* was able to achieve: Artusi's *gustemi*, units of taste, succeeded in creating a code of national identification where Manzoni's stylistic features and phonemes failed" (xvi). Camporesi's remarks are echoed (and re-dimensioned) by Giorgio Manganelli, according to whom Artusi "did not compile imperative recipes, but told them. In this way he gained the housewives' hearts. . . . And so he invaded the womanish, maternal center of the Italian unconscious"; in fact, "Artusi" became, in time, "a domestic object, like a pan, a pot, a terracotta jar."[22] Primo Levi, too, proposes Artusi's book as a beautiful example of didactic literature, written by "a man of pure heart" who "passionately loves the art of the kitchen despised by hypocrites and dyspeptics, sets out to teach it, says as much, does so with the simplicity and clarity of someone who knows his subject deeply, and spontaneously produces a work of art."[23]

I wanted to quote so many positive evaluations of Artusi's work because times change, and his unifying function appears today overwhelmed by the two equally centrifugal currents of internationalization and of the return to regional or local cuisines (with their own dialects). A cookbook of Italian regional cooking like Ada Boni's valorizes precisely those local traditions that Artusi was necessarily obliged to sacrifice to his unitary project, and the interest shown by anthropologists like Alessandro Falassi and Ulderico Bernardi respectively for Tuscan (actually, Chianti) and Venetian cuisines is quite significant.[24] Yet Artusi's influence was not, historically, an easy one and did not fully succeed, as it might appear from Camporesi's conclusive *boutade*.

At the beginning of this century, in *L'imperio*, Federico De Roberto staged a dinner of parliamentary representatives who, while eating spaghetti with clams, heatedly debate the necessity of "unifying the Italian cuisines," or at least of "federating them," and they put forth "a national meal, an Italian dinner par excellence," but they agree only on the opening dish of macaroni, and then remain divided among "mullets Leghorn style, fried soles with calamari, beef stew with risotto, Modena *zampone* with spinach purée." The use of the French term prompts a character to translate, "con passato di spinaci," to which another one retorts, with a pun in rather bad taste ("passato" also means "past"), "then I am in favor of the beans' future."[25]

The entire post-unitary literature fundamentally follows *verismo*, the Italian version of realism in which regionalism is preeminent, leaving a long-lasting mark also on the years to come, a mark that, passing through Antonio Fogazzaro's use of local types (*macchiettismo*), reaches the present. A delightful example is a page from *Il giardino dei Finzi-Contini* by Giorgio Bassani, in which Micòl tells the narrator that as a young girl she preferred *il brógn sèrbi*, the green plums, "to the best Lindt chocolate": "And so apples were *i pum*, figs *i fìgh*, apricots *il mugnàgh*, peaches *il pèrsagh*. There could only be dialect for speaking of these things. Only the dialect word allowed her, naming trees and fruits, to curl her lips in the grimace, half-tender, half-scornful, that her heart prompted."[26] In this quotation one cannot really speak of *macchiettismo* because all the dialect words are an integral part of Micòl's character, and at the same time they betray the narrator's sentiment toward her. But the dialect remains, objectively. On the other hand, in the same novel, the first dinner the narrator has at the *magna domus*, in the dinner room in Art Nouveau style, with all the family seated around the table and Micòl's place empty but ready for her, has nothing to lose in comparison with an Artusi dinner: "a soup of rice and chicken livers in broth, minced turkey in galantine, jugged tongue with black olives and pickled celery stalks, a chocolate cake, fruit and nuts: walnuts, hazelnuts, pine nuts, raisins."[27] And in reading *Casalinghitudine* by Clara Sereni, a book made up of recipes elaborated by the female narrator as an integral part of her life and as a means of affirming her own personality against the pressures of the career and the family, one can see that even here tradition and innovation, gastronomy and literature are the inescapable poles and links of one same experience.[28]

REALISM

If alimentary referents become verbal and culinary signs in gastronomy, with even greater reason they become so in literature, and particularly in the novel, where they constitute an integral part of the technique used for representation, narration, and characterization, and hence are meant to establish (and to make us understand) the quality and the value of the text, its literariness. In other words, to deal with the uses of food in the novel means also to cut up a large strip of the verbal tissue that allows an in-depth critical analysis, both metonymic and metaphorical, valid for the entire text.

It is worth outlining briefly some of the uses, or functions, of the representation of food in the novel. First, obviously, there is the realistic function. It produces the verisimilitude of the text by guaranteeing its coherence at the referential level and by intimately linking the literary expression with the pretextual, historical or sociological level. One may say that in this function the choice of foods, meals, and table manners is almost compulsory, in the sense that Manzoni must make the Lombard Tonio eat polenta *bigia*, and Verga must make the Sicilian Malavoglia family eat fava bean soup. A Tonio eating a fava bean soup would be perceived as a historico-geographical incongruity (a lack of verisimilitude). The same would happen in the case of a too-sumptuous meal for a poor character (unless it signals a great occasion), or vice versa of a too-frugal meal for a noble or rich character (unless there is a moral or economic justification). But one should also remember that a text requires certain choices: to mention no food at all, or a particular dish, for example, without, however, renouncing what Roland Barthes called "the reality effect," in other words, the verisimilitude of the scene (D'Annunzio is a master in such an art). And much depends on the ideology of the writer, for instance, on his/her intention of confirming the model of reality he/she faces or of criticizing it or of proposing an alternative one.[29]

The "mimetic" function had its great season in the nineteenth-century novel, especially the *verista* novel (one immediately thinks of Giovanni Verga and Luigi Capuana, but also of Matilde Serao's *Il paese di Cuccagna*), with echoes in the twentieth century (for instance, the Carnia and Friuli region of Paola Drigo's *Maria Zef*: polenta, mountain cheese, vegetable soup with pork fat, pork liver, and grappa liquor) and also in a surge of neo-realism (from Carlo Cassola to Vasco Pratolini). This is the function that allows the novel, in an immediately recognizable and evident manner, to reflect the changing contemporary reality. This reality has actually changed in recent years at an incredibly quick pace even in the culinary field: take, for example, the vogue of nouvelle cuisine, or the revival of the so-called Mediterranean diet, with the triumph of that pasta so opposed by Filippo Tommaso Marinetti and the futurists, or the remarkable worldwide diffusion of American fast food, with its related reduction in consumption time, simplification of table manners, and leveling of tastes.

Such changes have occurred, beginning in the fifties, because of many concurrent factors listed by Camporesi in a complex picture: the crisscrossing of regional cultures between the north and the south of Italy with internal migrations; the quick processes of industrialization; the rational organization of distribution with the success of the supermarket at the expense of the small store; the serialization of consumption; the spreading of new techniques of preservation, presentation, and packaging of alimentary products; the influence, the stimuli, and the control exerted by multinational corporations on the tastes and the mentalities of masses of consumers. (I am also tempted to insert an iconic commentary—the vogue of Andy Warhol's "Campbell Soup" series of paintings.) Furthermore, numerous social changes have occurred: "the modification and confusion of established roles, the new image of women, the reform of family laws," and last but not least, "the making of a youth universe, which lives and nourishes itself in ways quite different from those of the family tradition": soft drinks instead of wine, a cold or grilled sandwich instead of dinner. All this brought about "the leveling of the alimentary calendar" and the common incapacity "to distinguish between weekdays and festive days, between 'sacred' and profane cuisine, between Sunday and Monday, between Friday and Saturday," with an irreparable "eclipse of the sacred" and the loss of "value as a symbolic communication" of the various dishes and meals of the traditional cuisine, the expression of a "pagan-Christian agricultural civilization." In short, in Italy, too, "a Eurocuisine is probably being born, capable of satisfying the tastes of the average European, the new man who travels easily by airplane."[30]

Of course the contemporary novel reflects such developments and such changes, beginning with the lexical choices of certain titles, like

Snack Bar Budapest by Silvia Bre and Marco Lodoli, or *Hot Dog* by Luigi
Fontanella, unthinkable in Italian up until a few years ago for lack of the
corresponding referents in extratextual reality. Among the many possible examples, I have chosen some from *Atlante occidentale* by Daniele
Del Giudice,[31] a text that seems particularly interesting and meaningful.
Its meals take place predominantly in cafés, cafeterias, pizzerias, and
even "a place halfway between a pub and a cafeteria, already crowded
with couples or with young people in separate wooden benches, bend-
ing over tropical drinks with curved straws" (86). The foods are those of
the international cuisine (the Eurocuisine for the new man who travels
easily by airplane?), that is, "the elaborate and untrustworthy dishes of
diverse national cuisines that arrive all the way there," in the self-service
cafeteria of a research institute in Geneva, Switzerland, "losing flavors
and properties in a sort of esperanto": a local duck, cheeses, "the roast
beef, the small bowl with a spicy sauce, various vegetables in the appropriate sections of a dish like that for children, the coca-cola carton, the
cutlery wrapped in the paper napkin" (45). Even at home the characters
eat in a style that is midway between the refined and the nonchalant:
fresh "mozzarella" cheese just arrived from Italy, "slices of deer ham and
goose salami" in trays with "pâté canapés and lettuce leaves" (35), a "rice
salad" with just a bit too much Tabasco sauce (107–8). Precise and impassive, the narrating voice registers the habits and the daily gestures
changed by mass catering and by the rhythms and exigencies of contemporary society.

NARRATIVITY

Usually meals are social occasions in extratextual reality, and novelists
rightly use them, in the possible worlds they create, in a narrative function, that is, to introduce characters on the scene of the narration (as
Carlo Emilio Gadda does with the dinner at the Balducci house at the
beginning of *Quer pasticciaccio brutto de via Merulana*), to make the characters meet (as Italo Svevo does with the "dinner of veals" in *Senilità*), to
follow them in their movements or in the passing of time (as Elio Vittorini does with Silvestro in *Convesazione in Sicilia*). At times it is not
even necessary to have an entire meal in order to fulfill the narrative
function successfully: for instance, for Paola Drigo a simple bottle of
grappa is enough to build the tension and the dramatic resolution of
Maria Zef. In all these cases, even if it is present, the realistic function
is in the background, and the building mechanism and the dynamism

of the action are highlighted—one can say that food is also a vital element for the story being told.

From this point of view, in particular, food can be a privileged catalyst of the relations need-desire and desire-satisfaction, both in a strictly alimentary sense and in the area of eroticism (in which, incidentally, the "erotic" meal of Henry Fielding's *Tom Jones* is memorable, in the book as well as in the film version by Tony Richardson). As far as the Italian novel is concerned, there are Mena and Alfio in Verga's *I Malavoglia*, Tancredi and Angelica in Giuseppe Tomasi di Lampedusa's *Il Gattopardo*, and many pages by Italo Calvino.

Food is also quite naturally at the center of the juxtaposition between scarcity and excess. Even without taking into consideration the pathological manifestations of anorexia (especially "religious" anorexia, which is the focus of the beautiful historical-novelistic rendering of Fulvio Tomizza's *La finzione di Maria*)[32] and of bulimia (which does not appear to have received particular attention as a literary subject, although cinema has given it a bitter triumph in *La grande bouffe*), the juxtaposition scarcity-excess constitutes a valuable narrative element. In fact, both hunger and gluttony produce dissatisfaction (albeit from opposite directions), and dissatisfaction produces movement, activity, and hence a story, or storytelling. The pages on the bread riots in the Milan of *I promessi sposi* remain paradigmatic in this connection. But a book like *Le avventure di Pinocchio* is *entirely* based on such a juxtaposition. As Perella notes, "the close alimentary association between money and eating, between poverty and starving, is the ground for the potentially tragic reality of Pinocchio's world," and of Italian society of the time as well.[33] Here it is worth quoting the well-known supper at the Red Crawfish Inn:

> The poor Cat, suffering from a badly upset stomach, was only able to eat thirty-five red mullets with tomato sauce and four portions of tripe à la Parmesan. . . . The Fox also would have been glad to pick at something; but seeing that the doctor had put him on a strict diet, he had to limit himself to hare in sweet-and-sour sauce, meagerly garnished with plump pullets and prime cockerels. After the hare, as an entremets he ordered a small fricassee of partridges, rabbits, frogs, lizards, and dried sweet paradise grapes. . . . It was Pinocchio who ate least of all. He asked for a quarter of a walnut and a small piece of bread crust, but he left everything on his plate. With his mind fixed on the Field of Miracles, the poor boy had got a case of anticipatory indigestion from gold coins.[34]

It is lightness, this quality so dear to Milan Kundera and Calvino,[35] that allows Collodi to make his irony so effective by turning it into a moral

lesson at the expense of the puppet: the Cat's heavy stomach is juxtaposed with Pinocchio's metaphoric indigestion of heavy but hypothetical gold coins, while in the middle there are the "meager" (more
precisely, the "very light" in the original) garnish, the picking, the self-
limitation, the small fricassee (into which there enter also the fantastic
ingredients of frogs and lizards, that are in fact absent in a true recipe,
such as the corresponding one in Artusi's cookbook).

Furthermore, food can become the occasion or the pretext to affirm
or establish positions of authority or subordination (like Don Rodrigo's
guests in *I promessi sposi*), or of rebellion (like Cosimo di Rondò faced
with a dish of snails in Calvino's *Il barone rampante*), or even of fantastic
and free play (Marcovaldo, also in Calvino, as well as Emilio Salgari's
exotic heroes are memorable[36]).

Another fundamental function, connected with narrativity, is the one
that could be called connotative. It is used to define the characters at the
social as well as psychological or affective levels: I am thinking of
Renzo's capons and of Don Abbondio's small flask of wine in Manzoni's
novel, or of the innumerable dishes of the protagonists in Federigo
Tozzi's *Tre croci* (such as thrushes and quails, Parmesan cheese and
pears, eels and mullets, roasted woodcocks and Tuscan beans), which
are listed not with joy but with the anxiety of not being able to possess
them, and which in the end determine the economic, social, and moral
ruin of the three brothers—the sign of their ineptitude, the abyss into
which they let themselves fall. The examples could go on, but just one
more should suffice, the coupling (a "judicious" coupling, I hope) of two
meals distant in time and geography: one is prepared by Diodata for
Gesualdo in Verga's *Mastro-don Gesualdo*, the other is cooked by Giulia
for Michele in Gina Lagorio's *Golfo del paradiso*:[37]

> The girl had prepared a fresh fava bean soup with an onion, four fresh eggs
> and two tomatoes she herself had picked gropingly behind the house. The eggs
> were frying in the pan, and the full flask of wine was standing before him.
> Through the door a cool breeze that was indeed a pleasure came in, together
> with the chirping of the crickets and the scent of the sheaves in the yard.

> So as to erase that image that had hurt her, of him as an old man who had
> surrendered to the others' compassion, she decided she would cook for lunch
> a dish of spaghetti with pesto. During the summer she had prepared a great
> deal of pesto with the basil from the orchard, and had preserved it in jars. On
> the freshly boiled pasta, al dente as Michele liked it, the pesto was still fra-
> grant with an intensity that was enough by itself to make one want to eat and
> to discard the winter blues.

In both these texts it is clear that the realistic function, even though it is present (a Sicilian fava bean soup in the former, Ligurian pasta with pesto in the latter; and also, respectively, the scent of sheaves and the fragrance of basil), remains in the background in comparison with the primary connotative function. In Verga, the rustic supper connotes first of all Diodata's loving care, silent loyalty, and love; it also points to Gesualdo's simple, solid tastes, which will be juxtaposed later in the course of the novel with the artificiality and coldness of the Palermitan noble setting, where he will end up dying (of stomach cancer, almost a *contrappasso* to his greediness for the possession of material things). The scene is a country idyll, a simple and heavenly pause juxtaposed to the hellish pressure of action—fatigue, works, engagements, and incessant concerns for the protagonist in search of riches and climbing the social ladder.

In Lagorio, Giulia's pasta is a concrete manifestation of her love for her old husband, a painter (it is a reaction of life against the thought of the inexorable passing of time), it reveals her relationship with nature (characterized by immediacy and foresight, along the cycle of seasons), and finally it connotes the sense of harmony with the world felt by the couple: they look for and enjoy beautiful, well-made things—he, colors and canvases, she, oven and pans (she is also famous for other dishes she prepares, like a flan of wild mushrooms and potatoes or a rosemary tart). The fundamental difference between the connotations of the two texts is not so much in the social conditions of the characters as in the inner life of two women: Diodata's is elementary, completely resolved in external gestures, objectified and unsaid; Giulia's is less simple, more nuanced, emphasized, and expressed.

It is obvious that any aspect of narrativity, as such, can be transformed into metanarrativity every time the text reflects upon itself. I have already mentioned Rajberti's case in mid-nineteenth century, but the author who exploits this function to the fullest is Calvino, especially in some of the beginnings of the novels that make up *Se una notte d'inverno un viaggiatore*, like "Fuori dell'abitato di Malbork."

FIGURES AND MEANINGS

Food is also used in literature for two purposes, which on the surface may appear antithetic but which are actually complementary and necessary for all verbal signs: one is cognitive, the other tropological. As a cognitive pretext, food is used to stage the search for meaning that is carried out every time one reflects on the relationship among the self, the world, and others—or among the subject, nature, and history—and such a reflection is made somewhat easier by the fact that precisely in food (just as in certain landscapes) nature and history tend to be conjoined.[38] It is a truly fundamental relationship that is incessantly explored not only by the disciplines already mentioned, such as anthropology and sociology, but also by other ones like historiography, science, philosophy, and psychoanalysis.

The human body had great importance in the popular culture of the Middle Ages and the Renaissance, and this importance has been studied by scholars from widely differing perspectives, with complementary results. For example, Mikhail Bakhtin studies the valorization of "the lower bodily stratum" and the carnival in Rabelais, and Piero Camporesi and Carlo Ginzburg analyze the intricate network of magic-superstitious beliefs—including the alleged relationship between putrefaction and divinity—which devalued the body systematically and prompted "strange" hygienic, alimentary, sexual, and religious practices.[39] Such is the background for the progress of medicine (from anatomy to physiology—the figure of Marcello Malpighi suffices here) and the philosophic materialism of the eighteenth century. Undoubtedly, both phenomena helped greatly to modify the world view and to focus attention on a wider and more open interior landscape, with all the related "reality effects," even in literature.

In particular, Gaston Bachelard describes the prescientific attitude of the sixteenth and seventeenth centuries as characterized by a preeminence of the senses of smell and touch over sight, according to Lucien Febvre's historical reconstruction. This means, in Ezio Raimondi's precise comment, that "things are not contemplated in order to establish relationships; on the contrary, a relationship with things is sought in order to have and possess them. Such an attitude is so overt that in extreme cases the knowledge of the real coincides with the typical possessive operation of eating." Hence, in many books of the period, "where science continues to coexist with the fallacies of a naive and linguistically analogic realism, one of the most frequent images ... is that of the possession of a certain matter, in that such matter is swallowed or assimilated thanks to a reciprocal expansion: the myth of digestion is linked with the 'libido' of the alchemist."[40]

Therefore it should not be surprising to find, at the base of Hegel's master-slave dialectic, the explicit ingestion of food as possession and transformation of the world, as a primary, biological example of an animal desire that precedes the more appropriately human desire but prefigures it with its own action. Alexandre Kojève comments that, being "born of Desire," this action "tends to satisfy it, and can do so only by 'negation,' the destruction, or at least the transformation, of the desired object: to satisfy hunger, for example, the food must be destroyed or, in any case, transformed." Such a "negating" action inexorably reflects also upon the environment and others, including the "other" in social and love relationships: René Girard's concept of "mediation" derives precisely from Hegel's "Desire of Desire."[41] Or, at a more common level of experience, the electronic game called Pac-Man is entirely based on a devouring aggressiveness (that is, negating the other). Here the master-slave dialectic takes on the connotations not only of a game, but also of the contemporary, consumeristic, and even imperialistic mentality.

The oral phase of Freudian psychoanalysis also gives an explanation of the relationships among the self, the world, and others: it is based on the "organization of the libido" in the birth and development of human sexuality, and on the fact, underscored by Freud, that many of its aspects persist "alongside of and behind the later configurations and obtain a permanent representation in the libidinal economy and character of the subject."[42] In the Italian novel, some of the protagonist's dreams in Italo Svevo's *La coscienza di Zeno* are true textbook cases: "I had a curious dream: I was not only kissing Carla's neck, I was positively devouring it. But though I was inflicting terrible wounds on it in my mad lust, the wounds did not bleed and the delicate curve of her neck was still unaltered under its soft white skin. Carla, prostrate in my arms, did not seem to suffer from the bites."[43] It is a dream in which the impossible cannibalism actually appears to combine in itself both the oral phase of Zeno's libidinal economy and his (Hegelian) desire for an absolute possession and mastery. The dream is repeated and emphasized later on, with the variation that there is a child, significantly, who "dreamed of possessing that woman ["a beautiful woman, perfect in shape and dressed in black. She had fair hair, great blue eyes, and exquisitely white hands; she wore patent-leather shoes on her small feet"], but in the strangest manner; he was convinced that he would be able to eat little bits off her at the top and the bottom!"[44] In this case there is no doubt that the novelistic character repeats and filters the author's own attitudes: in his *Diario per la fidanzata*, on January 19, 1896, Ettore Schmitz writes a "poem in bad prose" for Livia Veneziani where he states: "My spouse is a bonbon and I hope that by eating it my rotten teeth will heal. . . . My spouse is a ripe fruit that Mother Nature threw into my lap, and there may it rest. All the parts that my teeth and my old stomach will not be able to appreciate will remain there unwelcome, created in vain, my damnation, because I shall be there on guard, suffering and making [her] suffer."[45]

But perhaps, in the context of the present analysis, the most effective example of how, through its own means, literature examines human experience (the intertwining of self, nature, and history) may be Silvestro's search for "the lost human kind" in Elio Vittorini's *Conversazione in Sicilia*.[46] This search is carried out also through foods, which are bearers of meaning—from the Sicilian cheese the protagonist eats in order to identify with his fellow countrymen to the orange the little Sicilian and his baby-wife peel and eat "desperately" (15–16), to the smoked herring Concezione prepares for her son on a copper brazier:

> "It tastes good, you'll see," she said.
>
> "Yes," I said, as I inhaled its odour. I did not feel indifferent, I liked it, and I recognized what my meals used to taste like in my childhood. . . . She kept examining the herring, first the one side, then the other, fully cooked yet none of it burnt. Of the herring, too, my mind perceived its image in the past and its present shape. Thus everything possessed a two-fold reality: the memory and the present actuality. The sun, the cold, the copper brazier in the middle of the kitchen, and my awareness of this corner of the earth where I was, everything possessed this two-fold reality. That was why perhaps my presence here was not a matter of indifference to me, because it was a journey to something that had a two-fold reality, . . . and a fourth dimension acquired during the journey. (42 and 44)

This text could not be more explicit: it is the odor of the herring, this rustic madeleine, that brings the memory of childhood back to Silvestro, together with other flavors equally lost and found again: peppers during the summer, fava beans with cardoons, and "lentils cooked with onion, dried tomatoes, and bacon," and "a sprig of rosemary," too (42). It is the herring, juxtaposed with the rather disgusting boiled meat common in northern Italy, that makes Silvestro acquire the taste for life again, the taste of belonging to a reality in which nature and history, the countryside and "the men from the sulphur mines," have their place (45), and in which the initial "abstract furies" of the protagonist are going to be finally soothed.

The second, literary use of food is tropological, inherent in the very structure of the culinary sign and of the verbal sign: it is the analogic transformation (metaphor), or the displacement by contiguity (metonymy), or the linking by comparison or similitude, or the arbitrary attribution of significance (symbol), whereby a given food is also other than what it is literally, and this other (a rhetorical figure) often contains within itself an entire discourse. A discourse may be moral, ideological, affective, or social, but when it is expressed within a rhetorical figure it is first and foremost a literary discourse—that is, an inquiry, a knowledge, and an expression that are literature's own, and not historiography's or gastronomy's. Interdisciplinarity moves between different areas, but also requires a precise definition of boundaries. It is again the Vittorini of *Conversazione in Sicilia* who gives the most convincing examples. The oranges are a metonymy of the desperation of the Sicilian hired hands; the dialogue on eating habits in America has to do with a symbol of hope, an "idea of the kingdom of heaven on earth" (18) for many generations of emigrants; Concezione's "old honey" is the metaphor for the spiritual nourishment she spreads around, including the herring and the melons for her son, and the freshly baked bread for the wayfarer, with a Biblical gesture (73); and the wine of the drunkards is a sort of anti-nourishment that only "live water" will be able to oppose (123 and 126). The value of such figures is made explicitly evident in Silvestro's reflections on the lost human kind, against the background of the "slaughter perpetrated in the world": "Kill a man, and he will be something more than a man. Similarly, a man who is sick or starving is more than a man; and more human is the human race of the starving" (88). And again, with the power of the rhetorical questions: "Is not hunger the whole pain of the world that goes hungry? Is not the man in hunger more of a man? More a member of the human race?" (91).

CHOICES

Having established some fundamental characteristics of the literary uses of foods as verbal signs, it is necessary to question the fact that focusing on the Italian novel as a privileged area of research implies, necessarily but painfully, relinquishing other areas. For instance, I shall not deal with non-novelistc genres, like poetry (from Giacomo Leopardi, who mentions "ice creams and drinks" in "Palinodia in onore del marchese Gino Capponi," to Giovanni Pascoli's "La piada," from Guido Gozzano's Signorina Felicita's kitchen with its "consoling scents of basil, garlic, lemon verbena" to the "pâté destined for pestilential gods" in Eugenio Montale's "Il sogno del prigioniero"). And I shall not deal with other literatures—not the epic struggle against hunger by Lazarillo de Tormes, not Robinson Crusoe's careful and didactic production and accumulation of foods, not Madame Bovary's wedding banquet or Marcel's madeleine, not Leopold Bloom's kidneys or Mrs. Ramsey's *boeuf en daube*, not the numerous and precisely detailed meals and drinks of Ernest Hemingway's alter egos or the desecrating opulence of Günther Grass' "flounder."[47] And last but not least, as far as Italian literature is concerned, I shall not deal with texts written before the nineteenth century.

From the beginning, Italian literature is rich with situations and characters that would be worth analyzing in depth for their meaningfulness in relation to the many functions and connotations of nourishment. Of course there are the gluttons in Dante's *Divina Commedia* and Count Ugolino's macabre and tragic "fierce meal" in *Inferno*;[48] and Boccaccio, who on the one hand has another, albeit involuntary, fierce meal by Guiglielmo Rossiglione's wife, and on the other hand plays with Calandrino, who believes in the "land of Bengodi" (literally, Enjoywell), a land of Cockaigne filled with mountains of grated Parmesan cheese and macaroni, sausages to uphold vineyards, rivers of wine.[49] There are also Boiardo's and Ariosto's Renaissance chivalric costumes, Pulci's gigantic meals by Morgante and Margutte, Folengo's *Maccheronee* with its exuberant, popular abundance (a worthy precursor to Rabelais). Giambattista Basile's *Pentamerone*, plebeian and baroque, fabulous and cultivated at the same time, is memorable, as are Giulio Cesare Croce's stories about Bertoldo, the peasant who "died amidst grave pains for not being allowed to eat turnips and beans." And one should pay attention to the theme of hunger (which reflected harsh living conditions) and its playful sublimation in the characters of the "Commedia dell'Arte," the eternally hungry servants like Pulcinella, or Harlequin, the servant of two masters.

The novel has in its background such a richness of motifs, characters, and images, and rather than discarding them, it takes them up for its own purposes. For instance, the theme of hunger is clearly turned upside down in comparison with the "Commedia dell'Arte": it is a serious problem, to be faced and solved for the very survival of the characters— not by chance, with the origin of the novel, we also find the picaresque genre, with Lazarillo de Tormes and El Buscón. In the Italian novel, beginning with Manzoni's pages on the Milanese famine, the problem of hunger is felt in all of its importance, even if of course every author articulates it according to his/her sensitivity and times, and from the angle that is most congenial. Thus, for instance, Verga shifts to the south of Italy the attention for the living conditions of the poorest strata of the population, beginning an entire "southern" trend in literature that will include well-known representatives, from the Ignazio Silone of *Pane e vino* to Corrado Alvaro and Francesco Jovine, while Vittorini belongs to it but emphasizes universalizing and symbolic intents and results, as already noted. On the other hand, Collodi takes up in part the playfulness of the "Commedia dell'Arte" but uses his puppet Pinocchio, hungry from the very first page of his story, for didactic and moral purposes (and not only through the little figure of the Talking Cricket!); and for his part, Luigi Malerba revives certain grotesque and lacerating tones of medieval literature in his *Il pataffio*, a successful novelistic and linguistic pastiche in which a fake "macaronic" style highlights the endless hunger of its ragged protagonists.[50]

Unfortunately, hunger is not a thing of the past but is present in this century, notably during the Second World War (see Miriam Mafai's *Pane nero*) and above all as an enormous stain on mankind's progress in the Nazi Lagers, where it was used as a weapon for genocide; more recently, there are the recurrent famines in African countries. Literature has witnessed these phenomena, in particular, the Lagers: among the many possible examples, Piero Caleffi's *Si fa presto a dire fame* is emblematic in its very title, "it's easy to say hunger"; and in *Se questo è un uomo* Primo Levi emphasizes the primary importance of the search for food for the survival of the prisoners, not only physical but also spiritual survival, because it was in the extreme conditions of a hunger leading to death that man had to succeed in saving not only his body but his dignity, his solidarity toward other men, his own humanity.

The example of Levi clearly indicates the ample and flexible sense with which I intend to use the term "novel" in my research. I agree with Bakhtin's conception of the novel as the hegemonic form of modernity, born and developed alongside the ascent of the bourgeoisie, open to the most diversified formal experimentations.[51] Hence I consider legitimate to analyze critically some narratives that are not traditionally classified as novels, precisely because the novelistic genre allows such territorial invasions. Beside Levi, I shall also examine Calvino's "Sotto il sole giaguaro," which is not classified as a novel because of its brevity and its combinatorial status.

A re-reading of the Italian novel *sub specie culinaria* seems then a critical endeavor of great interest, which promises confirmations as well as discoveries from an unusual angle. I do not intend to perform a systematic, historiographic inquiry. I want to analyze some crucial moments and texts that can give a sense of the richness, diversity, and developments of the novelistic genre in Italy, from Manzoni onward. I have chosen those texts that focus with greatest effectiveness on the uses and meanings of foods and eating, from the referential to the figurative. The culinary sign in Manzoni's *I promessi sposi* is used to construct a micro-history but is also the tool for a realistic project tied to a profoundly religious and ethical view. In Verga's *I Malavoglia*, the culinary sign is seen within the chorality of the village *langue* and transformed from a cliché into a modern invention, ahead of its times. In Gabriele D'Annunzio's *Il piacere*, it is the basis of a refined and deliberate communicative-expressive strategy. In Tomasi di Lampedusa's *Il Gattopardo*, it subtends a whole series of historical-political representations and judgments that seal an entire heredity from the nineteenth century. And while Carlo Emilio Gadda uses the culinary sign in an epistemological discourse ranging from the neurosis of *La cognizione del dolore* to the laughter of *Quer pasticciaccio brutto de via Merulana*, Calvino employs it throughout his oeuvre in a complex and varied discourse, which sums up in its multiple registers all the functions examined so far, and expands the boundaries of what literature can say originally in its cognitive inquiry. And Primo Levi, the soft-voiced and peremptory witness of Auschwitz, calls attention to the seriousness of food—which is sacred, civilized—in his moral discourse in defense of humanness.

WHERE FLAVORS AND STORIES ARE COOKED

Like its French cognate *cuisine*, carefully analyzed by Louis Marin, the Italian term *cucina* derives from the late Latin *cocina*, which stands for *coquina*, from the verb *coquere*, "to cook," and it means: (1) site, room appropriately equipped for the preparation and the cooking of foods; (2) the furniture and equipment with which a kitchen is set up; (3) the stove or appliance with plates for the cooking of foods; (4) the act of cooking; (5) the way in which foods are prepared; (6) the foods themselves. By extension or analogy, the term *cucina* may also mean the equipment necessary to prepare the dyeing compounds in dyeing-works; the site where milk coagulates in a dairy; and the editorial work for the preparation of a newspaper. It is a truly extraordinary semantic range, in which the various relationships linking the term to its meanings "also animate every dimension of the object that this word signifies," so that, as Marin notes for *cuisine*, in the very term *cucina* there is an echo of the way in which "the various possible worlds pertaining to basic foods are constantly displaced and transformed into rigorously regulated systems of cookery."[52] Not only this, but the metaphorical-metonymic potentiality inherent in the term is so strong that it can be naturally expanded to the most diversified areas or lexical fields—as, for example, in my own syntagm "where flavors and stories are cooked."

Precisely because the semantic range of *cucina* is so powerful in generating meaning, it is worthwhile, even before dealing with the foods or meals privileged by writers, to look at the places where food is prepared, at the kitchens some of them have chosen, which are an integral element of their novels and of their world view.

The starting point could well be a statement by the narrator of Ippolito Nievo's *Le confessioni d'un italiano*:[53] "for me who have not seen either the Colossus of Rhodes or the Pyramids of Egypt, the kitchen of Fratta and its hearth were the most awe-inspiring monuments that ever burdened the surface of the earth," not even comparable to the Cathedral of Milan or the Church of St. Peter in Rome, but only to Hadrian's Mole (4). Such awe-inspiring comparisons with famous monuments are instrumental in projecting the following description into an epic, mythical, hyperbolic dimension:

> The kitchen of Fratta was a vast place, with an indefinite number of walls very varied in size, which rose towards the heavens like a cupola and delved under the earth deeper than an abyss; obscure, even black, with a secular layer of soot, whence shone like so many huge diabolical eyes the shining bottons of saucepans, dripping pans and flasks; cumbered in every direction with immense sideboards, colossal dressers and endless tables, it was haunted at all hours of the day or night by an unknown number of black and gray cats, which gave it the appearance of a witches' laboratory. (4)

The hyperbolic dimension begins to make sense: it is the young Carlino who is talking, so that the adjectives "immense, colossal, endless" are to be related to a diminutive viewpoint, of a person who does not know well the reality surrounding him ("indefinite, unknown"), and in fact, he can liken it to "a witches' laboratory." Indeed, at the beginning of the novel the kitchen of Fratta is the whole world for Carlino, and it is a fabulous world, around whose hearth with its "two gigantic andirons bossed with bronze" there is "a grave sanhedrin of fateful and somnolent figures" (5)—from the Count of Fratta to Carlino himself, who is, however, often relegated to the function of a live spit. Here, in this monumental and sooty place, in this "acherontic gulf" (4), Carlino moves his first steps and makes his initial experiences.[54] Only in chapter 3 will he enlarge his horizons: "The first time that I escaped from the kitchen of Fratta to wander in the outside world, it seemed to me beautiful beyond all measure," because "Nature prefers light to darkness and the sun in heaven to flames in a chimney-place," and also because "in this world of grass, of flowers, of jumping and somersaults" Carlino is freed from all the constraints and the norms imposed by the Signor Count, the Monsignor, Fulgenzio, and everybody else: "though I lived in the kitchen as a vassal, two paces outside and I felt myself master and could breathe at my ease" (67–68). Therefore, surely, Carlino is born to life in the kitchen (almost the womb of Great Mother Earth) and acquires self-awareness and autonomy as a person by comparing the kitchen with the world "of grass, of flowers, of somersaults": it is a truly beautiful "myth of origin," appropriate for a novelistic and romantic character.

Federico De Roberto must have remembered the kitchen of Fratta when he described a similar one in *I Vicerè*, where, however, he deals with a convent and not a castle, and where the hyperboles have quite a different function from Nievo's, beginning with the initial comparison of kitchens "as spacious as barracks," in which there is no trace of monumentality but rather a preparation for mere quantity ("not fewer than eight cooks, apart from kitchen-hands"):

> Every day the cooks got four loads of oak charcoal from Nicolosi to keep the ovens always hot, and for frying alone the kitchen Cellarer would consign to them every day four bladders of lard of two *rotoli* each, and two *cafissi* of oil; enough for six months at the prince's. The pots and grills were big enough to boil a whole calf's haunch and roast a swordfish complete; two kitchen-hands would each grasp half a great cheese and spend an hour grating it; the chopping block was an oak trunk which no two men could get their arms round; and every week a carpenter, paid four *tarì* and half a barrel of wine for this service, had to saw off a couple of inches or it became unserviceable from so much chopping.
>
> The Benedictine kitchen had become a proverb in town. The macaroni pie with its crust of short pastry, the rice-balls each big as a mellon, the stuffed olives and honey-cakes, were dishes which no other cook could make.[55]

Here the exaggerated and distorting hyperboles are not even attributable to a healthy, Folengoan corporality, but are dictated by the narrator's moral indignation against the waste and the opulence displayed in these kitchens. De Roberto's attitude is partly due to the anticlericalism that accompanied the struggles for the Italian unification, but it also has universal validity because of the type of public morality (including lay as well as religious powers) it implies and advocates.

Universal and moral considerations are also present behind the description of Concezione's kitchen in *Conversazione in Sicilia*:

> I looked about me in the kitchen, and saw the stove with the cracked earthenware pot on it, and next to it the bread-bin, the water jug, the sink, the chairs, the table, and the old clock said to be my grandfather's on the wall; and looking about me I was filled with fear. With fear, too, I looked at my mother. Enveloped in her blanket amidst her possessions, she was like each one of them: redolent with time, of past humanity, of infancy, and so on, of men and sons, yet nothing to do with history. There, inside the kitchen, she would continue her days, forever roasting herrings on the brazier and her feet clad in my father's shoes. I looked at her and was afraid. (148)

In this humble kitchen in which each object is simply mentioned, Silvestro performs the recovery of the lost human kind that had brought him to the trip and the various conversations in Sicily; and both this private and humble kitchen and the viewpoint of the onlooker indicate the importance of the individual in Vittorini's narrative and symbolic discourse—and in the twentieth century in general. Humankind is made up of many particular individuals, each with his/her own life, tastes (the smoked herring, again), gestures, and habits, and family, "nothing to do with history"!

Therefore it is not surprising to find another private, "tiny" kitchen, in Calvino's *Se una notte d'inverno un viaggiatore*:

> The appliances are in their place, useful animals whose merits must be remembered, though without devoting special worship to them. Among the utensils a certain aesthetic tendency is noticeable (a panoply of half-moon choppers, in decreasing sizes, when one would be enough), but in general the decorative elements are also serviceable objects, with few concessions to prettiness. The provisions can tell us something about you: an assortment of herbs, some naturally in regular use, others that seem to be there to complete a collection; the same can be said of the mustards; but it is especially the ropes of garlic hung within reach that suggest a relationship with food not careless

or generic. A glance into the refrigerator allows other valuable data to be gathered: in the egg slots only one egg remains; of lemons there is only a half and that half-dried; in other words, in basic supplies a certain neglect is noted. On the other hand, there is chestnut purée, black olives, a little jar of salsify or horseradish.[56]

This passage deals, of course, with the kitchen of the female Reader and the glance of the male Reader who is already "favorably disposed" toward her, if not just in love. What a difference from the kitchen at Fratta! That one was enormous just as this is tiny; that one was fabulous as this is practical; that one was seen as a myth (the place of narrativity) as this is looked at carefully as the place that can reveal the other (the female other) and hence as a possible accomplice in a story (a love story) not yet narrated in its entirety: it is the site of metanarrativity, and it is this, more than the electric appliances and the refrigerator, that makes it modern.

So, from the kitchen at Fratta to that of the female Reader, it is possible to trace a critical and cognitive itinerary that goes from the nineteenth-century peasant society to the individualistic one of today. The food and the attitudes connected with it that these "novelistic" kitchens imply and point out are part of a rapidly, at times even vertiginously changing mentality and set of customs. In this sense there is no doubt that the novel is an extraordinary cognitive tool that allows the reader to understand the anthropological, social, cultural, and psychological structures surrounding and conditioning alimentary phenomena. The discourse on food inevitably becomes a discourse on pleasure and on power, on the most secret individual as well as on the most visible classes; in short, it becomes a discourse on the world. Paraphrasing Hans Blumenberg, I could state that the "reading" of food is a heuristic tool indispensable for "the readability of the world."[57] At the same time, in literary and particularly novelistic texts, food is the material sign of human dialogism, conviviality is also the discovery of the other, and the rituality of eating stands out even more clearly than in custom.[58]

By talking about hunger and satisfaction, foods and table manners, appetites and eros, the novel tranfers into its microcosm and illuminates data of experience that make up every life; but in doing so it also talks, metaphorically, metonymically, and metanarratively, of itself, of its own being as literature, a system of verbal signs that construct possible worlds. Therefore once again literature obliges the reader to reflect upon its double nature: involved in the world and in life, savory with sauces and juices, fragrant with freshly baked bread; and at the same time autonomous, self-referential, a nourishment for the spirit and the mind. An interdisciplinary analysis is absolutely necessary to make this autonomy and this involvement stand out.

Upon such bases, then, I can begin my in-depth critical exploration of the uses of food in the novel, and of the flavors that the novel, the literary genre of modernity, can offer the reader, eager to gain knowledge and wisdom.

The Juice of the Story:
Alessandro Manzoni, *I promessi sposi*

A REREADING of the Italian novel *sub specie culinaria* must begin with the fountainhead of the genre, Alessandro Manzoni's *I promessi sposi*, which was soon compared by Wolfgang Goethe to "a good fruit in its full ripeness"[1]—an excellent auspice for my critical project. As a novel, *I promessi sposi* is certainly "a work combining history and invention," but it is perhaps worth pausing a moment on what type of history Manzoni had in mind.

With his interest in the study of economic and social phenomena, and in particular of mass psychology and the customs of the people juxtaposed with and privileged above the "Princes and Potentates, and mightie Personnages,"[2] Manzoni prefigures a fundamental attitude of the contemporary historians of the *Annales* school, from Lucien Febvre to Fernand Braudel.[3] This attitude culminates with the scholars of micro-history, a prime example of which, in the semantic area under consideration, is Carlo Ginzburg's *The Cheese and the Worms*.[4] Of course the paradox is that the "invention" part of the novel, concerning Renzo and Lucia, is at the same time, antithetically, the most "micro-historical" (potentially, for its detailed documentation) and the most motivated ideologically (for its religious conception of life, which translates into an ethical conception of history). Perhaps precisely such a paradox caused the silence of the novelist, his famous renouncement or repudiation of the historical novel as a genre: it is therefore logical to recall that *I promessi sposi* was the origin of (and ideally culminated in) *La storia della colonna infame*, and that both these works, in their respective ways and genres, dig into and foreground the responsibility of the individual.

In any case, the "Historie" that stands at the beginning of the novel with its impossible "definition" is the clear and revealing sign of the romantic narrator's intentionality. If, on the one hand, he recognizes the centrality and importance of the historical phenomenon, on the other he chooses a critical and innovative stance vis-à-vis history, a stance that is at least in part a forerunner of contemporary trends. It is then necessary to examine the novelistic manifestations and developments of such a stance in the micro-historical area ranging from hunger to food and to table manners with precise textual analyses.

It is even too well known that in the Manzonian novel, the pages on the famine, "sustained by an authentic economist's passion," especially in the dialectic between shortage and price rise, are absolutely central in that they support the whole structure of the narrative by determining the facts and the destinies of the characters.[5] What I want to emphasize here is that the famine is the historical and precise manifestation of hunger, a hunger that is spread out in a capillary manner, a paradigmatic hunger that is the sine qua non antecedent of food. Let us see at the very beginning of the novel how Renzo is presented as "a silk-weaver" and at the same time the owner of "a small piece of land," "so that he could call himself prosperous for his state in life, and though that year was even leaner than the ones before, and a real famine was already beginning to be felt, our young man . . . was now well enough supplied not to have to struggle against hunger" (19). Hence his situation is one of relative privilege, especially if it is compared with that of the beggars and the peasants whom Fra Cristoforo sees a few pages later in the serene Lombard countryside, or, on a more personal level, with Tonio's condition:

> [Renzo] found him in the kitchen with one knee on the hob of the fire, holding the rim of a pot on the hot embers with one hand, and stirring with a wooden spoon a small mess of grey *polenta*, made of buckwheat. Tonio's mother, brother, and wife were at table; and three or four small children were standing in front of their father, awaiting, with their eyes fixed on the pot, the moment when its contents was poured out. (84)

Raimondi and Bottoni have rightly remarked that "through the details of this interior," which is a "still life of the poor" (as Roberto Longhi might say), "a descriptive-ornamental event à la Scott functionally corresponds to the social status of the character; but the details are also used for the interiorization of the persons."[6] In fact the meager, grey polenta is clearly insufficient for the family, and the compassionate eye and moralistic attitude of the narrator do not fail to point out the consequences:

> The size of the *polenta* was in proportion to the year's harvest, not to the number and appetites of those sitting round the table. And each of them

seemed to be thinking, as they gave side-glances of ravenous hunger at the common dish, of the appetite that would survive it. As Renzo was exchanging greetings with the family, Tonio poured the *polenta* onto a beechwood board standing ready to receive it, where it looked like a small moon in a big halo of mist. (84)

The most upsetting effect of hunger lies in those "side-glances," in that "ravenous" and unsatisfied desire that pits each member of the family against the others, tacitly but eloquently—while the "beechwood board" is the sober but precise sign of the reality of the entire scene. No wonder then that Renzo does not accept the invitation to remain and that in fact he in turn invites Tonio to the inn, thereby withdrawing "a competitor, and the most formidable competitor of all, too, for the polenta," with great satisfaction for the women and the children, "who reach the age of reason on this subject very early" (85).[7]

Later Renzo witnesses the bread riots in Milan in well-known and exemplary pages that could have interested the Elias Canetti of *Masses and Power*, and on which I shall pause long enough to emphasize how hunger produces its semantic opposite, "abundance" or "plenty." Renzo's first reaction in finding out that the white dust he thought was snow is flour is significant: "There must be a great glut in Milan—said he to himself—if they scatter the gifts of God about in this way" (180); and soon afterwards, at the sight of bread loaves on the ground: "Is this the Land of Cockaigne?" he asks himself, thus giving a narrative voice to that popular belief in a gastronomic utopia, to that true anthropological mythologem dealt with by Giuseppe Cocchiara and taken up by Camporesi.[8] In the long run, Renzo's good sense and goodness are not denied; when he is safe in the Bergamo territory, after "the meal and the good deed" (268), he contemplates the time when famine has gone, and "plenty has come back at last," and for him, plenty is concretized in the idyllic image of a "picnic on the bank" of the Adda river (269).

Renzo does another good deed when he gives his bread to a hungry family in Milan, ravaged by the plague. One should also remember the pensive remark by the tailor's wife on "the very poor, who can only just manage to get vetch bread and millet *polenta*" (365), so that at the end of the meal her husband sends a poor neighbor, a widow, "the food on the table" in a plate wrapped in a napkin tied "at the four corners," together with a loaf of bread and a flask of wine (369). Finally, the narrator does not neglect the organizational and logistic aspects of the hospitality given by the Unnamed to the refugees from the war (bread, soup, and wine), and of the assistance by the friars in the lazaretto: especially memorable are the touches of tenderness amidst the horror—the goats used as wet nurses for the newborn babies, and the humble bowl of soup offered by Fra Cristoforo to Renzo. These latter examples, all based on the primary referent of hunger, are particularly significant because they illustrate the Manzonian ideology of Christian charity at the very heart of the narrative action. It is as if Manzoni equated charity with the act itself of nutrition, with an intentionality that goes well beyond realistic mimesis and will recur in other episodes and situations in the novel.

It is now appropriate to turn to some realistic descriptions of the characters who belong to the lower classes, with their precise and meaningful alimentary connotations.[9] The narrator pauses with "the little flask of Don Abbondio's favourite wine" (15), with Perpetua who replies to her master's call "with a big cabbage under her arm, and a look of brazen unconcern on her face" (27), with "those four capons—poor things!" whose necks Agnese "was going to wring" for the wedding banquet, and which Renzo has to take instead as a homage or sacrifice to the lawyer, Doctor Quibble-weaver (33–34: Verga will remember the scene when he makes the Malavoglias bring two hens to Don Silvestro). Similarly, after the wedding has been postponed, Lucia is shown "sadly preparing the supper" (80), and Agnese takes Menico into her kitchen and gives him "his lunch" before sending him to Pescarenico (93). Also revealing is Renzo's appetite during his numerous walks in the Bergamo region and under the final downpour. Such connotations effectively reinforce the peculiar traits of the characters: Don Abbondio's peacefulness, Perpetua's shrewdness, Agnese's practicality, Lucia's homeliness, Renzo's vitality.

Such connotations become even more precise in some episodes concerning the two principal characters. When Renzo invites Tonio and Gervaso for supper at the inn to pass the time away before surprising Don Abbondio, the whole action seems to unfold around a humble and well-known dish of the Lombard cuisine, the *polpette* (meatballs—also celebrated after Manzoni by Giovanni Rajberti and Carlo Emilio Gadda), and to receive from it a kind of realistic validation. The innkeeper comes to the fore "with a coarse table-cloth under his arm and a flask in his hand" and is very effective in eluding the concerned questions by Renzo, who has noticed some unusual clients in the inn: "It's enough for us if our customers are decent folk; who they are and who they aren't doesn't matter. And now I'll bring you a dish of meat-balls, the like of which you never tasted;" in the kitchen, "as he was fetching the pan with the aforesaid meat-balls," the innkeeper is a bit less effective in eluding similar inquiries by a bravo; he then responds to Renzo's persistent questions: "But what the devil makes you want to ask so many questions, when you are a bridegroom, and ought to have your head filled with quite different things? And with those meat-balls in front of you, which would revive a corpse?" (101–2). But Renzo is indeed too concerned to enjoy those meat-balls, and in fact "was sparing in his eating and drinking, and was careful to pour out just enough wine for his two witnesses to make them lively without losing control of their wits" (102).

Renzo will be much less sensible at the Inn of the Full Moon in Milan during the bread riots. As soon as he has entered the inn, together with a guard whom he does not know but who is well known to the innkeeper, Renzo empties a glass of wine "in one draught" and turns to the landlord:

> "What can you give me to eat?" he said to the landlord then.
> "I've got some stew. Would you like that?" said the innkeeper.
> "Yes, fine. Some stew." (217)

The repetition underlines the typical dish of Milanese cuisine, the stew, or *stufato*, which, as such, is much more appealing for the "foreigner" Renzo. He begins to eat it with the "bread of Providence" he had picked up in the street and put in his pocket; he talks aloud and is taken to be more and more of an instigator, especially when he refuses to tell his name to the innkeeper and as he gulps down ("we are sorry to say," 220) I don't know how many more glasses of wine.

The rest of the episode is all too well known. In any case, after his arrest and his escape, Renzo walked toward Bergamo and stopped in front of "a bunch of leaves hanging over the door of an isolated house outside a little hamlet;" after entering, "he asked for something to eat; was offered a piece of *stracchino* cheese and some good wine; accepted the cheese and declined the wine," because of "the tricks it had played on him the night before" (247). Later on, famine and plague already over, when Renzo goes back to his town, food again has a prominent role in reflecting the difficult return to normalcy:

> At about midday he stopped in a little wood to eat some bread and meat he had brought with him. As for fruit, there was more of that at his disposal along the road than he could eat—figs, peaches, plums, apples, as many as he wanted. All he had to do was to go into a field and pick them or gather them

off the ground, where they lay as thick as hail. For it was an unusually abun-
dant year, particularly for fruit; and there was scarcely anyone to bother
about it. (514)

One should also remember the scene when a town friend, alone because
his entire family has been wiped out by the plague, welcomes Renzo

> as best he could at such short notice and in such times. He set some water on
> the fire, and began making *polenta*; then he handed the ladle over for Renzo
> to stir. . . . He came back with a small pail of milk, some dried meat, a couple
> of cream cheeses [*raveggioli*], and some figs and peaches. And when it was all
> on the table and he had ladled out the *polenta* onto a board, they sat down to
> eat together. (521)[10]

As for Lucia, she is at the center of the narrative action when, freed by
the Unnamed and "paler, more dejected, more wasted than ever" (359),
is taken care of by "the good woman," the tailor's wife, who inquires
first of all, with "respectful sympathy," whether Lucia has eaten anything (361). As soon as they arrive home, the woman makes Lucia sit "in
the cosiest corner of her kitchen" and "quickly rekindling the fire under
a pot, in which a fat capon was floating, she soon brought the broth to
the boil; then, filling up a bowl in which she had already put some pieces
of bread, she was finally able to set it before Lucia" (364–65). Indeed,
the adverb "finally" seems to contain all the charity and the kindness
displayed by the good woman, who also explains that everybody is celebrating the visit of Cardinal Federigo (hence the capon!). When the
tailor arrives, the family sits at the table, and "the mistress of the house
went and fetched Lucia, led her to it, and sat her down; then she cut a
wing off the capon and put it before her" (367).
    From the series of the preceding quotations the coherence of the
narrative stands out: it is not so much or not only a realistic or mimetic
coherence as a functional one in matching foods, settings, and characters. The novelistic importance of inns as places for necessary stops during journeys is clearly shown throughout *I promessi sposi*, so much so that
the inn should be considered as a true chronotope. And it seems right
that Renzo is the one who connects such places since he repeatedly
carries out the development of the "adventurous" action; equally right
is the fact that Lucia is at the center of homely scenes, which are also
necessary as a juxtaposition with the "Gothic" from which she has escaped.[11] Foods are chosen and named with equal referential precision,
both historically and sociologically: *polpette*, *stufato*, and *stracchino* are

unmistakably Lombard, even today after more than a century since the Italian unification; and broth and boiled capon constitute a festive meal, which is a counterpoint to the more usual and daily polenta, perhaps served with a soft ripened cheese like *raveggiolo*.

Before dealing with aristocracy and its alimentary habits as they are represented in *I promessi sposi*, I wish to examine an image that is projected with exceptional symbolic power from the beginning to the end of the novel. When Fra Cristoforo asks forgiveness from the brother of the man he has murdered in a duel, he asks for a bread as a seal of the forgiveness just granted: "The nobleman, deeply moved, ordered this to be done; and a footman in full dress soon appeared carrying a loaf of bread on a silver dish, and presented it to the friar" (57). It is truly an emblematic image: on the one hand the silver dish connotes the passage from the primary necessity of food to the luxury and the taste for pleasure—and the footman in full dress is indispensable for the solemn occasion, but also for the "good manners" of nobility; on the other hand, the same silver dish gives a religious connotation to the bread, emphasizing the eucharistic symbolism of charity and forgiveness brought by Christ into the world. Such symbolism is so important that Fra Cristoforo will always keep this bread-symbol on himself throughout the novel, in "a little box made of common wood, but turned and polished with a certain Capuchin refinement," and will give it to Renzo and Lucia (reunited in the lazaretto and in their forgiveness of the dying Don Rodrigo) as a "relic" and a viaticum for their "journey" together in life (573). This is a superb example of consonance between word and thing, or of a true consubstantiation between name and person, since "Cristo-foro" is, literally, "the carrier of Christ," as the etymology indicates.

It is appropriate to recall here Louis Marin's analysis of the interpretation of the eucharistic formula given by the Port-Royal logicians. Jesus destroys the bread (indicated by the deictic "this") as bread, and transforms (transubstantiates) it into his own divine "body," thanks to the strength of the word, of the linguistic utterance "is": "This is my body." Hence the formula means that the bread (and the wine) "are no longer things, but signs instead. They are a kind of sign-thing that hides the body of Jesus Christ as a thing and reveals it as a symbol." In fact (as Arnauld and Nicole, quoted by Marin, said) the image of bread "helps us to conceive of the way in which the body of Jesus Christ is the food of our souls and of how the faithful are united among themselves" precisely by the common food.[12] At the same time, the formula is also in a certain sense "the matrix of all signs," that is, it is the paradigmatic model of the linguistic (and semiotic) theory of Port-Royal, which strove for the *adequatio rei et intellectus*: "it was possible in 1683 for the Port-Royal logicians to believe that there existed a perfect adequation between the Catholic dogma of consubstantiation on the one hand and a semiotic theory of meaningful representation on the other."[13]

I believe that in Manzoni, too, this paradigmatic model is taken up and repeated, first of all, and in particular, precisely in the choice of "Cristoforo," which is a squared verbal sign of Christ's presence (in that it re-presents him twice, in the bread and in the name), and secondly, and in general, in the choice of realism, which is the complex of verbal signs in which the things of the world are re-presented, made present, with a truly miraculous "naturalness." With his eucharistic name and bread, Cristoforo goes through the novel from beginning to end, and in so doing, he expresses its religious and literary ideology with great effectiveness: it is Manzoni the Biblicist who abhors the violence done to human beings, points out the expiation of guilt, and insists on individual responsibility—with accents that perhaps only Primo Levi will be able to take up again and equal in much more serious historical circumstances. And incidentally, at this symbolic-religious level of the text of *I promessi sposi*, it is worth recalling the words with which Cardinal Federigo welcomes the Unnamed: "this banquet of Grace" (344); the entire episode is in fact properly crowned by a saying by Isaiah: "The wolf also shall dwell with the lamb; and the lion shall eat straw like the ox" (350).

In general, the narrator is not interested in the foods of the aristocracy; he is content to give the indications indispensable for suggesting settings and atmospheres. For example, "to the majestic, but cold and limited prospects called forth by the idea of being head of a convent," little Gertrude's friends "would oppose the varied and glittering visions of weddings and banquets, of parties and balls" (137); when she is practically a prisoner in her father's palace, Gertrude "was made to go up to the top floor, every time a visitor was announced," and "there she also ate, when there were guests," with the servants (141); once her resistance has been broken, the machinery that has been set in motion against her turns at a dizzying speed, not leaving her any time to retract: "They made a hurried supper, so as to get to bed quickly and be ready early the following morning" (149). Analogously, in the pages immediately preceding the bread riots, "the unfortunate Commissioner" is shown "munching a scanty, bitter little meal, without any appetite and without any fresh bread" (198), unaware of the imminent storm.

The meals of the aristocracy play a particular role: they are used to create favorable conditions for variously important decisions. For example, Don Rodrigo and Attilio have "luncheon" while discussing what measures to take against Fra Cristoforo (169); as a consequence, the "right honourable uncle" invites the Father Provincial to dinner with "a galaxy of guests chosen with exquisite subtlety:" there were some kinsmen who "by their very bearing, natural assurance, and lordly haughtiness, managed, without even trying, to impress and renew every minute an idea of superiority and power," and a few clients who "began at the soup to say 'yes' with lips, eyes, and ears, with their whole head, with their whole bodies and souls, so that by the time the fruit came round they were reduced to forgetting how anyone ever managed to say 'no' " (288): as a matter of fact, soon after this dinner poor Fra Cristoforo is sent away from Pescarenico.

Among the signs of the Unnamed's imminent conversion, there is also his concern for Lucia's hunger: "You must need something to eat. They'll bring you some right away," and immediately afterwards, with a necessary and reassuring clarification: "A woman will come to bring you food" (319). Of course Lucia does not even touch "the good things" brought to her in "a basket," while the old woman who guards her avidly enjoys the "lovely morsels" (320). Once the Unnamed is converted, Cardinal Federigo invites him to dinner and sits him "at his right-hand side, in the midst of a circle of priests" (367), and the reader can image that such a meal must be "frugal," as was customary for the cardinal, who preferred to show "liberality" in building the Ambrosian Library (333–34).

Only on three occasions does the narrator name particular foods or drinks. When Gertrude bends under the Prince's psychological torture and hints at her "willingness" to become a nun, she is immediately rewarded: "She was installed in an arm-chair, and served with a cup of chocolate, which was the equivalent at that time of being given the *toga virilis* among the ancient Romans" (151); one could add, with Parini, that she has become a *giovin Signora*.[14] When Don Rodrigo feels the first symptoms of the plague, he attributes them to "a *vernaccia*!" he had drunk, but he, too, falls prey to the plague and notices its first signs "as he was carousing in a tavern" (510). The third instance occurs with a client of the Inn of the Full Moon, who replies to Renzo's words, "A great mania those gentry have for using the pen!" with this explanation:

"The reason is this. . . . That as those gentry are the ones who eat all the geese, they've got such a lot of quills, such a lot that they've got to find something to do with them" (221)—a comic variation on an exact sociological referent.

The narrator, then, is not interested in the food of the aristocracy. Don Rodrigo's "banquet" at the beginning of the novel is perceived by Fra Cristoforo as "a confused din of knives and forks, of glasses and plates, but above all of raucous voices trying to shout each other down" (64), while great care is reserved for the actual arrangement of the guests: Don Rodrigo "at the head of his table," Count Attilio, his cousin, "on his right," "on his left, at the other side of the table," the mayor ("the very man whose duty it was, in theory, to see that justice was done to Renzo Tramaglino and restrain Don Rodrigo"); "opposite the mayor" Doctor Quibble-weaver, and "opposite the two cousins" were "a pair of obscure guests" (65). Once the social hierarchies have been established with such meticulous precision, it is no wonder that at the end of the novel Don Rodrigo's heir, the Marquis, invites to dinner Renzo and Lucia, who are finally married, but does not sit at the table with them, "and even helped to wait on them" before "withdrawing to dine elsewhere with Don Abbondio," because, the narrator comments, "I have said that he was a humble man, but not that he was a prodigy of humility. He had enough to put himself beneath those good folk, but not enough to be on an equality with them" (599). In other words, here the wordly habits codified in good manners triumph over the (inadequate) goodness or morality of a single representative of a class that remains privileged. As Raimondi has noted, "instead of being resolved, the antithesis of inequality is presented again in its adversative aspect: it is reinforced, not extenuated, by the paradox of a 'beneath,' which is easier than an 'above' when the latter means an 'equal'; therefore 'the same table' is only a metanarrative hypothesis or utopia."[15]

A first and partial reason for Manzoni's relative lack of interest in the food of the gentry is to be found in the juxtaposition proposed by the text between noblemen who are either "bad" (Spaniards or Hispanophiles: Don Rodrigo, the "right honourable uncle") or "good" (Milanese and Catholic: Cardinal Borromeo and the Unnamed, once converted), as Mirto Stone points out.[16] In the case of the bad ones, the author dedicates his attention to the social and ritual use of meals, which are reduced to mere occasions for displaying power, reaffirming hierarchies, preparing abuses, and demonstrating arbitrariness. In the case of the good noblemen, on the contrary, precisely because they are proposed as models their foods do not have any importance as such, and if anything, it will be the frugality or religious connotation of the food (the "banquet of Grace") that occupies the scene entirely.

But the decisive reason is that the primary and truest interest of Manzoni as narrator is in the habits and ways of the lower classes, the *gente meccaniche*; therefore the aristocrats' inclination to transform the fulfillment of a need into a social ritual (or even into an aesthetic sublimation) remains necessarily marginal in his novelistic project— marginal, but not less functional. Historically, such literary reason corresponds (independently of Manzoni's intentions) to the beginning of the aristocracy's decline and to the first achievements of a slowly rising, controlled bourgeoisie. Raimondi effectively remarks that Manzoni "introduces the humble reality, impervious to idyll, of *stufato*, *polpette*, and grey polenta into an aristocratic literature, for which hunger existed only as a playful, not as an economic theme."[17] And one might add here the textual echo of a sentence by an unknown customer at the Inn of Gorgonzola, uttered "in a voice as modest as the proposition was daring": "We have mouths of our own to eat with, and to say our reason, too, and once the ball is set rolling . . . " (251). This sentence is all the more meaningful in that it makes explicit at the novelistic level the ambiguity inherent in orality, divided between eating and saying, words and foods. This ambiguity is the very basis, the inescapable structure, of the relationships between need and power, individuals and society, society and history: the "daring proposition" effectively and literally joins *sitos* and logos ("to eat" and "reason"), to take up Marin's terminology again.[18]

But the aristocratic Manzoni does not limit himself to steering literature in a crucial turn toward realism, that is, toward an absolute fidelity of the word to the thing, of the literary sign to its referent. He does not forget that referentiality is only one among the possible dimensions of the literary word. Therefore even in the alimentary and culinary area, the metaphorical use of terms is superimposed upon the referential one, without concealing it; in fact the metaphor integrates the referential usage profoundly into the text. I shall give a few examples (in italics) that seem interesting. The fearful Don Abbondio is immediately compared to "an animal without tusks or claws, who yet was reluctant *to be devoured*" (9). Fra Cristoforo, the hero of conquered pride, is associated with metaphoric expressions such as "*ingozzarne* una" (original, p. 69: to swallow something), "to *swallow* every insult" (76), "with the look of one *swallowing* a very *bitter medicine*" (76), or "Patience! It's a hollow word, a *bitter* word" (89). The abbess and some of the nuns at Monza "avevano, come si suol dire, *il mestolo in mano*" (original, p. 177: had, as they say, the ladle in their hands). The "great big secret" of Renzo's and Lucia's attempt at the surprise wedding stays in talkative Perpetua's heart "like *very new wine* in an old, badly hooped cask, fermenting and gurgling and bubbling up, just not blowing out the cork, but swishing round inside, and coming frothing or seeping out between the staves, . . . for people to *taste* it and tell more or less *what wine it was*" (171). In all these instances, the metaphorical language is used to introduce or reinforce certain character traits, just as was the case with the "realistic" connotations of a little flask of wine or a big cabbage.

The narrator uses figures of speech from the spoken language at crucial moments in a way that has made the task of the English translator very difficult indeed—so that I will go back to the original Italian in some important instances, such as the scene in Milan when the rioters besiege the bakeries continuously "per godere quella cuccagna, finché durava" (original, p. 237: to enjoy that Cockaigne, that plenty, while it lasted); later on, a tax exemption is "another windfall" (603), again "una cuccagna" (original, p. 724) for Renzo and Lucia. Other popular ways of speaking are spread throughout the novel: "wolf does not eat wolf" (213), "[he] takes the bread from his own mouth to give to the hungry" (368),"[he] gets it just for a crust of bread" (597). Also: "la guerra che allora bolliva, . . . diciamo qui quanto basti per infarinarne chi n'avesse bisogno" (original, p. 509: the war that was boiling then, . . . let us say what is enough to enflour those who should need it), or: after making her vow, Lucia feels "a boiling-up of thoughts that do not go with words" (365), Don Abbondio gives some advice to the Marquis, "anche se non era sua farina" (original, p. 719: even if it was not his own flour), and Donna Prassede is used "to temper the bitter with the sweet" (417). All these are examples of linguistic realism inserted into the literariness of the text.

Similarly, there are those "certe ragioni senza sugo" (original, p. 116: certain reasons without any juice, that is, without any sense) that Don Abbondio opposes to Renzo, or the "poco sugo" (original, p. 193: little juice, that is, little taste) Gertrude finds in her vengeance against a maid servant: "chewing over and savouring the satisfaction which she had received, [she] was surprised to find it so tasteless, compared to the longing which she had had for it" (149); or, again, "il sugo del senso" (original, p. 486: the juice of the sense) that Federigo extracts from Don Ferrante's "flowers" (389). In these latter instances, the Italian uses the alimentary term "sugo," juice, in a way that sounds impossible, or certainly awkward, in English.

But let us consider the ending of the novel. Renzo and Lucia reach the conclusion that when troubles come, "whether by our own fault or not, confidence in God sweetens them and makes them useful for a better life" (604; original, p. 725). It is a conclusion in which the alimentary metaphor contained and, as it were, forgotten in common language (sweetens, "raddolcisce"), by being coupled with a spiritual referent like "confidence in God," effectively lowers divine transcendence to the thoroughly human and corporeal level of immanence. This mixture of sublime and low is a very beautiful example of that "Christian" and "humble" realism analyzed by Auerbach, in a different context, in *Mimesis*. Furthermore, at the intertextual level Lucia's words echo the corresponding language of the Bible: "*Gustate* et videte quoniam *suavis* est Dominus; beatus vir qui sperat in eo" (Psalms, 34:9). Perella refers to this passage as a suggestive example of the Christian and mystical doctrine of the "spiritual senses" juxtaposed with the corporeal or "external" ones of man.[19]

At this point the narrator intervenes and revives another alimentary metaphor made common by usage, thus further emphasizing the *sermo humilis* on his own, without the Biblical echo: "This conclusion, though it was reached by poor people, has seemed so just to us that we have thought of putting it down here, as the juice of the whole tale" (604). It is worth remembering that in *Fermo e Lucia*, the bodily and essential "juice of the whole tale" was "il costrutto morale di tutti gli avvenimenti che abbiamo narrati,"[20] the moral construct of all the events we have narrated, a language that was more solemn and philosophical, but infinitely less immediate and effective, than the one used in *I promessi sposi*. With such a lowering of the lexical register, the small "story" of Renzo and Lucia is definitely sealed within the initial "Historie," which, however, will be concluded, unlike the former, only in the Last Judgment. By sharing the conclusion reached by his characters and making it his own, Manzoni "has given the impression of writing the history of the people that had been forgotten by official historiography up to that time; but he has also given the impression that History in general was a moral History and that therefore it had a significance, a direction: the achievement of justice."[21] This remark by Norbert Jonard clearly indicates the novelty of Manzoni's historiographic operation and its characteristics, which are above all ethical: the novelist's motivations are not necessarily to be shared by the historian or the critic. But precisely for this reason I should emphasize that the "juice" of this "story," which as far as food is concerned is a true, *ante litteram* micro-history, is appropriately popular and at the same time literary,[22] like the work it concludes and the genre to which it has belonged from the beginning.

Finally, "the juice" also foregrounds "the story," that is, the novel. In fact, it performs a clearly metanarrative function because the dialogism between the author and his characters is reinforced and emphasized by the final sentence of the novel, which deals precisely with "the story" or tale whose "juice" I have examined so far, calls on "the man who wrote it" and the one "who patched it together" (605), and appeals to the readers' benevolence. Bakhtin could not have asked for more.

It remains to be seen how other Italian novelists followed (or did not follow) the road indicated by Manzoni. But this is another story, whose juice is still to be tasted.

How to Make a Stew:
Giovanni Verga, *I Malavoglia*

HUNGER remained constantly in the background of *I promessi sposi*, and in the famine episode it was a determining element of the narration even though it did not affect the protagonists closely. On the contrary, in Giovanni Verga's *I Malavoglia* (1881), it becomes the daily and obsessive concern, the human and historical condition with which its characters must struggle.

In an essay that does not seem to have received due attention in Italy, Sergio Campailla examines the enormous importance held in Verga's work and world view by the body and its inherent alimentary function. Starting from an analysis of a painting by Brueghel the Elder, "The Big Fish Eats the Small Fish," and applying it, through the Darwinian notions of "the struggle for life" and "the survival of the fittest," to Verga's texts, Campailla points out "the meagerness of the inventory of foods" they present, the "system of metaphors" that underpins them ideologically and poetically, and the insistence on parts of the body such as the belly, the eyes and the mouth, relevant at the referential but above all at the metaphorical level, also in connection with "trophic eros."[1]

Campailla's remarkable essay will be the starting point for my own analysis, which, however, will be oriented in a different way. A primordial and Darwinian hunger is at the root of the Malavoglia family's story in Sicily in the years 1863–1875. Hunger literally means how to supply food for the family's mouths, how to "earn the daily bread." There is no doubt that Verga's analysis, focused on the poorest stratum of society, has detected the economic factor as the dominant motif, the one that conditions first of all the satisfaction of hunger, but also affects all areas of behavior, beginning with sentiments. It is almost a commonplace in Verga criticism by now, from Luigi Russo on. But one example seems particularly appropriate, with its clear evidence: La Locca, who lost Menico in the shipwreck of the boat named *Provvidenza*, is desperate on her landing as she faces the Malavoglias; she "had been shrieking since morning in that cracked, crazy voice of hers, demanding that they give her back her son and refusing to listen to reason." Cousin Anna's lapidary comment is, "She's acting like that because she's hungry."[2]

Let us see then the inventory of foods in *I Malavoglia*. "The anchovies to be salted" (8) are one of La Longa's household chores from the very beginning. Salting anchovies is the basic activity that returns to accompany the life of the fishermen and the pages of the novel[3] because the abundance or the scarcity of the catch, the fluctuations of the prices on the market, and the fears, or just the hygienic precautions caused by cholera, are all factors influencing the family budget. Pounding salt, preparing the brine, checking it, pressing the anchovies in small barrels, counting them all lined up in the yard, are the best moments in the life of the village, a true "providence" sent by Saint Francis (157). These are also the best moments in the life of the Malavoglia family, when all together, while salting anchovies, they "made the time pass by telling stories and asking riddles, good enough for the children" (162)—and these stories, with the reactions they cause in the listeners, are admirable tools for revealing the inner traits of the characters. In fact, at the end of the novel, before the definitive departure, 'Ntoni evokes precisely these moments: "Do you remember the fine talks we used to have in the evening while we were salting the anchovies?" (257), but he forgets that at that time he told the story of the two sailors who had "come back from Trieste, or Alexandria in Egypt or, anyway, some far-off place," bringing with them images of fabulous cities, "up there" where "the people spend their time enjoying themselves all day long instead of salting anchovies" (162–63).

But let us have a close look at what the fishermen of Aci Trezza eat. Before the *Provvidenza* leaves with the ill-fated load of lupins, Maruzza "silently set about preparing the boat for the voyage, storing the fur-lined coat, the fresh bread, the jar full of olive oil, and the onions under the footboards and in the locker" (14). The minute, realistic details underscore how fundamental these foods are, and in fact they are mentioned several times in the novel. For instance, when Master 'Ntoni goes to look at the house by the medlar tree, now Uncle Crocifisso's property, he enjoys the sight of the onions in the orchard, "whose blossoms were like a sea of white plumes" (155). When Alessi and Nunziata speak about their future, their dialogue is entirely based on similar alimentary referents, at least on the surface:

"Now they've planted onions in the garden, and they've come up as big as oranges."

"Do you like onions?"

"I've got to like them. They help you eat your bread and they're cheap. When we don't have any money for soup, my little ones and I always eat them."

"That's why they sell so many onions. Uncle Crocifisso didn't plant cabbages and lettuce at the house by the medlar and has sown only onions, because he has another garden at his own house. But we'll plant broccoli and cauliflowers, too. . . . They are good, aren't they?" (186)

The simplicity of the foods mentioned in this dialogue is equal to the seriousness of the two young persons who will continue the Malavoglia lineage. Their dialogue acquires an even greater importance if we remember that it is the latest of a series begun by Nunziata and Mena concerning Alfio, continued by Alfio and Mena, and then by Alfio and Nunziata—a series in which the alimentary, and therefore economic, referents are essential for the development and resolution of sentiments.

The fava bean soup is familiar to almost all the characters in the novel: not only to the Malavoglia family, but also to Comare Grazia Piedipapera, Nunziata, Alfio Mosca, and La Locca; in particular, Alfio Mosca's words to Mena show the importance of soup: "I'm here eating my soup; because when I see all of you at the table under the light, I no longer feel so lonely, so lonely that I don't even want to eat" (29); and those of Nunziata to Alessi: "The hearth in the kitchen needs fixing. . . . The last time I cooked the soup there, when poor Comare Maruzza hadn't the heart to do a thing, I had to put stones under the pot to hold it up" (186). Through their minimum common denominator—the soup—, these examples emphasize the centrality, almost the sacrality of the home hearth. And even at the end of the novel a bowl of soup will underscore 'Ntoni's estrangement: "They put a bowl of soup between his knees, because he was hungry and thirsty, and he ate it in silence, his nose in his plate, as if he hadn't seen God's bounty for a week. But the others lost their appetite, they had such a pang in their hearts. Then 'Ntoni, when he had eaten and rested a while, took his bag and got up to leave" (255).

One should note that, notwithstanding their poverty, the Malavoglias are able and willing to give "some fava beans" (80) as alms to La Locca because they believe in the patriarchal values of a charity that is no longer Catholic and, so to speak, metaphysical (as in Manzoni), but simply humane, anthropological (lay)—and juxtaposed with Uncle Crocifisso's economic calculations and dehumanizing profits.[4] Hence the alms of these few fava beans are the sign of the intrinsic morality of the donors and reveal a fundamental, positive trait of their character.

In the Malavoglia domestic economy an egg is a luxury: hens are kept so that eggs can be sold at the market, and "they'll help pay off the debt, too" (81), or duck eggs are put "under the hen, and ducklings sell for eight soldi each" (81); the gift of two hens to Don Silvestro, the town clerk, in order to obtain his legal advice must have been a considerable sacrifice (certainly greater than that made by Renzo and Lucia with their capons for Quibble-weaver). Still, in order to help with the family budget, La Longa "had set up a small stand in front of her door and was selling oranges, nuts, hard-boiled eggs, and black olives" (154), and at the time of cholera she "went to the villas of the city folks selling eggs and fresh bread while the men were out at sea, and she managed to earn a few pennies" (171), but cholera "trapped" her, too (171), and she died. Later on, La Mena "with the money from the chicks . . . would also buy a pig, so as not to waste the hulls of the prickly pears and the water they used to cook the pasta" (244). Everything is useful, nothing must be wasted.

The provisions of the Malvoglia household are the bare necessities: "wheat, fava beans and oil for the winter" (158); the sobriety of their life is reflected also in the engagement party for Mena and Brasi, where "wine, roasted chick peas, fava beans and chestnuts" are offered (105 and 114). There is plenitude, paradoxically, only on the occasion of some misfortune, such as, for instance, Bastianazzo's death: "The neighbors brought something, as is the custom, pasta, eggs, wine, and all God's good things, and only someone with a happy heart could have eaten it all. Even Compare Alfio Mosca had come, holding a chicken in each hand" (40). As Campailla remarks, this is certainly "a variation of the custom, so rooted in Mediterranean societies, of funeral banquets, which are set up also to try to comfort and—if possible—to compensate the survivors for the loss of a beloved person."[5]

In sum, in the society of Aci Trezza, plenty of food is reserved for very few, like the parish priest, don Giammaria, who "is having fried spaghetti for dinner tonight" (28)—a dish that, although it appears to be utilizing the leftovers from lunch, still includes pasta rather than fava beans. Abundance is attributed to the outside world, those "Christians" who "had learned to eat meat on Friday too, like so many Turks" (13), or even to "the poorhouse" where they allegedly eat "meat and pasta every day" (230). In fact "meat and pasta every day" is 'Ntoni's favorite phrase, and he repeats it as a refrain in his dreams of evasion and richness, or when he flashes images of city life for the benefit of Master 'Ntoni. His first letter from Naples is worth recalling: "He said that the women in those parts swept the streets with silk skirts, and that on the quay there was a puppet show, and they sold pizzas for two centesimi, just the kind the rich folk ate, and that without money you couldn't live there" (11). But the world of the city is not, obviously, that "Land of Cockaigne" 'Ntoni dreams of;[6] in the novel, it is only used to feed the characters' dissatisfaction, so that it is both a pole of attraction and a paradigm of negativity.

In all the examples analyzed so far, and in other possible ones,[7] food clearly appears as a referent that is pinpointed with geographic, historical, and sociological precision. At the cost of emphasizing what is obvious, I again emphasize the difference between the (southern) fava bean soup in Verga and the (northern) polenta in Manzoni. From this point of view, there is no doubt that Verga continues the project of Manzoni's realism, and in fact pushes it to extreme consequences, at least in the sense of the absolute primacy given to the physiological needs of nutrition—the true survival of the lower classes, with a materiality and immanence unkown to Manzoni.

But there is another aspect of these alimentary referents that seems to turn their realistic function into a constructive one à la Tynyanov:[8] their repetition, or at least the repetition of the most important ones, is the sure indication of a structural function, of a textual weaving, that has little to do with realism. Repetition produces the leitmotiv, the scansion of the story, the rhythm of the narrative. I believe that Verga's particular geniality was that of joining precisely the "low" referents of food with a "high" literariness, as the great creator of texts he was. But before analyzing such repetition and its function in *I Malavoglia*, it is necessary to deal with another equally important phenomenon necessary for a true understanding of Verga's art.

Next to the paucity of the inventory of foods in the novel, there is the enormous proliferation and diffusion of the metaphorical usage of alimentary referents filtered through sayings, proverbs, idiomatic expressions, and comparisons, all of which enter into the linguistic texture of *I Malavoglia* in a refined orchestration (Bakhtin would say polyphony) of returns, resumptions, and variations among the characters, and between them and the narrating voice. Already the prevalence of metaphors would prevent the definition of the prose in which they appear as realistic, given the fact that realism, if one listens to Roman Jakobson, is governed and defined by metonymy and synecdoche, while poetry is characterized by the flowing of metonymy into metaphor (and vice versa).[9] But let us have a close look at the text.

The first area in which the metaphorical process develops is the tranference of sentiments and moods to the bodily level. For example, when 'Ntoni is enlisted in the Navy and leaves, La Longa has "a bitter taste in her mouth" (11), and analogously, almost a direct derivation from the proverb "a bitter mouth spits gall," La Zuppidda "really had a bitter mouth, because of that Barbara of hers, whom she hadn't been able to marry off" (22). When she hears about the lupins deal, La Longa remains "dumbfounded, as if that huge sum of forty onze had hit her in the stomach" (14), and Alfio looks at the empty house of the Malavoglias "as if his loaded cart were weighing on his stomach" (240). La San-tuzza's "mouth spills honey" because it is necessary "if you keep a tav-ern" (43); when he listens to 'Ntoni, who wants everybody to be rich, "Master 'Ntoni stared at him, and turned those words over in his mouth, trying to swallow them" (166). When the Malavoglias are com-pelled to sell their tools, "Master 'Ntoni felt as though they were rip-ping the guts out of his belly" (182); returning from the military service, 'Ntoni believes that "if nothing else, he had filled his belly with good sense" (189), and when he is thrown out of the tavern, his mouth is "filled with bile" and he would like to "stay there all day long" so that his rivals "would eat their hearts out" (217). Or again, "a hungry belly won't listen to reason" (219)—quite an appropriate proverb for the subject under examination.

The second area is metaphoric-synecdochic, and concerns "earning one's bread" (an expression that recalls the picaresque origins of the novel, in that the verb *buscarsi* derives from El Buscón): all the charac-ters must earn it, even the few privileged ones who eat "the King's bread" (174). But in particular "earning one's bread" has to do with 'Ntoni from the very beginning: "After he's tasted the bitter bread they eat elsewhere, he won't complain about the soup he gets at home" (11)—these simple words also hide an intertextual echo from Dante—to the last pages: "I'll go far away, where I'll find some way to earn my bread, and nobody will know who I am" (256).[10]

The third area includes many comparisons having foods or kitchen objects as their points of reference. "That's how you marry off a girl. Otherwise you're stuck with her, like an old pot" (69), and so Mena, who does not marry, will go to live "in the attic of the house by the

medlar tree, like an old pot put away on the shelf" (253); 'Ntoni, already
called "cucumber" by the village girls when he was imprisoned, is "getting as fat as a capon" (239); Don Silvestro "said he bet he'd make
Barbara fall at his feet, like a ripe pear" (97). The same type of comparison is applied not only to the characters, but to the landscape as
well: "the sea hissed and sizzled all around like a fish in a frying pan"
(134), the rain "spluttered and hissed like a fish in a frying pan" (224),
and even the stars "looked like sparks running along the bottom of a
black frying pan" (61). This area is particularly interesting because
it reveals Verga's representative strategy with absolute clarity: it is
through these typical comparisons ("like a fish in a frying pan") that the
text shows its primacy (as text), while it presents the reader with a fundamental fact in the life of the fishermen: they eat fried fish, which is such
a basic element in their nourishment that it is taken for granted, it does
not even appear in the "realistic" list of foods, and it is left to the
reader's inference to extract it from the metaphorical texture and insert
it in its proper place in the fictional reconstruction of the world of Aci
Trezza.

But perhaps the most important area is that of the verb *mangiare*, to
eat, already examined by Campailla in part for *I Malavoglia* and in general for Verga's ideology.[11] Let us consider the following expressions:
"the train left, whistling and snorting so much that it ate up the singing
and the last farewells" (11); "sun and water were uselessly eating up the
Provvidenza" (14); "Menico . . . shouted something which was eaten up
by the rush of the sea" (15); "his grandfather cried, straightening up
with an effort, because of those pains that ate up his back" (94); "But
when the sea was rough and threatened to gulp all of them down in one
big mouthful—them, the *Provvidenza* and all the rest—that boy had a
heart greater than the sea" (132); " 'Ntoni . . . let himself dangle over
the sea which was howling below and wanted to eat him" (136); "the
Provvidenza . . . did not bring them anything and ate up the pay they
gave to Nunzio" (180), or, on the contrary, she "came in with her belly
full of God's bounty" (135); "Then another bad year would come, another cholera epidemic, another disaster, and eat up both house and
boat" (190).[12] What is remarkable to me in all these examples is that the
metaphorization of the verb "to eat" (or to gulp down) is an integral part
of another rhetorical figure, prosopopeia, the personification of inanimate things (like the sea or the *Provvidenza*) or of abstract entities (like
the bad years or a disaster). Prosopopeia is one of the most ancient and
common rhetorical figures used in spoken language, and my examples

are quite eloquent in giving an idea of its importance. They are truly central and irreplaceable if one wants to enter Verga's art and ideology, his narrative impersonality in *I Malavoglia*. And like the "realistic" alimentary referents, these personifications are also repeated numerous times, they scan the narration and the destiny of the characters, they bind the text in an extraordinary verbal and rhythmic unity, and they foreground the text's literariness.

In fact, the language of *I Malavoglia*, with its personifications, predates any single event and individual conscience and allows the reader's identification with the individual members of a given speaking community. Verga can "regress" in language because in it there is already codified the author's "long-reaching view," the life experience of generations of human beings.[13] Hence language is the true narrating voice, the humanly omniscient voice of this novel, its rhythm, its deep and secret music. As a further confirmation, I want to quote another series of prosopopeias from the page of 'Ntoni's final departure, an important page also because it takes up and cyclically repeats the ending of chapter 2:[14]

> Only the sea was grumbling the same old story for him, down below there among the Fariglioni rocks, because the sea is homeless too, and belongs to all those who listen to it, here and there, wherever the sun rises and sets, though at Aci Trezza it grumbles in a special way, and you can recognize it at once when it gurgles and breaks among those rocks, and it seems the voice of a friend. (257)

Here, in this page, which Giacomo Debenedetti calls "one of the greatest poetic stanzas not only in Italy and not only in the nineteenth century,"[15] the sea is no longer threatening and deadly, it does not want to "eat" 'Ntoni anymore, but is comforting and friendly ("grumbling the same old story for him"), just like the voice of the Adda River for Renzo in *I promessi sposi*. In fact, the sea allows 'Ntoni to recognize his destiny of a man without his *paese*. Already imbued with the pathos of separation and a piercing nostalgia, this recognition will perhaps enable 'Ntoni to "earn his bread" with better luck than he had in his previous efforts and futile revolts.

But the ultimate meaning of the personifications and repetitions selected and emphasized so far goes well beyond a purely stylistic or formalistic interpretation of Verga's novel. This meaning coincides in a truly singular manner with the conclusions reached by other critics, it confirms and completes them. I am referring to Debenedetti's reading, which focuses on the leitmotiv construction of *I Malavoglia* (considering the leitmotiv not so much in a Wagnerian sense as a formulaic style of an epic community, as a repetition that gives the sense of the collectivity), the mythical dimensions of the story, in short, the presence of "aspects of a symbolist narrative" in the naturalistic novel.[16] I am also referring to the contributions and the clarifications by Romano Luperini, Giancarlo Mazzacurati, and Vittorio Spinazzola;[17] and above all to the conclusions of Nino Borsellino, who points out the "musical flow" produced by "formulaic cadences" as the characteristic trait of Verga's style. After asking who the narrating voice is that gives "the illusion of reality, not its more or less verisimilar reproduction," Borsellino states that one cannot talk of a chorus, a narrator, the planes of the story (as other critics did). Faced with the "multiple orchestration" of *I Malavoglia*, one can only say that Verga has created "the *inner* language of the community, a language capable of reverberating in the interior voices of the individual characters": "it is the achievement of a utopia, like the *antérieur* language sought by Stéphane Mallarmé, the greatest of the symbolists," a language that is "absolutely prior, not traceable to a chronological measure to be defined by the relationship between the narrating writer and the narrated events," in sum "archetypal."[18]

All this points to a critical conclusion that by now, it seems, cannot be postponed: *verismo*, as it is expressed in the particular impersonality of *I Malavoglia*, is not "realism" at all. The sociological referentiality is the pretext, or the basic stratum, for a linguistic and literary operation that in any case, whether it is called symbolism or decadentism, projects Verga beyond his time and his "school." Already Calvino had quoted *I Malavoglia* (after Lev Tolstoi and together with Marcel Proust) as an example of a narration in which the "moving force" is no longer made up by "human actions and passions," but by "the impalpable flowing of life": and "in this flowing that is both nature and history, human individuality is submerged, loses the features separating it from the sea of the other."[19] But what remains implicit in Calvino's insight becomes a fundamental suggestion by Borsellino, for whom it is necessary to revalue "the pioneering function held in the history of the modern novel by the narrative technique of *I Malavoglia*."[20] This technique is rooted in the epic and in the impassive acknowledgment of the passing of time, without any influence by a (divine) Providence, without any exemplary meaning. In fact, in chapter 8 of *I Malavoglia*, just at the mid-point of the novel, we read: "Time had passed, and time carries away the bad as well as the good" (105).

Not by chance, "Time Passes" is also the title of the central chapter in *To the Lighthouse* by Virginia Woolf, one of modernism's peaks, a novel that, beyond the many and obvious differences, also presents some remarkable affinities with *I Malavoglia* in structure and style. It is significant that a critic like J. Hillis Miller asks in relation to Woolf the same questions (and offers the same solutions) as Borsellino had asked (and offered) for Verga.[21] Who is the narrator in *To the Lighthouse*? "The narrator, it appears, is a collective consciousness," at least in the sense that it is "dependent on the consciousness of the various characters for its existence"; and it lives their lives "from the perspective of that prospective death toward which they all move, and where the narrating mind already is," so that there is "an indescribable pathos in this instantaneous transformation, by the impersonal conventions of story telling, of flesh and blood immediacy into long-lost, impalpable ghosts" (174). In these remarks there is an undeniable echo from the conception of the narrator proposed by Walter Benjamin in his essay on Nikolai Leskov—in particular, the authority derived by the narrating voice from positioning itself from the viewpoint of death.[22] But, Miller continues, is this narrating voice really so impersonal, so depersonalizing? "One form of figuration persists through all the citations from 'Time Passes' I have made—in fact it permeates the whole chapter: personification, that trope of prosopopeia whereby we speak of the absent, the dead, or the inanimate as if they were alive, as if they were possessed of human consciousness and intent" (181). These personifications, present everywhere in the impersonality of the style, peremptorily indicate that the narrating voice in *To the Lighthouse* "is not a ubiquitous mind but language itself," because "the personifications present in ordinary language (so that without necessarily thinking about it one describes the wind as creeping around corners, venturing indoors, questioning, wandering, sighing) are the source of one's ideas of the personalities of 'real people' (Lily Briscoe, Mr. Ramsey, Mrs. Ramsey, and the rest)" (182).

I have already suggested how all these remarks are applicable to *I Malavoglia*, where the personifications (such as the sea grumbling or eating) make the reader perceive the personalities of the "real people" of Aci Trezza, such as 'Ntoni. In fact, in the case of the collective consciousness, these remarks are even more pertinent to *I Malavoglia* than to *To the Lighthouse*, and the implicit comparison between the two novels— however different and distant they are from each other—persuasively strengthens Borsellino's proposal to consider seriously Verga's pioneering function in the history of the modern novel. Yes indeed, the Verga of *I Malavoglia* (which is different from his other works, not to mention from works by Luigi Capuana, De Roberto, or Matilde Serao) is a modernist, and the truth hidden and revealed by *verismo* is the truth of common language, of the language of all of us, "inhabitants of time,"[23] with our bodies in need of nutrition, with our souls eager for knowledge.

I am sure that Verga alluded to this truth when he wrote to his friend Capuana on March 16, 1879: "I have a fever to do [that is, to write], not because I feel I have the necessary strength, but because I believe I am alone—with you and a few others—in understanding how to make a stew."[24] The alimentary metaphor chosen and used by Verga privately and almost jokingly (but not too jokingly) takes one back to the initial point, and while making one measure the distance from the Manzonian Renzo's stew (in which referent and realistic meaning were one), it also confirms the singular method of Verga's so-called *verismo*. Here the "low" referent is used to indicate a "high" meaning: "the stew" stands for "the true literary text," and the metaphor contains and accurately indicates the author's poetics and, at the same time, the literariness of his text. Both poetics and literariness are confirmed by another metaphor, again an alimentary one, in another letter by Verga to Capuana dated April 11, 1881, after the seeming "fiasco" of *I Malavoglia*: "it takes the whole tenacity of my conviction in order not to prepare the delicacies the public likes, so that afterwards I could laugh in its face."[25]

One can only enjoy Verga's "stew" one last time before turning to the elaborate "delicacies" D'Annunzio, for his part, was about to prepare.

CHAPTER 3

Tea for Two:
Gabriele D'Annunzio, *Il piacere*

A READER expecting to find descriptions of succulent meals, dainty dishes, or elaborate delicacies in Gabriele D'Annunzio's works would probably be disappointed. It is true that the author gives a clear signal of his intentions and interests when he states in the dedicatory letter to Francesco Paolo Michetti, which was the premise of *Il piacere* of 1889:[1]

> Medicean tapestries do not hang from the walls, nor damsels come together in our decamerons, nor Paolo Veronese's cupbearers and greyhounds wander around the tables, nor supernatural fruits fill the china and glassware commissioned by Galeazzo Maria Sforza to Maffeo di Clivate. [On the contrary,] our desire is less superb: and our way of life is more primitive, perhaps even more Homeric and more heroic, if we take into account our meals along the resonant sea, meals that are worthy of Ajax and interrupt our industrious fasts. (It. 2–3)

The reader is warned: these meals "along the resonant sea," although they may be "worthy of Ajax," are metonymic of a "more primitive" (if not exactly "more Homeric and more heroic") way of life, hence they are not even meagerly described. As if to say that the "pleasure" of the novel's title is everything except the pleasure of the palate.

It is also true that from another viewpoint D'Annunzio's warning is an ambiguous one because it overturns and negates that which will be the scene of the novel, dominated precisely by tapestries and precious china and glassware, if not by cupbearers and greyhounds, according to a strategy of "good taste" and "refinement" that is fundamental to an understanding of D'Annunzio's project. After all, Raimondi defines *Il piacere* as "the novel of aestheticism and of Parnassian décor, where the naturalistic touch is reshaped as scenography, as the sentimental diary of the Italian decadence of the beginning of this century."[2] Hence it is necessary to examine this strategy carefully.

One can begin with the aristocratic dinner served by the Marchesa d'Ateleta, a dinner that takes up no less than ten pages in the Italian edition of Classici Mondadori (46–55), without counting the arrival of the guests at the Roccagiovine palace and the postprandial conversations. In these ten pages food is hardly mentioned, while a detailed description is accorded to the table, the seating of the guests, their clothes, the elegant and sensual atmosphere that must surround and facilitate the encounter between Donna Elena Muti, Duchess of Scerni, and Count Andrea Sperelli: "[He had] a place at one end of the oval table, between the Baron d'Isola and the Duchess of Scerni with the Cavaliere Sakumi as his *vis-à-vis*. Sakumi sat between the Baroness d'Isola and Filippo del Monte. The Marchesa and her husband occupied the two ends of the table, which glittered with rare china, silver, crystal and flowers" (7). The seating of Don Rodrigo's guests at his table in *I promessi sposi* inevitably comes to mind, with the obvious difference that there, the places reflected precise hierarchies of power, while here they serve a strategy of erotic conquest among peers. And while there obsequiousness and hypocrisy were predominant, here elegance shines forth: "Very few women could compete with the Marchesa d'Ateleta in the art of dinner giving. She expended more care in the preparation of a table than of a toilette. Her exquisite taste was patent in every detail, and her word was law in the matter of elegant conviviality. Her fantasies and her refinements were imitated on every table of the Roman aristocracy" (7). For instance, it is she who originates "the fashion of hanging garlands of flowers from one end of the table to the other, on the branches of great candelabras," or "that of placing in front of each guest, among the group of wine glasses, a slender opalescent Murano vase with a single orchid in it" (7). These examples seem paradigmatic illustrations of a liberty or Art Nouveau style that could be found today on the shiny pages of *FMR*. But aside from the mundane and decorative milieu, or perhaps precisely because of it, the Marchesa d'Ateleta's "art of dinner giving" remains quite mysterious as far as the selection and the quality of foods are concerned. Readers, who are not among the guests, are told only that at first "a pale gold wine like liquid honey" is served, followed later on by "iced champagne" (9 and 12), and the former is used solely to underscore Elena Muti's elegance and desirability, who in fact is described "in the act of placing her lips to the glass." Not even the dessert is an exception to the rule of such a strategy:

> As was ever the case at the d'Ateletas', the dinner increased in splendour towards the end; for the true luxury of the table is shown in the dessert. A multitude of choice and exquisite things delighting the eye, beside the palate, were disposed with consummate art in various crystal and silver-mounted dishes. Festoons of camellias and violets hung between the vine-wreathed eighteenth century candelabras, round which sported fauns and nymphs. (13)

All those "choice and exquisite things," not specified any further, that make up the dessert, remain exactly what they are, "things" that are totally generic and don't even receive a name, empty signifiers that the bourgeois reader is invited to fill with imagined, or dreamed of, or desired signifieds. Sight triumphs, and "the palate" remains in the background, confined in an incidental clause between two commas. Such vagueness is of course a calculated one, but in the meantime the dinner is concluded: Elena Muti dips her fingers "into warm water in a pale blue finger-glass rimmed with silver" and suggests that her host "revive the ancient custom of having the water offered to the guests after dinner with a basin and ewer" (14).

Hence, D'Annunzio's strategy of representation corresponds perfectly to that phenomenon studied by Pierre Bourdieu whereby, as far as food is concerned, the high classes (aristocracy and grande bourgeoisie) show an "aesthetic" attitude that privileges form and style above substance; on the contrary, substance, sustenance, is primary and immediate for the lower (popular) classes, which stick to the nitty gritty of the function and necessity of nutrition.[3]

Not satiated, but titillated and made curious, will the reader be luckier at the restaurant—the Doney Restaurant, just opened, where Andrea goes with three young *signori* and four young ladies of the *demi-monde*, and where "oysters" (It. 248) seem a promise? Alas, even here the scene is dominated by explicitly sensual conversations, the guests themselves, and the setting, rather than food. So, for example, Giulia Arici, the voluptuous *linguatica*, is shown "laughing, holding a glass of Chablis in her fingers, which were long and refined enough" (187). Or, in the same episode, almost entirely missing from the English translation: "The conversations were becoming more and more heated in the wines, in the old French wines, smooth and burning, which gave wings and flames to words"—while on the table the china and the silverware "were not too vulgar" (the difference with the classy dinner at the d'Ateletas is obvious) (It. 254). At a certain point, Clara Green "closed her sigh within the circle of a glass filled with champagne," and the narrator comments: "That clear and brilliant wine, which exercises such a prompt and strange influence on women, already was beginning to excite the brains and the matrixes of those four diverse *etàires* in various ways" (It. 255). No wonder if one of them crushes a *fondant* with her elbow and presses it on her friend's mouth, while another one succeeds in eating a *fondant* on her *own* elbow (and a third *fondant* is given later on by Barbarella to Andrea—for his sick horse) (It. 305). For their part, the four men at the restaurant exchange opinions on their respective girlfriends, whom they compare with "certain marmelades from Constantinople, soft as a pastry" or a "Juleb with Parma violets between two Peek-Frean vanilla biscuits"; and the narrator, who is male like them, notices that "Giulia Arici's mouth attracted bites like a juicy fruit" (It. 255). The dinner is concluded with "small glasses of *vieux* cognac" and marks Andrea's return to, not to say plunging again into, "pleasure" after the necessary pause of his convalescence (It. 257), with all the related intoxications and melancholy.

While in the aristocratic dinner the complete lack of foods underscored the sublimation and a certain spiritualization of eros, in the dinner at the restaurant, by contrast, the choice of stereotyped foods (from oysters to *fondants*) and the insistence on drinks (from Chablis to cognac—*vieux* cognac, please) emphasizes a certain vulgarity of eros, barely kept in check by the play of clichés, allusions, and veiled references.

It is then logical that D'Annunzio should insist upon food, intertwining it with sex, only in a scene that is a true narrative turn in the plot of the novel, when Andrea, while having lunch at Caffé Roma with Galeazzo Secìnaro, has to listen to his story of how he had been able to "take" Lady Heathfield, that is, Elena Muti, Andrea's former lover: "He showed neither reserve nor scruples, omitting no single detail, and praising the acquisition to the connoisseur. He only broke off, from time to time, to put his fork into a piece of juicy red meat, or to empty a glass of red wine. His whole bearing was expressive of robust health and strength" (304). On the contrary, Andrea, the defeated lover, "could not bring himself to swallow a mouthful of food, to overcome the nausea of his horribly upset stomach" (304). This is a truly crucial point in the novel, not only for the plot but also for characterization and ideology. Andrea (who does not eat) and Secìnaro (who eats with appetite) are both aristocrats, aesthetes, womanizers. But the former is presented as a model to be followed and imitated, he is sublimated and spiritualized; the latter, no: he is crude, "not subtle" (It. 361), strong and vulgar (he puts his fork into a piece of juicy—bloody—red meat, and empties—does not "sip"—a glass of wine, which is not white, or even better, gold, but red: the sum of these connotations could not be more clear).

Therefore it is necessary to take a closer look at the alimentary habits of Count Andrea Sperelli, and to verify the model D'Annunzio wants to propose with this "genial amateur," who, Raimondi again remarks, "offers to the dissatisfied small bourgeoisie of the Italian provinces a repertoire of attitudes and gestures that translate the discoveries of the Parnassian and symbolist poets of Europe into a practical language":[4] "He rarely dined at home, but for special occasions—some *recherché* love luncheon or private little supper—he had a dining room decorated with eighteenth century Neapolitan tapestries" (177–78). This quotation contains all the elements of D'Annunzio's technique: food is a function of eros explicitly (a love luncheon, a private supper); it is secondary in comparison with the setting—the precious tapestries, which "represented episodes of Bacchic love" (178), "with a certain copious magnificence à la Rubens" (It. 240); it is further removed through the use of the English term "luncheon," less immediate and bodily than the equivalent Italian, and by the attributes (the luncheon is *recherché*, the supper little). Furthermore, when Andrea feels hungry and has his breakfast served in his room, his true act of eating is not even mentioned but is rather displaced metaphorically: "he couldn't stop satiating himself with the view" of the sun shining over Rome (It. 241).

The premises are clear. Food as such is devalued, and eros, luxury, and aesthetic refinement are predominant. Thus reduced, food is part of that minimal touch of realism indispensable for D'Annunzio to build his symbolist text, a text that nowhere as much as here is "texture": the tapestries and the upholsteries of *Il piacere* are true metatextual emblems, they are much more important than the referents of the surrounding society, no matter how precise they may be. For instance, international gastronomy was spreading in fin de siècle Italy, too (with many French and English terms, as we have seen), and the restaurant (next to the more traditional and popular trattoria) was beginning to establish itself as a bourgeois institution, which made available to a larger public the delicacies once reserved for courts and aristocracy.

It is no wonder then that if Andrea eats little and seldom, to make up for it he drinks a lot of tea. To drink is a sublimation in comparison with eating, and "to drink" is a metaphoric network to be found throughout

D'Annunzio and *Il piacere* in particular, as Niva Lorenzini has shown.[5] Tea is the "elegant" drink par excellence, with connotations that are at the same time exotic (Oriental, from India to China) and aristocratic (in that tea was adopted and spread by the British nobility). Tea scans Andrea's worldly life as well as that of other characters. It is served by itself or with cookies or canapés, or with some liquor, or perhaps after a fencing match: it is, in sum, a sign of social distinction (see, for example, pp. 36, 86, 179, 250, 267). But above all, from the very first page of the novel, tea is an indispensable element in Andrea's love affairs. He is introduced as he is waiting for a lover of his: "the small tea-table was ready, with Castel Durante Majolica cups and dishes, decorated with mythological stories" and "Ovid's hexameters" (It. 5), and his lover will indeed preside over the ritual of the tea:

> She began her delicate manipulations—lit the spirit-lamp under the kettle, opened the lacquer tea-caddy and put the necessary quantity of aromatic leaves into the china tea-pot, and finally prepared two cups. Her movements were slow and a little hesitating, as happens when the mind is busied with other things; her exquisite white hands hovered over the cups with the airiness of butterflies. . . . Seated quite close to her, Andrea gazed at her from under his half-closed lids, drinking in the voluptuous fascination emanating from her. (198 and It. 23–24)

This quotation is eloquently Dannunzian: starting from the precise gestures of the preparation of the tea and passing through the butterflies, it culminates in the metaphor of "drinking" not the tea so lovingly prepared, but Elena Muti's "voluptuous fascination"; and she, in turn, arrives at the end of the love visit without having touched her cup, which remains "on the edge of the table, cold, untouched" (It. 32)—almost an omen or a symbol of a problematic relationship and a sad failure.

The entire scene is repeated, with another female protagonist and different modalities, at the end of the novel. Maria Ferres prepares "some precious tea she had received from Calcutta" (286), while Andrea, looking at her, more and more intensely superimposes the image of the other lover, Elena, upon hers, and regrets the loss. "The little cups of fine Castel Durante Majolica still glittered on the tea-table" (286). After pouring "the boiling water on to the aromatic leaves" and inhaling the "delicious fragrance diffused . . . with the steam" (287), with "a mysterious smile" Maria offers a cup of tea to Andrea, who refuses it and asks to drink a sip directly from her mouth. The reader is immediately brought back to a scene a few pages earlier, when Andrea

and Elena had kissed one last time, and their mouths had remembered
"the rapture of bygone mixings, those terrible and yet deliriously sweet
meetings prolonged to anguish and giving their hearts the illusory sensation of a soft and fresh fruit melting inside. They held their breath to
prolong the sip" (245 and It. 296). This whole scene is a literal repetition of another page (It. 93) missing in the English edition, where it
is also stated that a kiss exhausted Andrea and Elena "more than an
embrace": such returns and repetitions (including the Castel Durante
Majolica teacups) are fundamental elements in the structure of the symbolist novel. Now that metaphorical "sip" is about to be concretized and
almost embodied in Maria Ferres:

> She smiled at her lover's whim. He was a bit convulsive, quite pale, his eyes
> altered. They waited for the tea to get cooler. . . .
>
> "Now, take in a good sip. Like that."
>
> She kept her lips tight, to hold the tea: but her great eyes, made even more
> shining by recent tears, were smiling.
>
> "Now pour it, slowly."
>
> He drew the whole sip, sucking it in through the kiss. As she felt her breath
> failing her, she gently spurred the slow drinker by squeezing his temples. . . .
>
> "What taste did it have? You have drunk even my soul. I am all empty."
>
> (It. 343)

In such a manner Andrea "performed the horrible sacrilege on the body
of the unknowing lover" (It. 346). It is not by chance that, as often in
D'Annunzio, the most sensual and physical scenes are spiritualized also
through the use of mystic or religious language (like "you have drunk
even my soul," "the horrible sacrilege"). D'Annunzio appropriates the
tradition of spiritual writers—from Gregory of Nissa to Origen of Alexandria and Richard of Saint Victor, who had systematized the carnal
references in the Holy Scriptures, and particularly the kiss, and considered them as images of the contact with the Divine. But even if it is thus
spiritualized, D'Annunzio's kiss remains heavily human and carnal, as
profane as any ever, and as such it should be appropriately placed in the
gallery of *The Kiss Sacred and Profane* Nicolas J. Perella insightfully set
up.[6] As far back as 1895 Enrico Panzacchi had peremptorily defined
D'Annunzio's "mysticism" as "a form of epicurism," in fact as "an entirely aphrodisiac mysticism, a need of the senses and of the lower senses
at that, not a spiritual need."[7] In any case, the mixing or contamination
of sacred and profane is certainly preeminent in symbolist art, and
D'Annunzio authoritatively belongs in this cultural context and shares
this aesthetic sensitivity.[8]

From the examination carried out so far the premises of D'Annunzio's metaphorical language stand out. The alimentary area is relatively meager in a wide linguistic gamut rich with diversified interests. Furthermore, the metaphorical valence is remarkably diluted precisely because it is mixed with the language of the most nuanced sensory and spiritual sensations.[9] Thus, for example, in the well-known incipit that sets the tone for the entire novel, "The year was dying, quite sweetly" (It. 5), the adverb is completely torn from its etymological origin in order to express a diffuse and delicate sensation—and analogously "sweet" will be a beloved mouth (It. 50) or tears and kisses (It. 92). The word "fruit" is also constantly connected with kisses and loves (It. 93, 119, 137, 246, 296) and is often accompanied by verbs like "eating" and "biting"; also, rhymes have "flavor" (It. 151), and a poetic composition is compared to pouring wine (poetry) in a cup (the metrical form) (103).

But instead of proceeding with a systematic analysis, I prefer to concentrate on two quotations that can be considered, in different ways, as the sum and the emblem of D'Annunzio's art. The first concerns the language used by Andrea Sperelli on certain occasions:

> In the *demi-monde* he adopted a manner and style entirely his own, using grotesque phrases launching the most ridiculous paradoxes or atrocious impertinences under cover of the ambiguity of his words, ununderstandable subtleties, enigmatic madrigals; and all this in most original language, rich in a thousand different flavours, like a Rabelaisian *olla podrida*, full of strong spices and succulent morsels. (185)

Rabelais? strong spices? succulent morsels? Please. The quotation is a true prolonged litotes, it calls attention to what D'Annunzio's language could do but does not do, because his own *olla podrida* does not include Rabelais at all—Rabelais is quite at the opposite pole, both linguistically and ideologically, from D'Annunzio.[10] As much as the one expresses a popular, vigorous, and physical culture, the other expresses an aristocratic, nuanced, and spiritualized one.

If anything, the reference to Rabelais may be useful to show with an exemplary clarity precisely the type of market analysis D'Annunzio lucidly performed:

> The commerce of narrative prose had never been as active as it is now. The sentimental appetite of the multitudes had never reached such a rapid comsumption of literary foods. . . . All the varieties and all the mixtures are offered to the buyers' taste in this great fair of cheap ideals: slightly *faisandé* game, from which the incipient corruption extracts an intense, essential

flavor, as well as pale slices of stringy meat boiled in water without aromas; humble transparent jellies as well as fricassees thick with spices that burn the palate; learned pastiches, in which all the delicacies are harmonized like a symphony, as well as light broths in which unknowable leftovers float.[11]

The commercial terminology (commerce, consumption, buyers, fair, cheap) is coherently intertwined with the metaphorical language (the "sentimental" appetite, and the most unappealing list of literary "foods") precisely because both of them are part of that "vulgar [and very modern] phenomenon," the great development of an "entertainment literature." It is this kind of literature D'Annunzio intends to exploit, with lucid calculation and far-reaching foresight, for his cultural project:

> Between the subtle, passionate, and perverse novel, which the lady tastes with voluptuous slowness waiting in the melancholy of her sitting room, and the novel of bloody adventures, which the plebeian woman devours seated at the counter of her shop, there is only a difference in value. Both volumes are used to satisfy the same need, the same appetite: the need for dreams, a sentimental appetite. In a different way, both volumes delude a restless aspiration to get out of mediocre reality, a vague desire to transcend the narrowness of common life, an almost unconscious longing to live a more fervent and complex life. Having noted the vulgar phenomenon, I draw its consequence: against any funereal prophecy, literature is destined in the near future to an extraordinary development.[12]

This is the reason why D'Annunzio writes, and his faith in the future of literature is based on the exact recognition of the "need for dreams" and of the "sentimental appetite" of the common people—both the bourgeois lady (in the melancholy of her sitting room) and the woman of the *popolo* (the plebeian shopkeeper). D'Annunzio will feed this need and this appetite with appropriate recipes, which will necessarily have to take into consideration the consumers' tastes, partly by satisfying them and partly by guiding them.

Raimondi, importantly, was the first to emphasize D'Annunzio's attention to "the Bovaryism fermenting in the hearts of modern masses" and to the consequences he drew for both consumeristic literature and high art. He wrote of D'Annunzio's constant search, carried out "with unquestionable even if dangerous geniality," for "a true correspondence between literature and the public, through a relationship that is at the same time a market law." In fact, "D'Annunzio's so-called instinct appears also to be essentially the result of a calculation, of an intelligence that, with its own inventions, both seconds and anticipates the anxieties, the hidden furies, of a society in a precarious balance."[13] Sensitive to historical-sociological data as well as to textual elements, Raimondi effectively and accurately defines the "horizon of expectation" on which D'Annunzio's work was being built.

As for me, I must emphasize that D'Annunzio's geniality is also eloquently revealed in the strategies I have analyzed so far: the appetite of the masses is sentimental, and the food to satisfy it must be not only literary, but also spiritual. It is exactly for this reason that food cannot have importance, and so much the less, preeminence, in D'Annunzio's work. In the manipulation of the masses implicit in his aristocratic ideology, every "vulgar" aspect, every bodily need, from sex to food, must be transcended or sublimated. In order to be believed, power must be admired and must surround itself, absolutely, with prestige, beauty, and luxury. And they in turn are transformed into power precisely because they effectively mask its most "poor" and "shameful" aspects.[14]

All this does not mean, of course, that when he speaks of food D'Annunzio does not reveal his voracious geniality as a describer of sensory and sensual perceptions. An exacting reader like E. M. Forster, for example, after about thirty years remembered by heart a sentence from the play *La città morta* spoken by a character who evokes some Sicilian oranges ("We ate oranges as if they were bread"—but the original is, "mordevamo la polpa succulenta come si morde il pane") and emphasized its strength: "It brought out the taste of the newly picked fruit and the feeling of it between the lips and the teeth; not pulp, not juice, but a unity, bread-like, divine."[15] Forster's memory mechanism simplifies the original text greatly by fusing the hendiadys "polpa succulenta" with the effect of the action expressed twice by the verb "mordere." But if Forster's memory is philologically imprecise, the critical observation derived from it is right, it is almost another proof of the evocative power of the Dannunzian text. Furthermore these oranges, introduced "amidst the aridities of Greece," give importance to the fate of the characters, "like the peaches and pears surrounding a Crivelli Madonna."[16] How different, by contrast, are the oranges Vittorini's Sicilians eat "desperately" in *Conversazione in Sicilia*. Or better, the fruit (the referent) is the same, and its connotations, its textual functions, its figures, and its meanings are different.[17]

But going back to D'Annunzio, Forster also recalls the numerous lists (of fruits, mottoes, perfumes, horses, villas, women, dogs) that point out the aesthetic sources preferred by the author, and adds a very pertinent remark: "Most of these, including the women, had to be renamed after the poet handled them, so that he might have an additional sense of power."[18] A similar itinerary, from carnal sensuosity to beauty and from beauty to power, characterizes D'Annunzio's entire aestheticism, which was conceived as a deliberate reply to the modern. In fact, this itinerary can be traced in other works by D'Annunzio. For instance in *Il fuoco* of 1900, the protagonist, Stelio Effrena, boards a fishermen's boat in the Venetian lagoon, carrying with him a loaf of bread "still warm from the oven," grapes, and "Malamocco figs"; he is inebriated by the sea breeze "in the purple splendor of the sail" and his experience is concluded by a thought and a sensation of power: "To create with joy! And the world was his."[19]

These considerations on power—political power in general and D'Annunzio's creative and cultural power in particular—confirm and reinforce the design that is the very foundation of the expressive and representative strategy of *Il piacere*. But it is now time to turn our attention to the second and conclusive quotation from this novel. On the surface, and considered literally within its context, this quotation concerns the judgment that Andrea Sperelli formulates about Elena Muti: "She covered the erotic needs of her flesh with ethereal flames and was able to transform a low appetite into a high sentiment. . . . In this way, with this ferocity, Andrea judged the woman whom he adored once. . . . That magic wine which earlier on had inebriated him now seemed to him a perfidious mixture" (It. 268). Undoubtedly, the double metaphor of the magic wine turned into a perfidious mixture is quite appropriate to express the feeling of the male character as well as the nature of the woman; and it is reflected back onto him, showing him completely similar to her.

But what could and should be added, at a different level of reading, is that the ferocious judgment of the character is to be applied metatextually to the author and his style. In *Il piacere*, indeed, it is D'Annunzio himself who wants and knows how to "transform a low appetite into a high sentiment." The juxtaposition between the two adjectives "high" and "low," related one to "sentiment" and the other to "appetite," expresses a hierarchy of moral and aesthetic values through a spatial metaphor that is fundamental for the structure of the text, according to a semiotician like Juri Lotman,[20] in that it reveals the text's ideology. Finally, and perhaps even more fundamentally, the metaphorical use of "appetite" must be strongly emphasized because it indicates that the transformation is a sublimation, and that to achieve it D'Annunzio's genius only needs a few cups of tea.

CHAPTER 4

A Wise Gourmet:
Giuseppe Tomasi di Lampedusa,
Il Gattopardo

A GOURMET and curious reader, wandering through the textual universe of Giuseppe Tomasi di Lampedusa's *Il Gattopardo* and searching for good food or even some delicacy, will not be disappointed. After the frustrations caused by D'Annunzio's ideological and communicative strategies, and perhaps after feeling his/her mouth watering through the first chapter of Antonio Fogazzaro's *Piccolo mondo antico*, with that aroma of truffles alternatively asserted and questioned, preparing the way for a northern, noble risotto, this hypothetical reader will find satisfaction for his/her appetite in the Sicily of the Leopard.

Beginning to whet this appetite, I could start by saying that the whole of *Il Gattopardo* is extremely rich with alimentary referents, and that even the minimal ones among them are important because they contribute to the representative coherence of the text and to the presentation of settings and characters.[1] For example, some Bourbon officers are "eating huge iced *granite*" in a Palermitan café (35), while in a pause during the voyage to Donnafugata Don Fabrizio "had found thirteen flies in his glass of *granita*" (73); Don Onofrio is the administrator of the Salina estate, and he is so honest that he has kept for an entire year a small glass of *rosolio* liquor "once left half-full by the Princess," because even if its contents had evaporated and were "reduced to a state of sugary rubber," still it was "an infinitesimal part of the Prince's patrimony" (79)—and the Prince does not hesitate to subject his legendarily faithful servant "to the torture of tea" (80).

Actually tea is not a favorite drink in this novel, whose setting is aristocratic but southern nevertheless: the more traditional coffee is preferred, from the "black coffee with Monreale biscuits" Father Pirrone has after his Mass (50) to "the nuns' light coffee" at the Monastery of the

Holy Spirit, served with their "pink and greenish almond cakes" prepared according to centuries-old recipes (105); even Angelica's maid,
instead of accompanying her in her visits to the princely palace, "would
vanish into the servants' quarters to drink coffee and make the unfortunate domestics gloomy" (181), and coffee is served again during the
visits of Father Pirrone to Uncle Turi, of Monsignor the Vicar to Villa
Salina, and of the cardinal of Palermo to the three Salina sisters. On this
occasion, the cardinal politely does not even touch the "sumptuous re-
freshments" prepared for him, accepts only a glass of water, and departs
leaving behind Don Picchiotti, who for his part accepts "a cup of coffee
and a *baba*" (317–18) before sifting through the relics. Also Don Fabrizio, as the true Sicilian he is, appreciates the goodness of a glass of
water at the Ponteleone ball, soon after noticing Don Calogero, who
discusses "a possible rise in the price of *caciocavallo* cheese" (259–60).

Every occasion and every character have the appropriate food or drink:
thus, punch, biscuits, and cognac are offered to Tancredi and Cavriaghi
when they arrive, dripping wet, at Villa Salina; when he returns home,
Father Pirrone is happy to find that "from the kitchen arose the centuries-
old aroma of simmering meat sauce made of extract of tomatoes, onions,
and goat's meat, for the *anelletti* pasta of festive occasions"—a dish he
greatly enjoys since his palate "had not been spoiled by the culinary delicacies of Villa Salina" (221–22). In order to describe Don Calogero's
avarice, Don Ciccio Tumeo recalls that "when his daughter was at
school he and his wife used to eat a fried egg between them" (138). And
to console his friend Cavriaghi, disappointed in his courtship of Concetta, Tancredi tells him that she, being "Sicilian to the very marrow,"
probably would never feel at home in Milan, "a *paesaccio* where one has
to arrange a week ahead for a plate of macaroni"—and the narrator
ironically comments that "Tancredi's little joke" was "one of the earliest expressions of national unity" (192). Also, the Piedmontese envoy
Chevalley finds that "the oil in the cooking [of Sicily] had upset his
insides" (195); among the causes of the ugliness of the noble Palermitan
girls the Prince sees gathered at the Ponteleone ball there are "the
dearth of proteins and overabundance of starch in the food" (255); and
even some Sicilians who had voted "no" at the plebiscite had done so for
personal reasons, because "during the upsets of the liberation period
they had lost some capons and sacks of beans, and had gained instead
some pair of horns" (that is, they had been cuckolded) (128).

Even in these brief examples of minimal referentiality, some characteristics should be noted that are going to be found again, coherently, at

the more demanding levels of the text: the connotations of the characters and the social classes, the references to history and settings, the connection with eros. Let us see then how food enters remarkably in *Il Gattopardo* in the description of the customs of the Sicilian nineteenth-century aristocracy, in the analysis of a precise historical-political situation, and in the characterization of the protagonists. I shall focus in particular on three episodes, or textual moments, which I have chosen for their clear structural and contextual importance: the dinner at Villa Salina, the solemn dinner at Donnafugata, and the buffet at the ball in the Ponteleone Palace.[2]

Luncheon is the major meal at Villa Salina, and it takes place in the first chapter, against the background of Garibaldi's landing in Sicily in May 1861, Tancredi's "revolutionary" choice, the Prince's sensual and Concetta's chaste desires. But this luncheon is not described in detail. The reader knows from the preceding description of the dinner, "served with the shabby grandeur then customary in the Kingdom of the Two Sicilies," that the Prince loves to exercise his authority and his "nutritive functions as paterfamilias" (28). In fact, he is surrounded by the emblems of his power, such as the large Capodimonte dishes "with a wide almond-green border, engraved with little gilt anchors" or the "prancing Leopard" surmounting the "enormous soup tureen"; and he dominates the table with a circular glance of his blue eyes, which "numb" his family "with fear" and make everybody respect the rules of etiquette according to a ritual that is essential to the very nature of aristocracy. Therefore, when it is time for luncheon, the narrator's attention is completely (and *pour cause*) focused on the dessert:

> At the end of the meal appeared a rum jelly. This was the Prince's favorite pudding, and the Princess had been careful to order it early that morning in gratitude for consolations received. It was rather threatening at first sight, shaped like a tower with bastions and battlements and smooth slippery walls impossible to scale, garrisoned by red and green cherries and pistachio nuts; but into its transparent and quivering flanks a spoon plunged with astounding ease. By the time the amber-colored fortress reached Francesco Paolo, the sixteen-year-old son, who was served last, it consisted only of shattered walls and hunks of wobbly rubble. Exhilarated by the aroma of rum and the delicate flavor of the multicolored garrison, the Prince enjoyed watching the rapid demolishing of the fortress beneath the assault of his family's appetites. (56)

It is a delightful and delicious description. The goodness of the dish is completely transfused into the allusive and metaphorical language, which harks back from the table to history (a bit earlier on the same page the Prince had been explaining that the barrels of the Royal Army's muskets "had no rifling" and were therefore extremely ineffective, and so he "managed to transform war into a neat little diagram of fire-trajectories from the very squalid and very positive chaos that it really was"), and from the table to the bedroom (the "consolations" the Princess had received).[3] Hence history, bearer of death, and eros, bearer of pleasure, are intimately connected and present in this scene, and the enjoyment felt by the Prince in tasting and seeing the others taste his favorite dessert is a synecdoche for his love of life, a love that is all the more intense in that he is the character who knows death more consciously than any other.[4] The fact that food, which is precisely an affirmation of life, plays such an evident and significant role—beyond any referential and realistic function—indicates Tomasi di Lampedusa's great psychological and artistic sensitivity. His definition of Stendhal as a writer characterized by a "delicate epicurism" could be applied to him as well, although tempered and completed by his own skepticism toward history.[5]

The second memorable scene is the dinner Don Fabrizio offers to the major citizens of Donnafugata, with "the stamp of solemnity" that dictates its modalities and emphasizes its social function:[6] "children under fifteen were excluded from table, French wines were served, there was punch *alla Romana* before the roast; and the flunkeys were in powder and knee-breeches" (92). Given his bourgeois guests, the Prince forgoes only one detail of the ritual, he does not dress up for the evening, so that the fact that Don Calogero arrives in tails causes a sensation: sensitive as he is "to presages and symbols," the Prince immediately understands that "that white tie and two black tails" are a true epitome of the "revolution" under way (92–93). Undoubtedly, the ugly but appropriate bourgeois tails moving in the noble Salina house are one of those little changes necessary "if we want things to stay as they are" (40), according to Tancredi's foresight. As for the menu: "The Prince was too experienced to offer Sicilian guests, in a town of the interior, a dinner beginning with soup, and he infringed the rules of *haute cuisine* all the more readily as he disliked it himself" (96). The juxtaposition between *haute cuisine* (obviously French in origin: one should also remember that the cook of the Salinas is "Monsú Gaston") and the "town of the interior" could not be more marked. It corresponds perfectly, in the nuanced and ironic language of the novel, to the historical development of European gastronomy and to that phenome-non, noted by Revel, whereby international cuisine and local or provin-cial (not national) tradition are the two poles that, with ever increasing strength, dictate the rules and influence tastes and preferences at the table.[7] At Donnafugata, then, in 1861,

> rumors of the barbaric foreign usage of serving insipid liquid as first course had reached the major citizens . . . too insistently for them not to quiver with a slight residue of alarm at the start of a solemn dinner like this. So when three lackeys in green, gold, and powder entered, each holding a great silver dish containing a towering timbale of macaroni, only four of the twenty at table avoided showing their pleased surprise: the Prince and Princess from foreknowledge, Angelica from affectation, and Concetta from lack of appe-tite. (96)

Here the irony of the narrator is not only linguistic (the Italian text has "brodaglia," a derogatory form of "brodo," for soup), but also, and above all, psychological: it is directed toward the reactions of the guests as indexes of their respective characters. In particular, this occasion also reaffirms the primacy of the Prince, whose "threatening circular stare" stifles the "improper demonstrations" of his guests' too-evident sur-prise. But before developing the characters at table, the narrator turns his eyes (and nose) to the monumental dish being served:

> Good manners apart, though, the appearance of those Babel-like dishes of macaroni was worthy of the quivers of admiration they evoked. The bur-nished gold of the crusts, the fragrance of sugar and cinnamon they exuded, were but preludes to the delights released from the interior when the knife broke the crust; first came a mist laden with aromas, then chicken livers, small hard-boiled eggs, sliced ham, chicken, and truffles in masses of piping-hot, glistening macaroni, to which the meat juice gave an exquisite hue of suède. (96–97)

I believe that not even Artusi, who masterfully describes a macaroni *pasticcio all'uso di Romagna*, could compete with Tomasi di Lampedusa's aristocratic and refined elegance ("burnished gold, fragrance, preludes, delights, exquisite hue of suède") in the presentation of his timbale, a recipe that, after all, originated in Italian Renaissance courts.[8]

The reader can only enjoy the sumptuous dish vicariously, following the guests at the Prince's table: the organist "was grateful to the Creator that his ability to shoot hare and woodcock could bring him ecstatic pleasures like this, and the thought came to him that he and Teresina could exist for a month on the cost of just one of these timbales" (97); the beautiful Angelica "forgot her Tuscan *migliaccini* and part of her good manners and devoured her food with the appetite of her seventeen years and the vigor derived from grasping her fork halfway up the handle" (97); in a vain effort "to link gallantry and greed," Tancredi "tried to imagine himself tasting, in the aromatic forkfuls, the kisses of his neighbor Angelica"; Don Fabrizio, although he, too, is "rapt in the contemplation of Angelica," is "the only one able to note that the *demi-glace* was too rich, and made a mental note to tell the cook so next day"; and the other guests "ate without thinking of anything, and without realizing that the food seemed so delicious because a whiff of sensuality had wafted into the house" when Angelica had entered it (97).

Not by chance, in fact, the description of the timbale and the guests is entirely played between gastronomy and sensuality. The dinner at Donnafugata is a narrative sign, a turning point in the plot of the novel, in that the aristocratic Concetta (without much appetite) loses her undeclared duel with the bourgeois (and voracious) Angelica. Tancredi is fascinated by the sensual aura of the girl, and tells a salacious anecdote about his military experience, when his friend Tassoni, a Garibaldi volunteer, had teased some frightened old nuns: "Nothing doing, sisters, . . . but we'll be back when you've got some novices," and concludes for the benefit of Angelica: "Had you been there, Signorina, we'd have had no need to wait for novices" (99–100)—at which, Concetta, proud and indignant, "turned her back on him" (101). Only at the end of the novel, fifty years later, during a visit by Angelica and Senator Tassoni, will Concetta learn that Tancredi's anecdote was invented, that maybe he was in love with her, and that her own attitude had made him give up— in fact, she will remember, indeed see the scene, "very distant but quite clear, as if through the other end of a telescope: the big white table [of the dinner at Donnafugata] surrounded by all those people now dead" (309). This image, evoked with great constructive mastery at the end of the novel, calls back circularly the beginning, retrospectively explains its narrative development, and concentrates its temporal and psychological pathos in a Stendhalian manner.[9]

But in the meantime, one must note that the presentation of the aristocratic meals is constantly tied to the concept of good manners: an indispensable concept, which has a central place in contemporary thought, from Lévi-Strauss to Elias,[10] and which is hinted at and em-

phasized in *Il Gattopardo* on numerous occasions and from various viewpoints, but always as a distinctive sign of an entire social class. In fact,
precisely through the customs, the codes, and the models expressed by
good manners, aristocracy has been able to exercise its preeminence and
power, even political power (not by chance are good manners and con-
servatism contiguous phenomena).[11] I shall mention only a few significant examples. Don Calogero is fascinated by the Prince's education
and elegance (a "well-bred man" who "eliminates the unpleasant aspects
of so much of the human condition") and slowly comes to understand,
among other things, that "a meal in common need not necessarily be all
munching and grease stains" (161–62); Father Pirrone, recalling the
rage felt by the Prince of Làscari for being "wrongly placed at one of the
Viceroy's dinners," concludes that "a human being who is put out only
by . . . protocol must be happy, and thus superior" (227); and even Don
Fabrizio concludes his dialogue with Chevalley with self-ironic words:
"we must go and dress for dinner. For a few hours I have to act the part
of a civilized man" (213).

   After the historical turning point of Tancredi's revolutionary choice,
recalled during the first dinner at Villa Salina; after the social turning
point of the ascent of the bourgeoisie, emblematized in Don Calogero's
tails at the solemn dinner at Donnafugata, and Concetta's defeat during
this same meal, the third episode on which I wish to dwell—the ball at
Ponteleone Palace, with its buffet—seals the definitive insertion of a
certain bourgeoisie (Angelica the fiancée of Tancredi) into the Palermitan nobility, at the very moment when this nobility celebrates its
ephemeral last triumph. Here one can measure in its entirety the difference existing between D'Annunzio's aestheticism (with the related expressive strategies: for instance the dinner by the Marchesa D'Ateleta
examined in the previous chapter) and Tomasi di Lampedusa's histori-
cism (made up of skepticism and epicurism).

   Tomasi di Lampedusa devotes only one paragraph to the description
of the "long, narrow table" for the buffet, with "the famous twelve
silver-gilt candelabra given to Diego's grandfather by the Court of
Madrid at the end of his embassy in Spain"; and in this paragraph, a
sentence deals with the aesthetic quality of the artifacts, one with their
possible economic worth according to Sedàra, and one with the memories of the Prince (265–66). Then comes the triumph of the aristocratic
buffet, which no reader of *Il piacere* has ever been able to experience, and
which is worth quoting extensively:

Beneath the candelabra, beneath the five tiers bearing toward the distant ceiling pyramids of homemade cakes that were never touched, spread the monotonous opulence of buffets at big balls: coralline lobsters boiled alive, waxy *chaud-froids* of veal, steely-tinted fish immersed in sauce, turkeys gilded by the ovens' heat, rosy *foie gras* under gelatin armor, boned woodcock reclining on amber toast decorated with their own chopped insides, and a dozen other cruel, colored delights. At the end of the table two monumental silver tureens held clear soup the color of burnt amber. To prepare this supper the cooks must have sweated away in the vast kitchens from the night before. (266)

With such opulence there is only the embarrassment of choosing. Each of the many high cuisine delicacies is presented with nomenclatorial precision, knowledge of both the ingredients and the procedures, care for the aspects and the colors of the final result. There is even an epic touch, just hinted at in the spatial dimension of the "distant" ceiling and in the conclusive plural nouns (the cooks in the vast kitchens). But the buffet is not concluded here. In fact, there is also the table with desserts, presented with a precise and at the same time baroque language in which a proper noun (*Mont Blanc*) generates, by metonymic-metaphorical coupling, a chain of geographic signifiers (hillocks, plain), followed by other musical metaphors, and completed by denominations that originate in a cultural, sensual-religious context:

Huge blond *babas*, *Mont Blancs* snowy with whipped cream, cakes speckled with white almonds and green pistachio nuts, hillocks of chocolate-covered pastry, brown and rich as the topsoil of the Catanian plain from which, in fact, through many a twist and turn they had come, pink ices, champagne ices, coffee ices, all *parfaits*, which fell apart with a squelch as the knife cleft them, melody in major of crystallized cherries, acid notes of yellow pineapple, and those cakes called "triumphs of gluttony" filled with green pistachio paste, and shameless "virgins' cakes" shaped like breasts. (266–67)

The Prince limits himself to picking two of the latter, again uniting gluttony and eros, discreetly and ironically: "as he held them in his plate," he "looked like a profane caricature of St. Agatha"—and his half-scandalized, half-amused thoughts are interesting, too: "Why ever didn't the Holy Office forbid these cakes when it had the chance? 'Triumphs of gluttony' (gluttony, one of the deadly sins!) and St. Agatha's sliced-off breasts sold by convents, devoured at dances! Well, well!" (267). Still later, the Prince has "a slice of *Mont Blanc* and a glass of champagne" (269), which are the background for his conversation with Colonel Pallavicino, with the related gentlemanly "skepticism," military memories, and socio-political prophecies about the disquieting future of united Italy (271).

The Prince's temperance is an indication of his character, as well as a structural device to develop the narration; and as such, it is also a prelude to the end of the ball, with the inevitable sense of satiety and even disgust that follow a too-intense or prolonged pleasure: "In the empty supper room were only dirty plates, glasses with dregs of wine which the servants glancing around would hurriedly drain; through the cracks in the shutters filtered a plebeian light of dawn" (271).

This quotation can be used as a link for a series of referents that associate food and death—such as the head of a kidnapped victim returned to the family "in a great big basket, under a layer of figs," or a priest killed in his church, "liturgically," so to speak, with "poison in the Communion wine" (198–99); or "our spiced and drugged sherbets," which in the Prince's peroration with Chevalley become "a hankering for voluptuous immobility, that is, for death again" (206). From their materiality, these referents point to the Prince's attitude toward death. He gives a valuable indication of it when he explains to Father Pirrone, at the beginning of the novel: "Let's leave the Bendicòs down there running after rustic prey, and the cooks' knives chopping the flesh of innocent beasts. Above this observatory the bluster of the one and the blood on the other merge into tranquil harmony. The real problem is how to go on living this life of the spirit in its most sublimated moments, those moments that are most like death" (54). The death evoked here is not the death of the flesh, the death that follows physical decadence and provokes disgust because of the putrefaction of viscera (like those of the dead soldier in the garden), but is its exact opposite, "life of the spirit": in his astronomic observatory the Prince always tries to overcome the disgust for physical death (the cooks' bloodiness) in his mathematical abstractions and contemplation of the stars.

However, daily life is filled with reminders of physical death. Even the *carnaggi*, the portions of rent paid in kind, remind the Prince of the "gutted soldier of a month before," because they include, beside cheeses and hens, also "six baby lambs" just killed, "with their heads lolling pathetically above the big gash through which their lifeblood had flowed a few hours before," and with their bellies "slashed open too, and iridescent intestines hung out" (57–58). The same thing occurs after the ball, when the Prince walks out of the Ponteleone Palace: "There was already a little movement in the streets: . . . A long open wagon came by stacked with bulls killed shortly before at the slaughterhouse, already quartered and exhibiting their intimate mechanism with the shamelessness of death. At intervals a big thick red drop fell onto the pavement" (272). It is also because of such a sad scene that Don Fabrizio turns to look at the stars, and particularly Venus, the "always faithful": "When would she decide to give him an appointment less ephemeral, far from carcasses and blood, in her own region of perennial certitude?" (273). One should remember that when the Prince had seen it the first time, after the hunt, "Venus still glimmered, a peeled grape, damp and transparent" (112): the grape is as desirable and appetizing as the carcasses and blood are disgusting, but both are part of a vital and spiritual experience and attitude that are extremely coherent, played between the contingent and the absolute.

Beside the referents carrying an existential and ideological meaning, in *Il Gattopardo* there is a whole series of comparisons, metaphors, metonymies, and symbols—more or less explicit, more or less elaborate, but all related to alimentary signs—that are fundamental and characterizing elements of writing, and at the same time, at the stylistic level, they complete the protagonist's vision of the world. Among them there stand out those which are a commentary or a judgment on what Manzoni would have called "Historie," here duly lowered to history: a basically motionless history of landowners, classes, and sovereigns, diverse but essentially similar, if not worse than their predecessors. For example: "the abolition of feudal rights had swept away [aristocracy's] duties as well as privileges; wealth, like an old wine, had let the dregs of greed, even of care and prudence, fall to the bottom of the barrel" (43); Tancredi's famous sentence, "If we want things to stay as they are, things will have to change," also means, for the Prince, that the "cherry-colored ribbon of St. Januarius" will be replaced by "the pistachio-colored ribbon of the Order of St. Maurice" (48–49); when Don Fabrizio drinks "to the health of our Tancredi" at the end of the dinner we examined, "the initials F. D. [Ferdinandus Dedit] which before had stood out clearly on the golden color of the full glass were no longer visible" (57), and along with them, the Bourbon rule symbolically disappears. Conversely, on the occasion of the plebiscite, in the study of the mayor Don Calogero Sedàra a small refreshment is served, with "some ancient biscuits covered mournfully with fly droppings and a dozen little squat glasses brimming with rosolio: four red, four green, four white, the last in the center"—indeed, "an ingenuous symbol of the new national flag which tempered the Prince's remorse with a smile. He chose the white liquor for himself, presumably because the least indigestible and not, as some thought, a tardy homage to the Bourbon standard" (130).

Other details are written with the same ironic and demystifying spirit: Don Ciccio Tumeo had voted "no" at the plebiscite, and he sincerely protests against the officially unanimous results: "Those swine in the Town Hall just swallowed up my opinion, chewed it, and then spat it out transformed as they wanted" (133); his conclusion, in tone with the language of his protest, is geared around the play on the word "Savoyards," meaning both the supporters of the new Savoy House and a traditional type of biscuits: "Now they are all Savoyards! But Savoyards, I eat them with my coffee, I eat!" and "holding a fictive biscuit between his thumb and index finger he dipped it into an imaginary cup" (It. 76–77). Certainly the Prince is no less effective when he mentally compares the offer to become a senator of the Kingdom of Italy to the gift of a *pecorino* cheese by a poor peasant: "The difficulty is that the cheese is nauseating" (202).[13]

Another type of quotation can be grouped around Angelica and Tancredi, beginning with the official marriage proposal made by Don Fabrizio to Don Calogero, which is compared with the act of swallowing a toad (109). Here alimentary referents are used in various combinations and at various levels, from the descriptive to the metonymic and the metaphorical. For example, on Angelica's large straw hat "bunches of artificial grapes and golden ears of wheat discreetly evoked the vineyards of Gibildolce and the granaries of Settesoli" (163), that is, the girl's substantial dowery. The metaphorical possibilities of the narrator's allusion are duly developed soon afterwards from Tancredi's point of view: "He really felt as if by those kisses he were taking possession of Sicily once more, of the lovely faithless land which the Falconeris had lorded over for centuries and which now, after a vain revolt, had surrendered to him again, as always to his people, its carnal delights and its golden crops" (178). Never as here is the nephew similar to his uncle: they are linked by the war language ("revolt, surrendered"), the masters' language ("possession, lorded over"), the language of eroticism ("carnal delights"), and that of economics ("golden crops"), unified by a tone that is both lyric and epic, ample and melancholic, expressive of an aristocratic spirit.

The whole courting of Angelica by Tancredi is carried out under an alimentary sign that has the narrative function of preparing and emphasizing the action: "the foreign peaches" the Prince loves, "big, velvety, luscious-looking" (90). In the dialogue between the uncle and the nephew, these peaches are "products of love, of coupling" (as the Prince says), "but legal love, blessed by you as their master, and by Nino the gardener as notary. Considered, fruitful love" (as Tancredi replies) (90–91). This is an extraordinarily dense and allusive page, in which the freshness and the beauty of the product of the earth stand for the beauty and the freshness of Angelica, a "peach" that, coming from the bourgeoisie, is "foreign" for the aristocratic protagonists and will become immediately the object of carnal desires as well as patrimonial calculations.

In fact, the care the narrator uses in underlining these peaches is noteworthy. They are brought by "a lackey carrying a tasselled box" (107) the first time Tancredi visits Angelica, and they arouse the curiosity and the gossip of the entire town, which had discussed at length "the aphrodisiac and seductive properties of those dozen peaches" and had even "consulted the most expert witches and abstruse treatises on potion" (141). There is also a sweet-and-sour side to this story, when, after two months, Concetta reminds the Prince of the "theft" of these peaches by Tancredi, and "then she suddenly looked dour, as if she were chairwoman of an association for owners of damaged orchards" (166).

But if the seductive peaches are also a metonymy for Angelica's beauty, they are not enough to describe and celebrate her adequately. Angelica is not perfect, far from it, but her "numerous" defects simply are not noticed by men, who are overwhelmed by her beauty from her very first appearance at Villa Salina, her triumphal entrance for the dinner at Donnafugata: "She was tall and well made, on an ample scale; her skin looked as if it had the flavor of fresh cream, which it resembled; her childlike mouth, that of strawberries" (94).[14] In order for the comparison not to pass unnoticed, given also its obviousness, it is recalled and emphasized later on when Don Calogero informs the Prince that Angelica and Tancredi "were seen to kiss on Tuesday, the twenty-fifth of September, . . . in your garden, near the fountain" (147)—that is, in the very place where the dialogue on the peaches between the uncle and the nephew had occurred. Don Fabrizio, a "man not yet decrepit," is stung by "carnal jealousy": "Tancredi had tasted that flavor of strawberries and cream which to him would always be unknown" (147). And again, at the ball, Angelica refuses all the invitations to dance except Tancredi's, showing her *carnet* completely taken by the "possessive signature: Falconeri" and dispensing "a smile from her strawberry lips" (here the comparison has become an epithet) to each young man denied the pleasure of dancing with her (252). I don't think it is necessary to contrive further with the network of this lexicon, which is both erotic and gastronomic.

Rather, it is worth emphasizing that in *Il Gattopardo* the fusion of the two lexical areas, of eros and food, is particularly effective because they are perhaps the fittest to express the richness and fugacity of life, all the more so in that the Prince is always and lucidly aware of death at the point of "courting" her, as Tancredi tells him (262). Hence it will not be surprising to find another alimentary comparison in the very chapter of the death of the Prince: "He did feel sleepy; but he found that to give way to drowsiness now would be as absurd as eating a slice of cake immediately before a longed-for banquet. He smiled. 'I've always been a wise gourmet.' And he sat there, immersed in that great outer silence, in the terrifying inner rumble" (284). By comparing a slice of cake to drowsiness and a banquet to death, these images turn upside down the cliché of the banquet of life and fully express the protagonist's character. His gluttony and wisdom tend to possess, as much as humanly possible and without illusions, the pleasures of the flesh and of the spirit, the golden domains of Sicily, the riches of the world. And his gluttony and wisdom also strive to understand the inevitable flight of time, and hence to enjoy pleasures and riches with the intensity that only the acceptance of death, this eternal and not by chance longed-for "banquet," can give. A similar imagery is to be found in the short story "Lighea," when the old senator Rosario La Ciura tells his young friend Paolo Corbera di Salina, the narrator, about the incredible encounter he had when he was a young man, too, with the beautiful mermaid Lighea, "daughter of Calliope." She spoke ancient Greek, was both beastly and immortal, and taught him everything that he could only long for in his normal, mortal life: "She was already bringing to my mouth that flavor of pleasure which compared to your earthy kisses is like wine to tap water."[15]

Skeptic and epicurean, Don Fabrizio Salina, too, meets his "Lighea," who comes to fetch him on his deathbed, finally, in the form a beautiful, desirable, longed-for feminine vision. And he is absolutely right: he is a gourmet because he is wise—he enjoys the pleasures of the world because he knows the disgust and the death of the body; and he is wise because he is a gourmet—he desires the absoluteness of death because he has felt the transitoriness and limitedness of earthly pleasures. The two terms are actually a hendiadys. A wise gourmet indeed.

CHAPTER 5

The Cornucopia of the World:
Carlo Emilio Gadda, *La cognizione del dolore*
and *Quer pasticciaccio brutto de via Merulana*

IN A DELIGHTFUL divertissement entitled "La casa," the engineer Carlo
Emilio Gadda tells about his architectural, building, and interior deco-
rating preferences.[1] He takes particular care in praising the chamber
pot, the "capacious terracotta vase of the poet Parini," which holds at
least "two liters" (136–37), as well as the wide "john" equipped with a
"superb throne" made of "mahogany board and anti-rust hinges, with
such dimensions and such a shape as to avoid any possible exorbitance"
of the parts sitting on it, and designed in such a way that "the water does
not spurt up with ice cold splutters on the user's glutei, after the fall of
the body" (147–48). On this throne he, "august like a king," will be able
to meditate "in sweet and free fantasies" (149).[2] More modestly, even
though equally comfortably, Mr. Leopold Bloom in James Joyce's *Ulysses* is satisfied with reading the newspaper while "asquat on the cuck-
stool," and continues reading "seated calm above his own rising smell"[3];
and his wife Molly develops a part of her famous monologue at the end
of the novel while using a chamber pot that does not have "a natural size
so that a woman could sit on it properly" (as she wishes),[4] but would not
lose in comparison with the Parinian terracotta vase preferred by the
narrator of "La casa."

In any case, once the "lower" bodily functions and the connected bourgeois and even idiosyncratic comforts have been so nicely foregrounded,
Gadda can feel at ease and talk about a delicious dinner he ate:

> I availed myself, with excellent appetite and exquisite refinement, of the fol-
> lowing dishes:
> —Homemade *cappelletti* in capon broth.
> —Carloforte lobster with tartar sauce.

—Private reserve pheasant in the oven with chestnuts.

—Salmis of young hare.

—Sweet fruits and iced grapes.

All this with moderate sipping of French and Italian wines. (155–56)

It is a festive, not an everyday menu, which could figure well, with its sequence of soup, boiled meat, roast, stew, sweets, and fruits, among the "Dinner Notes" suggested by Pellegrino Artusi in the appendix of his *La scienza in cucina e l'arte di mangiar bene*.[5] But this menu is remarkable above all because it indicates the author's primary interest in cookery, an interest that is here almost a pretext (if not pre-text) for his typically literary taste for verbal play and deformation, at the expense of the guests at table.[6] There is no reason to doubt his "exquisite refinement" in availing himself of all the listed dishes: both the refinement and the dishes are consonant with the figure of the writer, who nominates himself "Prince of Analysis and Duke of Good Cognizance" (152), jokingly, but not too much, and never forgets that he is an engineer, a Milanese, and a bourgeois.

A different, and more complex case will develop for a character who appears later on and who has his origins also in the habits and preferences described in "La casa" (beside, of course, "Novella seconda"): Gonzalo Pirobutirro d'Eltino in *La cognizione del dolore*.[7] Mediated by the hygienic-sanitary reflection of the good doctor, filtered through the "baroque tales" (42) of the folks of Pastrufazio, framed between the mountain peaks of the landscape, "gelid diadem of eternity" (40), and the "catty ground" of a "very tenebrous den" (44), Gonzalo's portrait stands out in the first part of *La cognizione del dolore* as that of a man who is "voracious, and greedy for food and for wine," and devoted to "crapulous banquets" (39):

> In 1928 people had said, the gentlemen and ladies of Pastrufazio among the first, that he had been on the point of death in Babylon after having swallowed a sea urchin; others said it was a crab, a kind of sea scorpion colored a scarlet color rather than black . . . ; some mythologized also about a swordfish or a brooch fish—oh yes! tiny, barely born—which he must have swallowed whole. . . . They said the tail then flapped for a long time outside his mouth, like a second tongue he could no longer retract, and came close to suffocating him. (42)

The hyperbolic exaggeration of this anecdote related orally has to do with the very nature of the "horrendous crustacean" that is not properly identified and can therefore take on the most diversified shapes, from the urchin to the brooch fish, without neglecting the comparison between the tail of the ichthyoid and the tongue of the glutton.

As for the latter, his "concupiscence" is described in a crescendo of moralistic connotations and physiognomic deformations whose effects are truly devastating:

> The almost fatal lobster assumed the proportions of a human infant: and he, with a nutcracker, and pressing hard—harder!—both elbows on the table, had fiercely crushed its claws, coral-colored as they were, and had removed from them the best part, his eyes supergleaming with concupiscence and then squinting more and more inwardly, since aimed on the prey to which he neared, his nostrils flaring desirously, the obscene sucker of that mouth!— foul entrail that he had in anticipation extruded to approach the longed-for voluptuousness. Such an animal, in Babylon, according to the legend, they hadn't seen before or since. And he had had the nerve, the sin vergüenza, to dip them in tartar sauce, one by one—that is, those appetizing and quite innocent strands or shreds (of a white or pink mother-of-pearl color like a marine dawn) that he had been gradually extracting, also with his fingernails, from the inner void of the two claws, crushed! shattered! And, having also used his hands, and his fingers, he brought them to his greasy and sinful lips with an extraordinary greed. (42–43)

Aside from the suggestion of a voracity that is absolutely anthropophagous (grammatically, the "human infant" seems to be the direct object of the greedy actions), this quotation is more a tirade than a description. This tirade is entirely based on the accumulation of ever more disgusting details (from the eyes squinting "inwardly" to the mouth, "obscene sucker" and "foul entrail"), on a declamatory emphasis (the numerous exclamation points, beside the language), and on a calibrated juxtaposition between the spoken lexicon of the speakers and the cultivated one of the narrator (in the original Italian, p. 81: "compagni" instead of "simili" and "diti" instead of "dita" on the one hand; and on the other, "papillando, properare, estroflesso, tréfoli, lacèrtoli, eripiendo"). Also, the climax of the literary comparison ("like a marine dawn") preceding the rhetorical assertion of "greasy and sinful lips" is delightfully irreverent. It is then a beautiful example of the plasticity and dialogic quality of the modern novel according to Bakhtin,[8] of that polylinguistic and polyphonic conscience that governs the interpersonal relationships of everyone involved, including the author with his characters.

But the tirade is not enough, and it is prolonged in the description of another dish, succulent and Pantagruelic more than Artusian, prepared

with such richness that it appears to absorb (or almost absorb) any rep-
rehension for the gastronomic excesses of the glutton:

> His snout and his porcine aspect were also adduced by the legend to support
> the above, as if in the course of a whole interminable summer he had dined
> on nothing but lobsters in tartar sauce, cod in white wine with spurts of
> mayonnaise, or two or three times on peje-rey; and roast pigeons in casserole
> with rosemary and little new potatoes, sweet but not too sweet, and tiny, but
> already a bit overcooked, stewed in the very gravy derived from those very
> pigeons: stuffed in turn, according to an Andalusian recipe, with oregano,
> sage, basil, thyme, rosemary, horsemint, and pimiento, raisins, pork lard,
> chicken brains, ginger, red pepper, cloves, and still more potatoes, inside, as
> if those others set around weren't enough—that is, those outside the behind
> of the pigeon; which had almost become a second pulp, they had become so
> incorporated with that behind: as if the bird, once roasted, had acquired en-
> trails more suited to his new position as roast chicken, but smaller and fatter
> than the chicken, because he was instead a pigeon. (43)

This description, too, plays on the accumulation of ingredients and epi-
thets, on their repetition, and above all on their mixture: the small potatoes, which are fused with "the behind of the pigeon," in particular seem
to evoke and underline, even more than a confusion of bodily functions
(ingestion, digestion, evacuation), the traditional belief in the goodness
of what is popularly called "the priest's morsel" in Italian and "the
Pope's nose" in English. Hence the text is ambiguous: on the one hand,
it does not obliterate food as enjoyment and satisfaction, but on the
other hand, it presents the protagonist as the embodiment, the epitome,
the allegory of Gluttony, one of "the seven deadly sins" that Gonzalo
carries "in him, all seven, in his belly" (36), and to which the preceding
tirade alluded with its reference to his "greasy and [precisely] sinful lips."

Therefore the immediate *contrappasso* will not come as a surprise:

> In that season of crustaceans and rosemaries, . . . the vindictive Powers of
> heaven chose that there should follow, for him, thanks to their rightful inter-
> vention, a long and very costly disease . . . : for it forced him to eternal fasting,
> and it reduced him to powdering the mucous membrane of the gastric system
> with powdered kaolin, or discipline of bismuth (subnitrate of bismuth), as it
> willed. (45)

"Poor human entrails!" the good doctor comments lapidarily (46), and
with that he seals the distance inexorably separating Gonzalo, the modern and bourgeois antihero, from the Renaissance man celebrated by
Rabelais and analyzed by Bakhtin:[9] one is dyspeptic, nervous, and tor-

mented as much as the other was sanguine, physical, in complete harmony with the cosmos.

One should start precisely from this cultural fact in order to understand the importance of food in the vision of the world preeminent in *La cognizione del dolore*. Gonzalo is at the core of a particular existential and narrative tension between the phenomena of the world and the abstractions of ideas, the body and the spirit, noise and silence, the grotesque and the sublime.[10] Furthermore, Gonzalo is a great bourgeois who is decayed financially and who pitilessly judges the idiosyncrasies and vanities of his class. Hence certain culinary images and certain bourgeois manners acquire a truly remarkable relevance in the novel.

Among the culinary images, the gorgonzola cheese is undoubtedly preeminent. Already Gonzalo has a certain reluctance to "permit the cheeses to enter the painful circle of his apperception" (75) and is hardly able to arrange them "in that outrageous field of nonforms" that includes "cicadas onions clogs, hebephrenic bronzes, paleo-Celtic Josés, Battistinas faithful through the decades, goiter-cretin from birth: all the Acheron of mala suerte that had spilled down from the sense and prescience of his fathers" (76). But let us see the initial description of *croconsuelo*, the fictional, falsely South American name of the very Lombard gorgonzola: "This is a kind of Maradagàl Roquefort, but a bit fresher: fat, sharp, smelly enough to make an Aztec vomit, with rich mold of a dark green in the ignominy of its crevasses, very tasty to spread with the knife on the water-lily tongue and to chew over for quarter hours in a foul mush; red wine was drunk over it to restore the trade-used tongue and recover saliva" (19). This cheese, so smelly and substantial, reappears with an obsessive frequency throughout the novel; for instance, when the woman tells the doctor that Gonzalo has crushed under his feet a gold watch and his father's portrait, she manages to mention the price of "a hectogram of croconsuelo" (59); or, during a visit by the doctor, Gonzalo himself links the cheese with saliva, a "low" bodily function that allegedly God would have given us precisely "to salivate properly that swinishness called croconsuelo—moldy, yellow, verminous . . . to chomp it properly, the stinking, the nauseating" (94).[11] I wish to emphasize again the distance separating Gonzalo, the modern antihero who cannot stand the worms in the cheese, from the man of the Renaissance, for example Menochio, the sixteenth-century miller studied by Carlo Ginzburg, for whom the cheese and the worms were part of a well-ordered, meaningful, and cosmological system.

In any case, in *La cognizione del dolore* Gonzalo's disgust prevails. Specifically, it is "the old obsession of the crowd: the horror of his schoolmates, of their feet, of their croconsuelo lunch" (203), and this horror is even stronger in his childhood memory of the carnival, "of runny nose, of revolt, of nougat, of jostling and fritters, of roast peanuts which precipitate the bellyache into shit," and above all of "the spun sugar" that, "in the brute's huge hands, terrified him," as he feels almost "an accomplice of the obscenity" (211). In sum, there seems to be no doubt that the croconsuelo is for Gonzalo the metonymy of disgust, the horror that the world and the others can inspire. It is just the opposite of the warm and hearty physicality of the gorgonzola sandwich eaten by Mr. Bloom at Nosey Finn's, in Joyce's *Ulysses*, when the character shows how much he appreciates "the feety savour of green cheese" among the myriad associations caused by the pub's atmosphere.[12]

But gorgonzola is not the only food used to connote the feelings of Gadda's characters. At least other two episodes of *La cognizione del dolore* are revealing. The first deals with the attitude of the mother who gives all sorts of foods to "the coffe-colored grandson" in order to entice him to study French: "figs, peaches, sweets . . . the idiot. . . . And chocolates. And she smiles at him, as if she were his Mama . . . and biscuits, words of praise" (97). The son's jealousy over these nutritive and affective gifts is all too evident, and this jealousy prevents the reader from believing the alleged "hunger" Gonzalo suffered as a young boy because of the excessive alimentary gifts the mother gave to unworthy strangers.

The second episode is the "rustic offering of a basket of mushrooms" made by Poronga the carpenter to the mother (197),[13] and the concomitant offering by the fish-selling Beppina, "known in the whole area for her custom of peeing in a standing position," of "a yellow tench, enormous, from the Seegrün, . . . its eyes clouded by an Acherontic lassitude and its mouth open and rotund" (198). The mother knows how to cook this "repugnant and marshy fish" (199), "with carrots and celery, over a slow fire," so as to achieve "a thing . . . full of bones, of celery, but rather good to the taste," to be given in turn to the poor women of Pastrufazio (141). Object of exchanges and social relationships, of maternal care and goodness, these foods are instead for Gonzalo yet another stimulus for his neurosis to click—his ancient obsession with the crowd, his horror for the dirt and the smells of others, already noted in connection with gorgonzola; hence he reacts almost "ferociously" toward his mother: "If I find you again in that pack of pigs,

I'll cut your throat and theirs too," he shouts, throwing both mush-rooms and fish away (214).

But Gonzalo's anger is turned also against himself. In a well-known tirade against pronouns, his own "I" becomes the specific target of his metaphysical fury against all the limitations of being, and this fury finds an appropriately sarcastic expression in an alimentary comparison: "When immensity coagulates, . . . when righteous wrath becomes heavy in a belly, . . . in mine, for example . . . which has as its end and only destiny, in the universe, the stuffing of tons of bismuth, . . . that's when the I is determined, with its fine monad upon it, like the caper on the rolled-up anchovy on the lemon slice over the Wiener schnitzel" (88–89). It is always the belly, Bakhtin's "lower bodily stratum," moreover condemned to stuff tons of bismuth, that is the object of an irrepressible disdain, especially in the materiality of the comparison and in the devastating coupling between monad and caper, which have two things in common. Not only are they the respective culminations of two different stratifications, but they are also and especially both proparoxytone words in Italian (the assonance between *coppa* and *cappero* should also be noted [It. 126] as a useful device to redimension the philosophical concept of monad, which was crucial throughout Gadda's *Meditazione milanese*).

And it is through the belly that Gadda's metaphysical fury is unleashed on the loved-hated bourgeoisie, including the Fat Bourgeois at the restaurant with all their vanities, in a choral picture in which nothing and no one are saved, a virtuoso performance that needs to be quoted extensively:

> Black waiters, in the "restaurants," wore tailcoats, though full of stains: and the slab of starch, with false tie. . . . "A mixed chocolate-vanilla for Madame, very well, Madame!" It was, from nape to heel, like a thrashing of sweetness, "the pure and hidden joy" of the hymn. And also in the men, for that matter, the secret itch of complacency. . . . And the strikes were forgotten, abruptly; the shouts of death, the barricades, the Communes, the threats of hanging from the lamp posts, the purple at Père Lachaise; and the black and clotting rennet on the Goyesque abandon of the outstretched, the spent. . . . For that moment of delight. Oh! sweet pang! Furnished us by the reverent tailcoat: "A lemon and soda for the gentleman, yes sir! Lemon and soda for the gentle-man!" The marvelous, sumptuous cry, full of obsequiousness and a touching concern, more intoxicating than an Elysian melody by Bellini, reechoed from commis to commis, from slab to slab, enriching with new dextrogyrate spells

the marquisian hormones of the orderer; until, having reached the pantry, it was: "a lemon and soda for that prickhead at Number 128!"

Yes, yes, they were very highly considered, those tailcoats. Serious gentlemen, in the "restaurants" of the station, and to be taken seriously, ordered of them in perfect seriousness an "ossobuco with rice." And they, with eager motions, agreed. And this, in the full possession of their respective mental faculties. (163–65)

This long quotation moves the text down from metaphysics to history and sociology, with more than a precise allusion to the great fears of nineteenth-century bourgeoisie, from the Parisian Commune to the repression of the Milanese popular riots by General Bava-Beccaris at the turn of the century. These allusions are cleverly mixed with echoes from literature (duly distorted: Manzoni's hymn was religious, and Carlo Porta's "Marquis" was a simple Marchionn), not to mention the pictorial reference to Goya and the operatic one to Bellini—all in between totally banal orders.

Already this page should suffice, but Gadda continues until the completion of the dinner in the restaurant: there is a knife that is not sharp enough and therefore an apple, "shiny, and green, as if De Chirico had painted it" (165), skids off the plate onto the floor and makes the waiters curse, and after the apple there is a cigarette, held "between index and middle fingers," as a crowning of the meal, "while the stomach was thrown into a state of joyful murmuring, and went ahead like a desperate amoeboid in mauling and peptonizing the ossobuco. The peristalsis came off with a triumphal progress. . . . So they remained. . . . In full exploitation of their cuffs, and of their cufflinks. And of their faces like ossibuchivore dummies" (168). Prepared by De Chirico and the neologism, there is no doubt that these "ossibuchivore dummies" remain as the final epitome of the derisory triumph of the great bourgeoisie.[14]

But Gonzalo is a decayed great bourgeois because his father wasted his patrimony in useless but prestigious donations (such as the one for the church's bells), and his mother wanted to maintain the appearances—and the expenses—of the villa in the countryside with its useless protective wall. That is the reason why the narrator pauses to describe Gonzalo's avarice, his bargaining with the innkeeper "after all this licking and lapping" (44)—and the plebeian locution seems to underline the pettiness of his behavior. That is the reason why the kitchen of the villa is dark, "empty and cold," with "a whiff of lard and leftovers" to emphasize the meager supper hastily prepared by the mother: an unspecified soup and some pickles, "three little greenish peppers, withered, arranged in a chipped plate, a coffee saucer" (152 and 163). All these connotations are important, not so much for a possible realism in the representation, as for the characters' psychology: the mother's sorrow, the son's "secret rancor" (170) and his "obscure sickness" (154), mentioned, in fact, together with his hypothetical and symbolic parricide (153) among such connotations.[15]

The protagonist's neurosis is the unifying element for the fragmented culinary episodes, each of which is developed in seeming autonomy and all of which are important for the structure (the minimal "plot") of the novel. What remains to be emphasized is that the food referents make up an extraordinarily variegated lexical network in the linguistic texture of *La cognizione del dolore*. They contribute remarkably to its expressivity (the signifiers) as well as to its meaningfulness (the signifiers-signifieds relationship). I shall briefly mention some absolutely incongruous (that is, grotesque, baroque) comparisons: "hacer una pera" equals "to carry out a great feat" (49); Gonzalo is "more awkward [in pulling himself together] than a seal frying pancakes" (50); his shoes, "shiny, very black, looked like two black peppers" (67); or there are certain "electricians nearsighted as artichokes" (158). But above all, the alimentary terminology seems to serve the purpose of deriding the protagonist and his confession-cognizance, marking him forever with the pompous and ridiculous names Pirobutirro and d'Eltino "or Del Tino" (65), which hint respectively at a pear and a vat, and thus inexorably bring his metaphysical tension and tendency toward the sublime back to a sensorial and corporeal phenomenology.[16]

Actually this phenomenology, this "cornucopia" of the world (75), fascinates the author,[17] and indeed triumphs in other major works by Gadda, where the urgency of inner experience is smoothed in a more detached, impersonal, and objective vision, focused on the one hand on the loved-hated Milanese bourgeoisie (*L'Adalgisa*) and on the other on the Roman bourgeoisie and lower classes (*Quer pasticciaccio brutto de via Merulana*).

It is first necessary to say that the "Milanese drawings" of *L'Adalgisa*[18] are also the indispensable subtext of *La cognizione del dolore*, so much so that two of them, "Strane dicerie contristano i Bertoloni" and "Navi approdano al Parapagàl," are integral parts of the novel. Even more importantly, in their autonomy and fragmentariness as individual "drawings" (connected, however, by numerous coincidences and ties among characters, families, and settings), they constitute Gadda's splendid effort to give the comprehensive and totalizing picture or fresco of a whole epoch, of an entire society. This effort is based predominantly on what I should call a chaotic but structural enumeration of cultural, sociological, and technical referents, of habits and manners, of traditions and tastes—particularly alimentary ones—from which the literary inventions of similes and neologisms spring forth.

I hope I can condense in a single paragraph the chaotic-structural enumeration that Gadda masterfully spreads throughout the pages of *L'Adalgisa*: asparagus (315), sherbets and watermelons (323), Maggi soup boillon cubes (325), boiled beef and risotto (326), gorgonzola and eel (327), "a slice of Margherita cake, or a large slice of Mafalda cake" for the inmates of the Regina Elena Hospital (330–31), lobster, truffles, and *pastasütta*, Milanese for *pasta asciutta* (375), *beignets* (422), chocolates (453), Barolo wine (454), capons, spinach, *sabaglioni* (with *s* instead of *z*) (455), sausage (458), radishes (503), berries (523), ice creams (538), lemonades and candies (546), prosciutto and melon, written à la Milanese *giambone* and *mellone*, with the latter duly cooled under the running water in the kitchen sink (522).

There is no danger that such an enumeration become a catalogue of items and data for a gastronomic micro-history: Gadda himself warns us, with a peremptory smile, that his aims are only "limitedly representative" (455). In fact, he often comments on the alimentary referents with clarifying philological notations—like the one concerning the linguistic usages of the terms *colazione*, *pranzo*, and *cena* in Italy,[19] which shifts the emphasis from the thing to the name; or, even more, with literary references, such as the "picaresque" idea of hunger (423), or a "Pantagruelic" butcher (333), or Rabelais's note, a true if brief treatise on *beignets* (427), which suggests much more than the frivolity of the subject actually says.[20]

Above all, Gadda uses alimentary referents as second terms in an impressive series of similes, comparisons, and couplings that are as baroque as any ever. I choose only a few particularly effective examples. Here is the air of Lombardy: "You feel yourself kept floating like a Pope without even bothering to swim: upheld by a greasy and brotherly climate, by a vivifying pitch. Like a sagacious broth: or a frying lard, which melts in the works, in the pan of civilized aids. . . . With full lungs . . . you breath and splash about in an Elysian ether, which is, however, sanguine and sausagey, a sort of ether-lard" (313). This is the "comfortable air" between the Sèveso and Lambro Rivers breathed by the working population of Lombardy, a "people with distant slaughters and hybridizations, . . . with that splash of curule lies on top to give it the flavor and appearance of a civilization, almost like powdered cinnamon on whipped cream!" (313). It seems that the author does not want to abandon himself completely to sentiment and reevocation, and that his sacred right to criticism finds vent and balance in the sequel of alimentary comparisons.

But here is the description of a concert at the Giuseppe Verdi Theater: "Stimulated by an antipasto of geese's honking, now the theater ingurgitated an amalgam of matrons, jurisconsults and manufacturers of suspenders, with the greed of a young, hungry wolf who swallows a galaxy of raw chops" (461); inside, "there were Jonian columns floured with stucco, pale as a ricotta cheese; capitals with some gold, with their crème-caramel luster" (462); and even in the performance of the concert there is "an equivocal huge caramel of chords in seventh, completely coated with the small sugared almonds of the triangle" (476). Indeed it appears that no aspect of the grand baroque theater of the world can escape the omnipresent gastronomic contamination and deformation.

These few examples, in any case, should suffice to convey Gadda's literary strength and inventiveness, culminating in certain neologisms that, in the semantic area under examination, are undoubtedly no less effective than the referents, the similes, and the analogies quoted so far. I am thinking of a "peppered" nose or of a deli-boy, "gorgonzolaing messenger" (314), or a "banqueted" and "enchampagned" lady (321), or a maid "all carroted with celeries and hiccups" (425).

The real presents Gadda with an extremely rich cornucopia of inviting and appetizing phenomena, as other texts by him confirm. I am referring in particular to "Una mattinata ai macelli" (a morning in Milan's slaughterhouse) and "Mercato di frutta e verdura" (the fruit and vegetable market): Gadda displays a minute attention to the sanitary, commercial, and organizational problems and technical solutions of wholesale food distribution; at the end, almost a seal for the "conclusive and peremptory nomenclature" of the various cuts of meat derived from the butchered animals, there is the statement, valid well beyond the context, that "Every history is achieved and determined in a philology."[21]

I am also and particularly thinking of "Risotto patrio. Rècipe,"[22] where already in the title the half-affectionate, half-ironic attribute and the foreign term seem intended to put a distance between the author and a subject matter that is even too close to him. "The preparation of a good risotto *alla milanese*" requires "quality rice" ("big grain Vialone" and not "long grain Carolina"), a fitting container (ideally one of those copper pans that by now can only be seen in Jacopo da Bassano's interiors), a wooden ladle, Lodi butter "*quantum prodest*" (for Gadda, Latin is important even in the kitchen!), a tender onion, broth made with "beef with carrots and celery, all of them from the Po Valley—not a retired bull with Balkan horns and soul," and saffron "Carlo Erba Milan brand, in sealed small bottles." As the reader can see, in times of European Economic Community, of international corporations, and massive importation of beef precisely from the Balkans to the Italian market, it is almost impossible to follow Gadda's prescriptions. The whole recipe plays and insists upon the rituality and purity of the Milanese tradition, so much so that certain additions, such as the marrow of beef bones or some spoonfuls of Piedmontese red, full-bodied wine, are "thinkable, in fact suggested or requested by hyperconnoisseurs and hypertechnicians," while others are barely allowed "by good risotto eaters": for example, grated Parmesan cheese "brings cordiality to Milanese sobriety and elegance"; on the contrary, neither fresh wild mushrooms nor truffles, although they are evidently used, "arrive at perverting the profound, the vital, the noble meaning of risotto *alla milanese*."[23] Gadda does not care to make this meaning explicit: but it is clear that his risotto—which is a "fatherland" dish, one should not forget—is a metonymy of the purity and the ideals the author has always longed for, beginning with his patriotism in World War One (documented especially in his *Diario di guerra e di prigionia*), but which he always found impossible to fulfill in reality and in life.

The reader, however, should not believe that a gourmet and a voracious writer like Gadda wants to limit himself to his native Milan: the recipe for risotto is only a fragment, a piece of a much larger mosaic, the last of his "Milanese drawings" after the large Roman and Italic fresco of *Quer pasticciaccio brutto de via Merulana*.[24] An adventure and detective novel, a suspense story, and a book about ideas and manners, language and dialects, *Quer pasticciaccio brutto de via Merulana* shares with *La cognizione del dolore* the formal incompleteness, a fluid structure with ample ramifications and digressions, a plurilinguistic conscience, and also the expressive and narrative importance of foods and alimentary habits. In the opening pages the protagonist of the novel, Dr. Francesco Ingravallo, the police commissioner, is introduced with "a slightly dull manner, like a person fighting a laborious digestion" (3), and "with one or two little stains of olive oil on his lapel, almost imperceptible however, like a souvenir of the hills of his Molise" (3).

The style of this novel is particularly rich at the expressive-analogical level, which includes the most diversified genres (from the sublime to the grotesque) and registers (from the high-literary to the dialectal-spoken). Thus, for example, if on the one hand the cardinals of the Holy Roman Church are "like stupendous lobsters" (11), on the other, the slashed arteries of Liliana Balducci's neck appear to the policemen "like red-colored little maccheroni, or pink" (69), and the victim's clotted blood is "all sticky like a blood pudding" (70). And if a secondary character is shown "amid a soufflé of cushions" (143), another one pedals an old bike that "was like a music box, with a creak-creak in its hubs. It was like a machine with broken teeth for eating torrone" (302). Still on the theme of alimentary analogies, there is "an old hulk of a car . . . rattly and slow," with "two slabs of corrugated iron for fenders," which "swayed and jolted as soon as the car moved, like two cabbage leaves hanging out of the cook's half-empty shopping bag" (367); a dog barks with "a pulpy drool like béchamel" (307), and another character yawns and tears form in his eyes, first the left and then the right one, "like the two halves of a lemon successively used by the oyster vendor" (363).

A true virtuoso performance deals with Zamira's hen, "a surly and half-featherless hen," which "on steady legs before the horrified corporal . . . revealed the Pope's nose in all its beauty: diaphragmed to the minimum, the full extent of the aperture, the pink rose-window of her sphincter, and plop, promptly took a shit":

> a green chocolate drop twisted *à la Borromini* like the lumps of colloid sulphur in the Albule water: and on the very tip-top a little spit of calcium, also in the colloidal state, a very white cream, the pallor of pasteurized milk, which was already on the market in those days.
>
> All these aerodynamics, naturally, and the consequent release of chocolate, or mocha, as may be, were exploited by Zamira to avoid answering. (285–86)

Seldom, I believe, has scatologic material been treated with such an elaborate and refined, such a polyphonic lexicon (as Bakhtin would say), which combines and fuses the following elements: gastronomy (chocolate, cream, pasteurized milk, mocha), photographic technology (diaphragmed), history of art (significantly, the baroque of "twisted *à la Borromini*"), chemistry (calcium, colloid sulphur, colloidal state), physics (aerodynamics), anatomy (sphincter); and conversely a series of onomatopoetic elements ("plop," followed by "plink!" on the next page), spoken idioms (like "the Pope's nose" and "took a shit"), and Roman dialect expressions that are necessarily lost in translation but are an integral part of the original ("pure isso," "pe no risponne," It. 254). It is a true microcosm in which Gadda's poetics is condensed and revealed,[25] and which culminates in the expressivity of the syntagma "green chocolate"—a true novelistic triumph of the lower bodily stratum in front of legitimate authority, the "horrified" corporal.

It is clear then that Gadda's discourse effectively employs foods in all their range for eminently literary purposes, and that the hen's shit is only an example, a stupendous one, of a stylistic-ideological achievement. But *Quer pasticciaccio*, as the title itself suggests, is also a true pastiche of elements and functions that, in their continuous mixture, contribute in a determining way to the succulent and exquisite textual result.

The supper at the Balduccis has a preeminent narrative function, emphasized by its strategic placement in the text, as the initial and final frame. It is used to outline Ingravallo's feelings toward Liliana and is entirely described through the notations about the setting, the characters, and the psychologies that are systematically made by the commissioner, alter-ego of the writer. Ingravallo is a polite guest who, however, wants to track back the "clues" and "signs" of the surrounding reality to the "meanings" of the interpersonal relationships between Liliana and her husband, and between her and her "nieces" and maids, in order to be able to discover all the "concauses" of her "erotic potential," which did not arrive at maternity and found compensation in the young substitutes:

> For her, from the Tiber down, there, there beyond the crumbling castles, and after the blond vineyards, there was, on the hills and mountains, and in the brief plains of Italy, a kind of great fertile womb, two swollen Eustachian tubes [two fat salpinges], streaked with an abundance of granules, the granular and greasy, the happy caviar of the race. From time to time, from the great Ovary ripened follicles opened, like pomegranate seeds. (16)

These are Ingravallo's thoughts at supper. They reach an epic dimension (the great Ovary), to be related once again to Bakhtin's material hermeneutics: in fact, the use of an anatomical and geographic, erotic and gastronomical terminology achieves a con-fusion of elements that is absolutely extraordinary in its analogical and metaphorical valence— while revealing Ingravallo's own erotism.

But the supper at the Balduccis is also (and perhaps above all) used to introduce the characters that will animate the novelistic action and the police investigation: Virginia, Assuntina, Valdarena, all variously suspected, for different motives, of the horrible murder of Liliana, or more or less directly involved in the theft in the Menegazzi house. Therefore it is not surprising that in this episode the alimentary referents are sober and marginal, just realistic enough: maccheroni, a "golden Frascati" (10), later specified as "an extra-dry white, five years old, now, from Cavalier Gabbioni Empedocle and Son, Albano Laziale" (15), and "drained spinach," noted only because it "deviated from the oval plate onto the candid whiteness of the immaculate tablecloth" (8) at the hands of the sloppy Assuntina. Only at the end of the novel will the spinach appear as a side dish, but in the meantime a revealing click has occurred in Ingravallo's inquisitive memory:

> And she, she was the one, the one (the pathway of time became confused and lost) who had presented the filled and badly tilted oval of the plate, a whole leg, all the kidneyed syncretism of a dish of kid, or of lamb, in pieces as it was, had allowed to roll out, on the whiteness amid the silver and the crystal, of a goblet, or no, of a glass, the tuft of spinach: receiving, from Signora Liliana, that heartbroken reproof of a glance, and a name: "Assunta!" (380)

Even in the functional and narrative sobriety of this episode Gadda's style shines: "the kidneyed syncretism of a dish of kid" fuses together a lexical neologism Joyce might have envied (his Mr. Bloom loved kidneys, too[26]), a philosophical abstraction, and a typical food referent (no longer from Milan but from Rome).

In any case, Gadda's way of positing himself in front of the opulent intricacy of the real has numerous manifestations in the novel. I shall quote only three among the many possible[27]: the "prosciuttophile" Commendator Angeloni,[28] ironic alter-ego of the author; the roast beef sandwich devoured by Sgranfia, a modern version of the *macchiettismo* going back to Manzoni and Fogazzaro and promoted here to the rank of example and emblem of popular vitality; and the local market with the stands and the vendors of *abbacchio*, a choral and cordial representation of a joyful, overflowing abundance.

Commendator Angeloni is an inveterate gourmet, portrayed with the small, elegant packages he buys at the delicatessen; shy and reserved, fearful and dignified, he is a witness who should be able to recognize "the shop assistant" (as he says) or the "grocer-kid or delivery-boy" (Ingravallo's words) (46), who on the day of the Menegazzi theft had brought him home a ham, in fact "a nice lean ham, . . . a little one, a mountain ham, just a few pounds. The small weight of the ham apparently seemed to him a singular attenuating circumstance" (47) for a crime he never committed and of which he was never accused. And so, with his ham, his "*brisavola*," his artichoke hearts, and "a bit of marinated eel, perhaps, or a spot of galantine" (47), or with an hypothetical and little-dignified *caciocavallo* cheese around his neck or "two flasks of wine, one tucked under each arm" (52), the bulky Commendator Angeloni crosses the scene of the detective novel like an Alfred Hitchcock who appears slyly in a quick frame of one of his films.

During his questioning, poor Angeloni is even obliged to do without his lunch, not a small sacrifice for him, so much so that the policeman Pompeo suggests to him, unsuccessfully, to send for "a healthy pair of sandwiches" stuffed with "rare roast beef" (44) by "er Maccheronaro" (the macaroni provider, in Roman dialect), the usual caterer for the police station. To make up for it, it is precisely Pompeo, called Sgranfia, who later on "devours" another, similar sandwich:

> Er Maccheronaro, in Via del Gesù, just a stone's-throw away, never overlooked a chance to demonstrate his friendliness: and he had paved it inside, with three such slices of prime beef that, on first seeing them, he had taken them for three slate roof tiles on a roof in Sampierdarena: nestling one against the other, all three supported by that big beam of double roll, the size of a carpet slipper, Madonna! the kind you can't even remember nowadays, now that the Empire has put its oar in. The panacea of panaceas for his empty stomach, lacking its soup, but already dewy in the gastric juices of an anticipated gratitude and no less predisposed peristalsis. (190–91)

Undoubtedly it is an extraordinary sandwich: its referents are geographic (Sampierdarena), geological (slate), architectural (paved, roof, beam), historical (the fascist Empire), and scientific (gastric juices, peristalsis). They epically enlarge the lexical basis of the Roman dialect. And this extraordinary sandwich is doubled by another, similar one, "a reprise of that shoe-sized sandwich he had had at seven: with paving this time, of roast beef and mortadella, in alternate slices, gently laid in that sofa of bread, by the expert, pudgy fingers of the Maccheronaro himself" (221)—to reiterate its material, Rabelaisian function in the novelistic context.

Still another sandwich, with a slice of roast pork and rosemary, mentioned by Ines Cionini during questioning, brings the investigators who are after the suspect Ascanio Luciani into the midst of the market in Piazza Vittoria:

The following morning precisely at ten Blondie was on the spot . . . : that is
the hour when the housewives are used to doing their marketing, with a view
not only to supper, but more especially to the midday dinner which is their
imminent care: the hour of the mozzarellas, the cheeses, the vermifugue onions, and the cardoon greens, patiently hibernating beneath the snows, the
spices, the first salad, baby lamb. Of people selling roast pork there was a tribe
at the stands in the square that morning. Starting with the Feast of San
Giuseppe is its season, you might say. With thyme and the bows of rosemary,
not to mention garlic, and the side dish or stuffing of potatoes with crushed
parsley. . . . Wrapped in the vortex of invitations and incitements to buy
and in all the conclamations of that cheesy festival, he moved slowly in front
of the lambish stands, passed carrots and chestnuts and adjacent mounds of
bluish-white fennel, mustached, rotund heralds of Aries: . . . and the smell of
the burnt chestnuts, at the end, seemed, from the few remaining braziers, the
very odor of winter in flight. On many stands yellowed, now without time and
without season, the pyramids of oranges, walnuts, in baskets the black Provence plums, polished with tar, plums from California. . . . He reached at last
the ancient, eternal realm of Tullus and Ancus where, stretched on carving
boards, prone or, more rarely, supine, or dozing on one flank at times, the
suckling pigs with golden skin displayed their viscera of rosemary and thyme,
or a knot here and there, green-black, within the pale and tender skin, a leaf
of bitter mint, set there as if to lard, with a grain of pepper which the cry
praised in the hubbub. (353–55)

Here one is far away from Gonzalo's neurotic reaction against the
crowd and the carnivalesque vulgarity experienced during his youth:
this market is the place of a cosmic and popular harmony in which
everyone is in unison with nature and history, in which time and the
seasons are immediately, sensuously recognizable, and in which the
whole world, from Provence to California, seems to take part. This
market is then the place of plenty, it is the mythologem of Cockaigne
concretized and made present, it is, to use Camporesi's words, "the
place of multiplication, of a permanent miracle, of a daily portent. It is
a catalogue of limitless availability of comestible things within reach for
all, it is a saturation display of edible objects to be swallowed in order to
make up for the daily dispersion of energy, the loss of vitality, the lipidic
and glucidic impoverishment."[29] In fact, one can even say that this market is the modern echo of an anthropological phenomenon studied by
Marcel Mauss: in some archaic societies, the potlatch (a ritual, gen-
eralized, ostentatious gift) is intrinsic to a ceremonial feast, and the

waste it implies is conceived as a reply to scarcity, as a joyful (although temporary) liberation from hunger.[30] At the same time, this market-Cockaigne-potlatch is the objective correlative, the dialectical pole of Gadda's writing, which is rich with lexical multiplications and verbal marvels; it is not really necessary to recall that, in reply to those who reproached his baroque style, Gadda countered with the "more reasonable and soft-voiced assertion" that "baroque is the world, and G. has perceived and portrayed its baroqueness."[31]

It is therefore inherent in the logic of the text that *Quer pasticciaccio* should find its privileged and emblematic place in the "cheesy festival" of the market of Piazza Vittoria, in the "great comestible fair" (361) where the policeman, instead of losing himself, moves as an expert and skillfully picks the suspect, without causing a scandal and while enjoying the fair and the comestible show to the very end. As a consequence, the provisional arrest of the suspect is preceded and followed by the two complementary halves of the market:

They came out of the confusion towards Via Mamiani or Via Ricasoli: there was a passageway among the stands of the fish-mongers and the chicken-vendors, where they sell the squid and the cuttlefish and all kinds of eels and meals from the sea, not to mention mussels. The character, and Blondie himself, looked at those mushy polyps of a pale, silvery mother-of-pearl (so delicately burnished in their inner veins), sniffed, though involuntarily, the odor of seaweeds from all the cool dampness, that sense of sky and chloro-bromo-iodic freedom, of bright morning on the docks, that promise of fried silver in the plate against the hunger that already could be called profound. Coils of boiled tripe, one upon the other, like rolled-up rugs, gentle anatomies of skinned kid, red-white, the pointed tail, but ending in its tuft, to signify— beyond contradiction—its nobility. . . . And the white clumps of romaine, or curly salad greens, live chickens with the eyes peering from a single side, and who see, each one, a quarter of the world, live hens, still and huddled in their cages, black or Belgian or straw-ivory Paduans: yellow-green dried peppers, or red-green, which made your tongue sting just to look at them, and made saliva come into your mouth: and then walnuts, Sorrento walnuts, hazelnuts from Vignanello, and piles of chestnuts. Farewell, farewell, a long farewell. (360–61)

In these necessarily extended quotations, the almost encyclopedic and technical catalogue becomes an accumulation, which is only seemingly chaotic, of individual alimentary referents. Accumulation functions as the supporting syntactic structure for the whole episode, which is also founded, on the lexical level, on the prevalence of the Roman dialect (unfortunately lost in translation, as I have already pointed out), and this prevalence is itself significant.

In fact, accumulation (of clues, proofs, concauses) is the supporting structure not only of this episode but of the entire police investigation (which is a cognitive inquiry) throughout the novel. It is not by chance, then, that *Quer pasticciaccio brutto de via Merulana* culminates, even though unfinished, in the quoted description of the market, where the policeman-author moves, with all his senses on the alert, among the noisy and inviting stands-aspects of the real.[32]

And if such a structure is the governing principle for the novel, the bourgeois form of art, the dialectal and spoken lexicon constitutes its expressive, popular, vital stratum, indispensable to celebrate the triumph of plenty, Gadda's gluttonous laughter in the cornucopia of the world.

Under Olivia's Teeth:
Italo Calvino, *Sotto il sole giaguaro*

ITALO CALVINO published "Sapore sapere" in the elegant, luxurious review *FMR* in 1982, where his text accompanies the stupendous, disquieting images reproduced from the Florentine codex, in the Biblioteca Medicea Laurenziana, of the *Historia General de las cosas de Nueva España*, a sixteenth-century treatise on the life and customs of the Aztecs written by Fra Bernardino da Sahagún in the Nahuatl language.[1]

Retitled "Sotto il sole giaguaro" (under the jaguar sun),[2] the story now appears in the book that bears its name. While the new title has lost the trajectory, in fact the cognitive short circuit of the two words *sapore*, flavor, and *sapere*, knowledge (as well as the related linguistic plays of the change of vowel and assonance), it has acquired an iconic figurality, which is also entirely literary: it is connected with the climax of the narrated story-inquiry, in which the sense of taste is transcended, becoming encompassed within a truly cosmic vision. According to a project interrupted by the author's death, this book should have been called *I cinque sensi* (the five senses), and a French work of the same period, Michel Serres's *Les cinq sens: Philosophie des corps melés*, may further indicate the effort made by contemporary culture to enlist the senses in the cognitive inquiry of reason.[3]

The protagonists of Calvino's story are an Italian couple touring in Mexico. This fact is interesting in itself: that they are a couple points to the core of Calvino's oeuvre, from the "difficult" idylls and loves of the earliest short stories on; it is a question of tourists, not explorers or travelers "abroad" (according to the typology Paul Fussell proposes for English literature, the tourist figures modern human experience[4]); as Italians, they reflect the recent economic growth of the country, which has led to cosmopolitanism more than to nationalism; and finally, the locale, Mexico, is the land that, maybe more than any other, unites anthropology and art and that, perhaps for the same reason, appears singularly privileged in the imaginary of Calvino's late works. In fact, Calvino wrote both the introduction to the Italian edition of C. A. Burland's *Montezuma: Lord of the Aztecs*, and the preface to the new edition of Emilio Cecchi's classic travelogue *Messico* of 1932.[5]

Calvino's story, then, prolongs and updates the ancient topos of the journey, which had a constitutive function from the very origins of Italian literature, with Dante's "prophetic," Petrarch's "inner," and Boccaccio's "evasive" journeys, according to Roberto Antonelli.[6] But what is most unusual and original in "Sotto il sole giaguaro" is that the male narrator and his female companion are intent upon a "gustatory exploration" based on a novel conviction they share:

> The true journey, as the introjection of an "outside" different from our normal one, implies a complete change of nutrition, a digesting of the visited country—its fauna and flora and its culture (not only the different culinary practices and condiments but the different implements used to grind the flour or stir the pot)—making it pass between the lips and down the esophagus. (12)[7]

Furthermore, the couple are united by an even more intimate and personal "complicity," the desire to communicate "through flavors, or . . . with flavors through a double set of taste buds" (9), a desire made more intense and urgent because "the physical bond" between the two companions "was going through a phase of rarefaction, if not eclipse," and hence, as the narrator specifies, its stage "was no longer the bed of our embraces but a dinner table" (10). The couple have all the complementary qualities to carry out the double cognitive exploration: "Olivia more sensitive to perceptive nuances and endowed with a more analytical memory, where every recollection remained distinct and unmistakable, I tending more to define experiences verbally and conceptually, to mark the ideal line of journey within ourselves contemporaneously with our geographical journey" (11).

Clearly, food is such a central and capillary subject in "Sotto il sole giaguaro" that the narrative cannot be separated from it. I shall focus on all the primary functions of food that the story analyzes, from the satisfaction of desire to the possibility of transgression, from the narrative sign to the cognitive tool used to outline the problematic relations among self, others, and the world (or among subject, nature, and history). Using Louis Marin's terms in a broad sense, I can state that "Sotto il sole giaguaro" deals with the dialectics between logos, *sitos*, and eros in an extremely original manner: gastronomy fuses anthropology and eroticism within itself, while the underlying discourse probes the nature of literature. But though Calvino's interest in food culminates in "Sotto il sole giaguaro," gustatory images and topoi are significantly present throughout his oeuvre, even in the early texts, some of which I will now examine.

At the beginning food is a narrative sign connoting the "difficult idylls" in various ways. For instance, in "Pesci grossi, pesci piccoli" the octopus that is cut up in order to "fry it" is not so much a realistic referent as the indicator of the perplexity Zeffirino feels in front of Signorina De Magistris, who has just stopped crying.[8] In "Un pomeriggio, Adamo" Libereso is juxtaposed with Maria-nunziata also because he eats only "artichokes, lettuces, tomatoes," since his father, who is an anarchist and vegetarian, "doesn't like us to eat the flesh of dead animals," while "the sugar ration" is sold "on the black market" (10): here food is a precise social and historical referent, as well as the narrative indicator of the interest aroused in the little girl by Libereso's diversity of eating habits.

The most significant short story of Calvino's early period is, without any doubt, "Furto in una pasticceria." Recounting a triumph (albeit a temporary one) of abundance over the scarcity of World War Two, it is rich with succulent descriptions like the following one, which is based entirely on soldierly metaphors: "[Gesubambino's torch] lit up rows of shelves, and on the shelves rows of trays, and on the trays rows of lined up cakes of every conceivable shape and colour, tarts filled with cream glittering like candle wax, and deployed batteries of *panettoni* and fortified castles of almond cakes" (134). Abundance, that is, excess after scarcity, results not in the satisfaction of desire but in dissatisfaction, duly underscored by an exaggerated and grotesque language, not at all realistic:

> He flung himself at the shelves, choking himself with cakes, cramming two or three inside his mouth at a time, without even tasting them; he seemed to be battling with the cakes, as if they were threatening enemies, strange monsters besieging him, a crisp and sticky siege which he must break through by the force of his jaw. The slit halves of the big sugared buns seemed to be opening yellow throats and eyes at him. (134–35)

The sudden possibility of satisfying a long-unfulfilled craving for food causes first "a frenzy" (Gesubambino "was biting into apple strudels, picking at raisins, licking syrups") and then "nausea," when "the doughnuts began to turn into soggy pieces of sponge, the tarts to flypaper and the cakes to asphalt" (136–37). The story includes many felicitous incidents, such as the birthday cake the tall Sicilian, Uora-Uora, receives squarely and beatifically on his face (138); the police who, "distractedly, they, too, began to nibble little cakes that were lying about, taking care, though, to leave the traces of the thieves," but they end up "all eating away heartily" (139); and especially the conclusion centered on Gesubambino (called simply "Baby" in the translation). Having stuffed his shirt with every sort of pastry he could grab, he succeeds in eluding the incoming police and flees safely to his lover: "When Baby got to Tuscan Mary's and opened his shirt, he found his whole chest covered with a strange sticky paste. And they stayed till morning, he and she, lying on the bed licking and picking at each other till they had finished the last crumb of cake and blob of cream" (139–40). Here alimentary enjoyment and erotic pleasure are indeed the same thing, in an explicit scene that had been carefully prepared at the center of the story: "He could not discover any way of enjoying everything completely. Now he was crouching on all fours over a table laden with tarts; he would have liked to undress and lie down naked in those tarts, cover himself with them, and never have to leave them" (136). Every single verb refers equally to both erotic and alimentary activity: it is the first example in Calvino of a complete identity between two different but complementary lexical areas, which will culminate in "Sotto il sole giaguaro" with a greater complexity and depth of meanings and implications.

For the moment, anyway, the author's interest in food is centered on realistic referents that may also become fantastic, and may also be tied to erotic elements or suggestions. Among the realistic referents that acquire fabulous aspects, there are many from *Marcovaldo ovvero Le stagioni in città*:[9] the poisonous mushrooms in the city, the city pigeon, the contaminated rabbit, the lunch box with "salami and lentils, or hard-boiled eggs and beets, or else polenta and codfish" (31), or again "sausage and turnips": this lunch box is willingly bartered for the plate of the rich boy who has been grounded because he does not want to eat "fried brains, soft and curly as a pile of clouds" (34).

Written between 1952 and 1963, the stories of Marcovaldo also trace a parallel history of Italian society from the postwar poverty to the economic boom, and of Calvino's writing from neorealism to the critical fable. Some of the later stories are particularly endowed with inventive and polemical force; for example, there are the vicissitudes of Marco-

valdo, who is deceived by the illusory promise of finding fresh and un-
polluted fish "where the river is more blue" (67), and who is overwhelmed by a spending frenzy amidst the consumeristic overabundance
of the supermarket (84–89). He accompanies his entire family just "to
watch others go shopping," since he has no money, but he is "overwhelmed by envy, heartbreak," in front of the others' carts overflowing
with merchandise, he is allured by the example of "all these good housewives who, having come in to buy only a few carrots and a bunch of
celery" (85–86), cannot resist the various temptations and grasp can
after can and box after box, and little by little he, too, fills his cart to the
brim: "Products with more and more undecipherable names were sealed
in boxes with pictures from which it was not clear whether these were
fertilizers for lettuces or lettuce seeds or actual lettuce or poison for
lettuce-caterpillars or else seasoning for lettuce or for the roasted birds.
In any case, Marcovaldo took two or three boxes" (86). By the end of the
shopping spree, in a comic but tremendously serious crescendo, "the
wandering of Marcovaldo and family resembled more that of caged animals or of prisoners in a luminous prison with walls of colored panels"
(88). It is useless, I believe, to underscore the abyss separating this
supermarket from the market of Piazza Vittoria in Gadda's *Quer pasticciaccio brutto de via Merulana*: the texts deal with two different ways of
shopping, and even more, with two opposite ways of organizing society—Camporesi has written important pages on this;[10] and the two authors deal with opposite and complementary ways of viewing the world
and writing.

Alimentary referents also fulfill numerous functions in *Il sentiero dei
nidi di ragno*.[11] Realistic function: Pin eats cherries and bread (51),
"bread and a piece of German ersatz chocolate made with groundnuts"
(139), a bowl of boiled chestnuts first with the partisans and then with
some peasants (115 and 137); he peels potatoes (60) and looks for
"water-cress for the cook's salad from the stream" (84); the partisans
also eat boiled chestnuts (109), or a generic rice (84).[12] Fabulous function: having eaten the realistic cherries, Pin spits the cores in order to
mark the way for Lupo Rosso (47), thus repeating the gesture of Tom
Thumb in the children's tale; or, when Mancino announces the menu
made up of "goat's meat and potatoes," he tells Pin about his job as a
cook, and their dialogue appears as an intertextual mixture of Vittorini
(with the insistent repetitions) and Salgari (with the exotic and the
adventurous):

"Twenty years, I've spent, cooking on ships; ships of every kind and every nationality."

"Pirate ships too?" asks Pin.

"Yes, pirate ships too."

"Chinese ships too?"

"Chinese ships too."

"Can you speak Chinese?"

"I can speak every language under the sun. And I know how they cook in every country under the sun; Chinese cooking, Mexican cooking, Turkish cooking . . ."

"How are you cooking the goat's meat and potatoes today?"

"As the Eskimos do. D'you like the way the Eskimos do?"

"Hell, Mancino, as the Eskimos do it!" (61)

Food also has a political function. I am thinking of the soup Lupo Rosso offers Pin when they are in prison (29), or of the talks of the partisans in which communism is explained as "going into a house and being given soup even if one is a tinker; and if they are eating panettone at Christmas then they'll give one panettone" (92). Then there is a symbolic function: the cousin's hand "seems made of bread" (51), is "soft and warm as bread" (142), and in the final page becomes "that huge hand of bread" (145)—friendship, protection, almost a vicarious but reassuring paternity.

Finally, there is the erotic function: in the rustic kitchen of the partisan camp the dominant character is Giglia, the young and sensual wife of the cook, Mancino, and Dritto loses his head over her. Instead of peeling potatoes, Giglia combs her hair (60), offers Dritto some chestnuts (114), even pretends to be peeling potatoes with him in order not to be disturbed by others (117), and plays and runs with her lover, revealing "that warm breast of hers in a man's unbuttoned shirt" (118). When she drinks water from a flask Dritto "looks at her lips" (118)— his gaze expressing desire and, laconic as it is, presaging a whole series of similar postures and gestures throughout Calvino's oeuvre and culminating, with much greater complexity, in the narrator's glance at Olivia's lips in "Sotto il sole giaguaro." Also the statement at the beginning of chapter 7 should be kept in mind: "The dreams of the partisans are short and rare, dreams born of nights of hunger, linked to food which is always scarce and to be divided among so many; dreams about chewing bits of bread and putting them away in drawers. . . . Only when the men's stomachs are full . . . can they dream of naked women" (74).

The relationship between food and eros could not be stated more effectively than it is here.

It is not by chance, then, that in a later story, "La nuvola di smog,"[13] the narrator's beautiful and refined girlfriend, Claudia, passes without being touched or affected, almost a dream materialized, amid the greyness and the dust of the city. The descriptions of a cafeteria with an ironic Risorgimento name and of a squalid bourgeois kitchen are eloquent:

> And I, torn between suffering and love, joy and cruelty, saw her mingling with this scene of ugliness and desolation, with the loud-speaker of the "Urbano Rattazzi", which blurted out: "One *cappelletti* in broth!," with the dirty bowls in Signorina Margariti's sink, and I felt that by now even Claudia's image must be stained by it all. But no, it ran off, along the wire, intact, aware of nothing, and each time I was left alone with the void of her absence. (129–30)

This story also includes remarkable descriptions of the small restaurants featuring fixed-price menus where the narrator often eats (132–35), and these descriptions should be ideally related, as a melancholic counterpoint or an elegy of alienation, to the ferocious satire of the bourgeois at the restaurant in Gadda's *La cognizione del dolore*, examined in the previous chapter.

But in the meanwhile, with the three novels making up the trilogy that is significantly titled *I nostri antenati* (our ancestors), let me jump from industrial and urban greyness to the vivacious and colorful world of fantastic invention.[14] The weight and the role of food are different in the three novels. In *Il visconte dimezzato* the very short references are used only to confirm the connotations of the characters: thus, for example, the halves of the poisonous mushrooms and of the octopuses (165 and 191) announce the bad half of the protagonist, while a beautiful apple pie (217) is what the unbearable "Good 'Un" (his good half) can offer Pamela; in the woods she eats moderately pastoral foods the young narrator brings her, "fruit, cheese and fried fish," and in return she gives him "cups of goat's milk and duck's eggs" (201). It goes without saying that the aesthetic lepers indulge in licentious carousals, while the austere Huguenots live on turnip soup and speculate in a miserly way on the price of rye in times of scarcity (225)—a narrative description that ironically echoes Max Weber's and R. H. Tawney's theses on protestant ethics and the spirit of capitalism.

On the contrary, in *Il barone rampante* food is the narrative spring on which the whole novelistic action is built: "*It was on the fifteenth of June, 1767, that Cosimo Piovasco di Rondò*" rebelled against his father's authority, "pushed away his plateful of snails," (3) and decided to live in the trees and never come down. In addition to its indispensable narrative function, here food is presented as the focus of power and of a possible rebellion. More precisely, the dinner table is the place where the power conflict is played, starting with good manners:

> Our meals in the Abbé's company used to begin, after many a prayer, with ordered ritual, silent movements of spoons, and woe to anyone who raised his eyes from his plate or made the slightest sucking noise with the soup; but by the end of the first dish the Abbé was already tired, . . . by the main dish we were using our hands, and by the end of the meal were throwing pear cores at each other. (4)

But the place where the conflict between opposing wills and personalities may be subtlest and most devastating is the family table; the fact that it is an eighteenth-century aristocratic family is purely accidental, as the insertions of contemporary bourgeois speech clearly indicate or suggest:

> Now, at table with the family, up surged the intimate grudges that are such a burden of childhood. Having our father and mother always there in front of us, using knives and forks for the chicken, keeping our backs straight and our elbows down—what a strain it all was! . . .
>
> The only person really at ease was Battista, the nun of the house, who would sit shredding her chicken with precise deliberation, fiber by fiber, using some sharp little knives, rather like surgeon's scalpels, which she alone had. . . . So it can be seen why our family board brought out all the antagonisms, the incompatibilities, between us, . . . and why it was there that Cosimo's rebellion came to a head. (4–6)

Battista's strange and evil cuisine finds its appropriate place in such a family setting: pâté toast of rats' livers, grasshoppers' claws "laid on an open tart in a mosaic," a porcupine with all its quills, in sum, "works of the most delicate animal or vegetable jewelry," such as, for example, "a pig's head from whose mouth stuck a scarlet lobster as if putting out its tongue, and the lobster was holding the pig's tongue in its pincers as if they had torn it out," or some beheaded snails, whose heads she had "inserted, I think with a toothpick, each in a wire-mesh; they looked, as they came on the table, like a flight of tiny swans" (9–10). No wonder indeed that Cosimo should rebel against such a cuisine, and the cruelty that it implies against "the poor tortured creatures" and that is implicit in every power.

Perhaps precisely the theme of power (which will fascinate Calvino so much when he writes an essay on Manzoni's *I promessi sposi*, defined as "the novel of ratios of power" in 1973, now in *Una pietra sopra*) can serve as the appropriate link with the third novel of the trilogy, *Il cavaliere inesistente*. The behavior of the emperor, who sits at table before everybody else and helps himself with his hands, "against all Imperial rules of etiquette," prompts a general remark, such as could be found in a treatise on the nature of political power: "Absolute power often slackens all controls and generates arbitrary actions, even in the most temperate of sovereigns" (72). However, in this novel the discourse on food is connected above all with that on eros in the two juxtaposed figures of Agilulf and Gurduloo. Food and eros are equally ideal and abstract for the knight, material and concrete for the squire, with their respective intertextual precursors Ariosto and Folengo, in addition, of course, to Cervantes.

It is no wonder then that the ancient and chivalric topos of the banquet is taken up and ironized by Calvino in order to prepare his literary bet of how to make a nonexistent knight "eat": "What had he come to do at table, he who had not and never would have any appetite, nor stomach to fill, nor mouth to bring his fork to, nor palate to sprinkle with Bordeaux wine?" (73). Agilulf "never failed to appear at these banquets" because "he had the right like all the others to a place at the Imperial table," and he "carried out the banquet ceremonial with the same meticulous care that he put into every other ceremonial act of the day" (73), in clear and total juxtaposition with the disorderly conduct of the other knights:

> The courses were the usual ones in a military mess: stuffed turkey roasted on the spit, braised oxen, suckling pig, eels, gold fish. Scarcely had the lackeys offered the platters than the paladins flung themselves on them, rummaged about with their hands and tore the food apart, smearing their cuirasses and squirting sauce everywhere. The confusion was worse than battle—soup tureens overturning, roast chickens flying, and lackeys yanking away platters before a greedy paladin emptied them into his porringer. (73)

Against such a noisy and chaotic backdrop, here is what the nonexistent knight does, how he behaves with a punctiliousness that in part justifies the length of the quotation:

At the corner of the table where Agilulf sat, on the other hand, all proceeded cleanly, calmly and orderly. But he who ate nothing needed more attendance than the whole of the rest of the table. First of all . . . Agilulf went on asking to have put in front of him fresh crockery and cutlery, plates big and small, porringers, glasses of every size and shape, innumerable forks and spoons and knives that had to be well sharpened. So exigent was he about cleanliness that a shadow on a glass or plate was enough for him to send it back. He served himself a little of everything. Not a single dish did he let pass. For example, he peeled off a slice of roast boar, put meat on one plate, sauce on another, smaller, plate, then with a very sharp knife chopped the meat into tiny cubes, which one by one he passed on to yet another plate, where he flavored them with sauce, until they were soaked in it. Those with sauce he then put in a new dish and every now and again called a lackey to take away the last plate and bring him a new one. Thus he busied himself for half hours at a time. Not to mention chickens, pheasants, thrushes—at these he worked for whole hours. (73–74)

I shall not follow Agilulf as he deals with the rest of the dishes and the variety of wines. Clearly, it is a very fine page, a delightful divertissement lively with its invention, which defines the character and at the same time provides an ironic commentary on good manners at table. And I shall not even follow Agilulf at the table and in the bedroom of the widow Priscilla (98–103): the behavior of the character and the narrative technique are exactly the same just seen in the long quotation about the banquet.

And Gurduloo? Not having awareness of being, he con-fuses himself with all the things of the world, also and above all the soup, which was simmering in the pots of the imperial army: "He had cabbage soup spattered, smeared, all over him from head to toe, and was stained with blacking. With liquid sticking up his eyes he felt blind and came on screeching, 'All is soup!' with his hands forward as if swimming" (54). And of course, when he is surrounded by the damsels of the court of the widow Priscilla, "Gurduloo was quite beside himself now. What with the warm bath they had given him, the scents and all that pink and white flesh, his only desire now was to merge into the general fragrance" (96).

Such light and entertaining passages are part of an extremely serious discourse Calvino is pursuing on the nature of desire. Excess always leads to a lack of satisfaction: Agilulf's formalism is empty, literally, while Gurduloo's corporality is unconscious; and on the other hand, the lack of satisfaction is the spring that renews desire, as the couple Bradamante-Raimbaut demonstrate in narrative terms.

But it is important to underscore another function of food in *Il cavaliere inesistente*: it is an occasion and an example of metanarrative discourse, of an unveiling of narrative codes and mechanisms that will become predominant—indeed, primary—in *Se una notte d'inverno un viaggiatore*:

> Beneath my cell is the convent kitchen. As I write I can hear the clatter of copper and earthenware as the sisters wash platters from our meager refectory. To me the abbess has assigned a different task, the writing of this tale. . . .
>
> Today perhaps the air is hotter, the smell of cabbage stronger, my mind lazier, and the hubbub of nuns washing up can transport me no further than the field kitchens of the Frankish army. I see warriors in rows before steaming vats. . . .
>
> All I have to do next is imagine the heroes of my tale at the kitchens. I see Agilulf appear amid the smoke and bend over a pot, insensible to the smell of cabbage. (49–50)

Let us leave Agilulf amid the pots of the imperial army and proceed along the galactic and biological itineraries of *Cosmicomiche vecchie e nuove*,[15] where food, although it expresses already-known problems, acquires partly different connotations. First of all, alimentary referents from the spoken language, once inserted into the cosmic context, affect a "comic" result, of a double or squared defamiliarization, I should say. How else could I define a full moon "with a butter-colored light" (3), or the smell of the moon, which was "like smoked salmon" (4), or being "packed like sardines" there where space did not exist (43), or the galaxy that "turned like an omelet in its heated pan" (38)? After such comparisons, neither the galaxy nor the omelet will ever be the same.

But even in interstellar spaces and in the depths of time, food is above all a fantastic and literary invention, often connected with eros, as for example in the description of the "lunar milk": "It was composed chiefly of vegetal juices, tadpoles, bitumen, lentils, honey, starch crystals, sturgeon eggs, molds, pollens, gelatinous matter, worms, resins, pepper, mineral salts, combustion residue. You had only to dip the spoon under the scales that covered the Moon's scabby terrain, and you brought it out filled with that precious milk" (6). This description is quite successful in itself as a beautiful example of chaotic enumeration; however it receives full meaning only if it is referred to Signora Vhd Vhd, whose breast "had an attraction as strong as the Moon's or even stronger" (9)

on Qfwfq; once she is on the moon she remains there forever, an un-
reachable object of desire, become herself "the color of the Moon," she
who "makes the Moon the Moon and, whenever she is full, sets the dogs
to howling all night long, and me with them" (16).

The same procedure governs the narrative development of "Tutti in
un punto," beginning with the invention of noodles, a passage John Barth
must have had in mind when he wrote that in *Cosmicomiche*, "along with
the nebulae and the black holes and the lyricism, there is a nourishing
supply of pasta, bambini, and good-looking women sharply glimpsed
and gone forever" (and Barth emphasizes the alimentary metaphor by
concluding that Calvino's fiction is "delicious and high in protein"):[16]

> We got along so well all together, so well that something extraordinary was
> bound to happen. It was enough for her to say, at a certain moment: "Oh, if
> I only had some room, how I'd like to make some noodles for you boys!" And
> in that moment we all thought of the space that her round arms would oc-
> cupy, moving backward and forward with the rolling pin over the dough, her
> bosom leaning over the great mound of flour and eggs which cluttered the
> wide board while her arms kneaded and kneaded, white and shiny with oil up
> to the elbows; we thought of the space that the flour would occupy, and the
> wheat for the flour, and the fields to raise the wheat, and the mountains from
> which the water would flow to irrigate the fields. (46)

And so on and so forth, until the whole universe and the whole of time
are thought of, in a retrospective-prospective movement that will be
remembered by Marco Polo in front of the Great Khan's chessboard,
and by Palomar faced by French cheeses. But the making of noodles
separates all the "boys" from Signora Ph(i)Nk$_0$—creating space between them, so that they are no longer "all in one point"—and inexorably leads to a desire that will be impossible to satisfy and will never be
reciprocated: "she [was] lost at that very moment, and we [were left]
mourning her loss" (47).

These are only two instances of that difference on which desire is
founded and which in *Cosmicomiche* ties Qfwfq to, and divides him from,
numerous female figures: Ayl, Lll, Vud, and (particularly remarkable)
the smiling Flw, who bites "the juicy pulp" of a pineapple (It. 124).
Because this difference is at the very origin of desire, of life, it is pursued
into the meanders of cells and of genetic evolution in the "Biocomics,"
that is, in most of the stories making up *Ti con zero*.

While in the stories on the universe and the millennia in *Cosmicomiche*
galaxies, nebulae and dinosaurs are interiorized by human conscience,
in the "Biocomics" it is the human individual who is projected and ex-

teriorized into the minimal but broad structures of matter. In other words, the boundaries between subject and object are blurred, perhaps because, as Michel Serres says, "each term of the traditional subject-object dichotomy is itself split by something like a geographical divide (in the same way as I am, who speak and write today): noise, disorder, and chaos on one side; complexity, arrangement, and distribution on the other. Nothing distinguishes me ontologically from a crystal, a plant, an animal, or the order of the world," since each one has its own "diverse systemic complexion": "but this is complexity itself, which was once called being."[17]

Calvino explores just this systemic complexity, more as a narrator than as a philosopher; and through the ubiquitous, nonchalant and perplexed Qfwfq he posits problems and values about the individual and the world at a new, suggestive or dizzying level of understanding.

Particularly successful in this context is "Priscilla," a touching love story involving the development and diversification of pluricellular organisms. Living "in a greedy expectation of what might come to [him] from the void" (T 77), the protagonist is constantly aware of proteins and nucleic acids inside himself and inside Priscilla, and of the changes he and his beloved undergo at every passing instant "because of the continuous renewal of the protein molecules in our cells through, for example, digestion or also respiration" (T 83). Priscilla is a lovely feminine creature who is very difficult to define because her identity is a totality, a systemic complexity, an entire "way of being" that is completely hers. For example, "the scent emanating from her skin" is due not only to her given "glandular constitution," but also to "everything she has eaten in her life" and "the brands of soap she has used"—in other words to "what is called, in quotes, culture." And she is she because of the things she has stored in her memory and of the things she has forgotten, which, however, "still remain recorded somewhere in the back of the neurons like all the psychic trauma a person has to swallow from infancy on" (T 84–85). This "way of being" cannot but differ from one individual to another because "we were born not from a fusion but from a juxtaposition of distinct bodies" (T 88), all the way down into the core of the nuclei, which, in duplicating themselves, actually perpetuate "the unbridgeable distance that separates in each couple the two companions" (T 88). Thus the narrator can, at most, remember the sweetness of "sunsets in the oasis" and a gesture by now well known to the reader, "a little nip" he gave Priscilla's curved neck when they were camels together, before she became an elegant Parisian girl (T 93).

The same yearning is expressed in even stronger and more extreme terms in "Il sangue, il mare," where the memory of "the primordial wave which continues to flow in the arteries" (T45) explains the aggressive impulses of Qfwfq toward his rival, Signor Cècere, as well as his "sanguinary" instinct to reproduce himself by coupling with Zylphia in order to multiply their "blood circulation":

> So there was in my impulse toward Zylphia, not only the drive to have all the ocean for us, but also the drive to lose it, the ocean, to annihilate ourselves in the ocean, to destroy ourselves, to torment ourselves, or rather—as a beginning—to torment her, Zylphia my beloved, to tear her to pieces, to eat her up. And with her it's the same: what she wanted was to torment me, devour me, swallow me, nothing but that. The orange stain of the sun seen from the water's depths swayed like a medusa, and Zylphia darted among the luminous filaments devoured by the desire to devour me, and I writhed in the tangles of darkness that rose from the depths like long strands of seaweed beringed with indigo glints, raving and longing to bite her. (T 55)

This truly beautiful page seems to recall and enlarge a thematics playfully expressed by Raymond Queneau, the founder of the Oulipo group Calvino knew and admired: in *Petite cosmogonie portative*, the living species are first cannibals, as descendants "de la cellule unique édentée et imberbe / qui découvrit que c'est dégustable un vivant" (from the single toothless and callow cell / that discovered that a living being can be tasted); then they evolve and discover sexuality, whereby all the animals "savourent la planète en y procréfoutant" (savor the planet while procreating-screwing on it—notice the felicitous French neologism-pun that fuses the genetic function with erotic pleasure).[18] But while Queneau's discourse builds a joyful and ironic cosmogony, Calvino's is more perplexed and tormented: Qfwfq and Zylphia's reciprocal desire to tear and devour each other under the medusa sun is already a preview, in the genetic depths, of the inquiry that Calvino carries out in the anthropological depths of "Sotto il sole giaguaro." The jump is not so vertiginous if one considers the final invitation of Signor Cècere, before the car accident, to stop and eat "a cold minestrone soup at the truck drivers' café" (T 56).

I shall stop, instead, for a moment at the court-inn of *Il castello dei destini incrociati*, where the combined topoi of the chivalric castle, the picaresque inn, and the banquet propitious to story-telling are used together with the spell of muteness in order to create the indispensable conditions and the appropriate atmosphere for the combinatorial experiment of a series of narrations developed by means of a Tarot cards deck. (Just for the record, the guests are served a pheasant timbale, amid "the sounds of chewing and the smacking of lips gulping wine").[19]

The combinatorial method achieves the most intense, rarefied, and elegant results in *Le città invisibili*, perhaps because it is governed by a deconstructive logic in which the Khan's power is juxtaposed with the curiosity and the knowledge of Marco Polo, an exceptional tourist who wanders along the imperial routes carrying the image of his native Venice always in his heart.[20] All the feminine names of the cities Marco describes indicate the constant metonymies of desire, a desire constantly different and constantly renewed that is at the root of all lives, even the most alienated, like those of the inhabitants of Chloe, who "are all strangers" and "imagine a thousand things about one another, . . . surprises, caresses, bites" (51)—a minimal but important signal of an extraordinary fantastic coherence in Calvino's texts, from Giglia to Flw and from Priscilla to Zylphia, as noted so far, and to Olivia in "Sotto il sole giaguaro."

In any case, in the multiple phenomenology of the world appearances, alimentary referents play a remarkable role. Both in the interludes between Marco and the Khan, and in the descriptions of the cities, these referents are in fact simply fragments of reality that are used systematically to build and deconstruct various models and aspects of cities. These referents are purely verbal fragments posited as a warranty of the possible reality of the world and experience—also, and perhaps above all, fantastic experience. So the reader may recognize or give features and substance to the "food stalls" of Diomira (7), the sign with the "tankard" that means "the tavern" at Tamara (13), or "the melon vendor's kiosk" (15), the "wineskins and bags of candied fruit, date wine, tobacco leaves" (17), or ginger, pistachio nuts, and poppy seeds, sacks of nutmegs and raisins (36), or "zebus browning on the spit and dripping fat" dreamed by the Khan (73), "the boats unloading baskets of vegetables at the market squares" (85), "the barrels of salted fish" and the "sacks of pepper" (103), or "cooks cleaning the lights of chickens" (117); or again one remembers "a wand of bread" held in hand by millions of Parisians (136), or "a piece of polenta dropped by a stonemason" and "a young serving-maid who holds up a dish of ragout under the pergola" at Raissa (148), or "the sober but tasty cuisine, which evokes an ancient golden age" for the righteous people of Berenice: "rice and celery soup, boiled beans, fried squash flowers" (161). Indeed, the appearances of the world have an inexhaustible richness and variety, and in front of them Marco's attitude is already a prelude to Palomar's systematic perplexity.

Other fragments of reality, other culinary images are part of *Se una notte d'inverno un viaggiatore*,[21] where they contribute in a substantial and decisive way to the disassembling of narrative mechanisms and codes. At the beginning of "Fuori dell'abitato di Malbork," "An odor of frying wafts at the opening of the page, of onion in fact, onion being fried, a bit scorched" (17). It is an exemplary beginning because it foregrounds the tension between the elements of representation and the formal ones, because it calls attention to the construction of the text precisely by decontructing it. Thus the frying oil is "rape oil, the text specifies; everything here is very precise, things with their nomenclature and the sensations that things transmit," and then the foods, the stove, the tools in the large kitchen at Kudgiwa, and everything, in this pseudo-Polish and pseudo-realistic novel, "is very concrete, substantial," and "the impression given to you, Reader, is one of expertise, though there are some foods you don't know, mentioned by name, which the translator has decided to leave in the original; for example, *schoëblintsjia*" (34). Or again, almost a quotation from an ironic treatise on narratology:

> What counts are the physical details that the novel underlines . . . and also the gestures, the utensils that this person or that is handling—the meat pounder, the colander for the cress, the butter curler—so that each character already receives a first definition through this action or attribute; but then we wish to learn even more, as if the butter curler already determined the character and the fate of the person who is presented in the first chapter handling a butter curler, . . . thus obligating the author to attribute to him acts and events in keeping with that initial butter curler. (35–36)

Suffice it to recall here some of the considerations already developed in examining other texts (such as Don Abbondio's little flask, or Angelica's foreign peaches). But the expectations arising from Calvino's ineffable butter curler are further confirmed and at the same time placed *en abyme* by the page on the kitchen of the (feminine) Reader: "The kitchen is the part of the house that can tell the most things about you: whether you cook or not, . . . whether only for yourself or also for others, whether you tend toward the bare minimum or toward gastronomy, . . . whether standing over the stove represents for you a painful necessity or also a pleasure" (142). It is a tiny kitchen, as my reader may remember from the introduction, but it is a functional, modern kitchen, equipped with all the necessary tools (even if a butter curler does not seem to be there). The narrator accompanies the (male) Reader with the eye and the attitude of an amorous detective after the traces (the objects become signs) of his beloved. So the various provisions—an assortment of herbs, the mustards, "the ropes of garlic hung within reach," the only egg left in the refrigerator with half a lemon, "and that half-dried," while "on the other hand, there is chestnut purée, black olives, a little jar of salsify or horseradish"—these provisions are so many indications of the character (but I should really say "the way of being") of the feminine Reader: "Observing your kitchen, therefore, can create a picture of you as an extroverted, clearsighted woman, sensual and methodical; you make your practical sense serve your imagination. Could a man fall in love with you, just seeing your kitchen?" (143). Certainly yes, and first of all the author, who in the meantime has confirmed the strict connection between food and eros, and has prepared the ground for another deconstruction and another connection concerning love relations: "Ludmilla, now you are being read. Your body is being subjected to a systematic reading, through channels of tactile information, visual, olfactory, and not without some intervention of the taste buds. Hearing also has its role, alert to your gasps and your trills" (155). All five senses are then necessary for a successful "reading" of the beloved; but they are not sufficient, in front of the other's systemic complexity:

> It is not only the body that is, in you, the object of reading: the body matters insofar as it is part of a complex of elaborate elements, not all visible and not all present, but manifested in visible and present events: the clouding of your eyes, your laughing, the words you speak, your way of gathering and spreading your hair, your initiatives and your reticences, and all the signs that are on the frontier between you and usage and habits and memory and prehistory and fashion, all codes, all the poor alphabets by which one human being believes at certain moments that he is reading another human being. (155)

This passage is a true comment by Calvino on himself, in a trajectory going in particular from Priscilla in the biocomics to Olivia in "Sotto il sole giaguaro." Speaking of whom, it is worth recalling that the male Reader "takes a special nip" at the feminine Reader's shoulder (155), and that the act of biting the beloved is imagined or stated twice elsewhere in *Se una notte d'inverno un viaggiatore*: in the pseudo-Japanese erotic novel (205) and in the pseudo-South American novel, where Jacinta replies to the narrator, showing her teeth: "As for that, I can gnaw you as clean as a bone" (231). The narrator of "Intorno a una fossa vuota," during his quest for his mother, eats "a dish of spiced meatballs" that burns his lips "as if that flavor should contain all flavors carried to their extreme"; and he reviews all the flavors he has tasted in his life "to try to recognize this multiple flavor," but he arrives "at an opposite but perhaps equivalent sensation which is that of the milk for an infant, since as the first flavor it contains all flavors" (226). In any event, the narrator's quest remains useless, and in this meal-synecdoche flavor (*sapore*) does not bring knowledge (*sapere*).

In three chapters of *Palomar*,[22] where the eponymous protagonist does his shopping in Paris, respectively in a charcuterie, a cheese store, and a butcher shop, Calvino surveys a great variety of foods. Actually, Palomar's gastronomic and cognitive itinerary evokes the motifs traced by Calvino's earlier texts: the connections between food and eros, between the mechanism of desire and satisfaction, between abundance and lack of satisfaction; and food as a metonymy of the world, at the center of the relations between human beings, nature, and history. By now it is apparent that Calvino's exploration can be considered anthropological even more than cultural or sociological.

Palomar explicitly identifies food with eros when he remembers a cassoulet, "a fat stew of meats and beans in which goose fat is an essential ingredient" (67), that awakens in him "an immediate fantasy not so much of appetite as of eros: from a mountain of goose fat a female figure surfaces, smears white over her rosy skin, and he already imagines himself making his way toward her through those thick avalanches, embracing her, sinking with her" (68). There is not even time to listen to the intertextual echoes—of Gesubambino with Tuscan Mary after the theft in the pastry shop, of Gurduloo amid the damsels at the court of the widow Priscilla, and of Qfwfq longing for Signora Vhd Vhd or Zylphia—because in the meantime, Palomar discovers that some cheeses "on their platters seem to proffer themselves as if on the divans of a brothel," so that they are called with "lowering nicknames" (72). And soon after, more subtly, he knows he is "conditioned by his alimentary background to perceive in a butcher shop the promise of gustatory happiness, to imagine . . . the pleasure of the tooth in severing the browned fiber" of a grilled steak (78). The (gustatory) happiness and the (tooth's) pleasure possess a remarkably sensual connotation in their ambiguity and polysemy.

But Palomar is also fascinated, irresistibly, by the "cornucopia of the world," by the "Pantagruelic glory" (69) displayed in the shop windows.

His fascination is expressed above all through the list and the catalogue: "salamis that hang from the Christmas wreaths like fruit from boughs in the land of Cockaigne," "game pâté," "galantines of pheasant," "the roseate, variegated beds of pâtés de foie gras, of head cheese, terrines, galantines, fans of salmon, artichoke hearts garnished like trophies," and "mountains of vol-au-vents, white puddings, cervelats" (68–69); then the various types of cheese, of which Palomar tries "a classification" according to shapes, textures, "alien materials involved in the crust or in the heart," although he knows that "true knowledge" lies "in the experience of the flavors" (73); and finally all the meat cuts, from the "vast ribs" to the "slender and agile contre-filets," from tournedos to rolled roasts, and "veal escalopes, loin chops," "legs and shoulders of lamb; farther on some white tripe glows, a liver glistens blackly" (77).

But since Palomar's gluttony is perhaps "chiefly mental, aesthetic, symbolic" (69), he is destined to remain disappointed: in the charcuterie the people appear to him "gray and opaque and sullen" (68), and he will almost "end up convincing himself that he is the profane one, the alien, the outsider" (70). As a consequence, ironically, instead of making "the elaborate and greedy order that he intended to make," he falls back "on the most obvious, the most banal, the most advertised" cheese of them all (74–75). At the butcher's his mood is one "of restrained joy and fear, desire and respect, egoistic concern and universal compassion, the mood that perhaps others express in prayer" (78).

To make up for his disappointment, he uses his eyes and his reflections to transform every food "into a document of the history of civilization, a museum exhibit" (70)—but a living, fertile museum, one that Duthuit would call "unimaginable."[23] In fact:

> Behind every cheese there is a pasture of a different green under a different sky: meadows caked with salt that the tides of Normandy deposit every evening; meadows scented with aromas in the windy sunlight of Provence; there are different flocks, with their stablings and their transhumances; there are secret processes handed down over the centuries. This shop is a museum. Mr. Palomar, visiting it, feels as he does in the Louvre, behind every displayed object the presence of the civilization that has given it form and takes form from it. (73)

Similarly, Palomar experiences the cheese shop as an encyclopedia and a dictionary: "the language is the system of cheeses as a whole," and "learning a bit of nomenclature still remains the first measure to be taken" in order "to stop for a moment the things that are flowing" (74).

Obviously, his personal relationship with cheeses, with the world, will be extremely complicated. Palomar responds in much the same way at the butcher shop:

> On the wall a chart shows an outline of a steer, like a map covered with frontier lines that mark off the areas of consuming interest, involving the entire anatomy of the animal except only horns and hoofs. The map of the human habitat is this, no less than the planisphere of the planet; both are protocols that should sanction the rights man has attributed to himself, of possession, division, and consumption without residue of the terrestrial continents and of the loins of the animal body. (77)

Here Palomar advances the same view that juxtaposes Marco Polo and the Khan, the same deconstructive and cognitive logic that contrasts with the western tradition of the dialectics of possession and power. Palomar's perplexity becomes emblematic of an attitude toward the world that is less arrogant and violent than logocentrism: if "butchering wisdom and culinary doctrine belong to the exact sciences, . . . sacrificial practice, on the other hand, is dominated by uncertainty, and what's more fell into oblivion centuries ago, but still it weighs obscurely on the conscience, an unexpressed demand" (76). Palomar embodies and expresses precisely this demand, with pensive irony, by partaking of "the man-beef symbiosis" with "a clear conscience and full agreement," but stressing again that "what is called human civilization should be called human-bovine," as well as "human-ovine" and "human-porcine, . . . depending on the alternatives of a complicated geography of religious prohibitions" (78). The insights and the interpretations that the anthropologist Mary Douglas develops on this subject are also quite pertinent to Calvino's discourse.[24]

In these passages from *Palomar* there is in full evidence an element that is lacking in the corresponding yet significant passages by Gadda on the slaughterhouse and the markets of Milan, examined in the previous chapter: the sense of the sacred. Perhaps it is this sense that explains Palomar's obscure fascination with the belly of the gecko on an illuminated glass, which allows him to see, "as if under X rays," a just-swallowed gnat "in its course through the viscera that absorb it"; he ponders:

> If all material were transparent—the ground that supports us, the envelope that sheathes our body—everything would be seen not as a fluttering of impalpable wings but as an inferno of grinding and ingesting. Perhaps at this

moment a god of the nether world situated in the center of the earth with his eyes that can pierce granite is watching us from below, following the cycle of living and dying, the lacerated victims dissolving in the bellies of their devourers, until they, in their turn, are swallowed by another belly. (58)

An infernal god: a terrible and sanguinary god similar to the ancient Mexican deities the Italian couple face in "Sotto il sole giaguaro"—the story to which I finally return after the long *excursus* through Calvino's oeuvre. All the examples collected and ordered so far should prove indispensable as antecedents that elucidate how the culinary obsession in the story works to give a global explanation of both the individual and the species, in a cognitive inquiry that inextricably combines gastronomy, anthropology, and eroticism on the literary page.

Early in "Sotto il sole giaguaro" elements of a cultural gastronomy are already oriented toward anthropology:

> In Tepotzotlán . . . we had savored dishes prepared (at least, so we were told) according to the traditional recipes of the nuns. We had eaten a *tamal de elote*—a fine semolina of sweet corn, that is, with ground pork and very hot pepper, all steamed in a bit of corn-husk—and then *chiles en nogada*, which were reddish brown, somewhat wrinkled little peppers, swimming in a walnut sauce whose harshness and bitter aftertaste were drowned in a creamy, sweetish surrender. (5)

The description of these doubly exotic recipes—exotic both in space (they are Mexican) and in time (they are ancient)—is based entirely on the minimal nuances of gustatory perceptions and sensations, hence it is made from Olivia's standpoint. Soon afterwards the narrator's conceptualization follows, even if both are unified in the first-person plural of the couple:

> After that, for us, the thought of nuns called up the flavors of an elaborate and bold cuisine, bent on making the flavors' highest notes vibrate, juxtaposing them in modulations, in chords, and especially in dissonances that would assert themselves as an incomparable experience—a point of no return, an absolute possession exercised on the receptivity of all the senses. (5)

But such a conceptualization must take history—micro-history—into account. It presupposes nuns who devoted their entire lives "to the search of new blends of ingredients, new variations in the measurements, to alert and patient mixing, to the handing down of an intricate, precise lore" (6); not to mention that those same nuns, through their recipes, wanted to express "their fantasies confined" within the convents' walls,

> the fantasies, after all, of sophisticated women, bright and introverted and complex women who needed absolutes, whose reading told of ecstasies and transfigurations, martyrs and tortures, women with conflicting calls in their blood, genealogies in which the descendants of the conquistadores mingled with those of Indian princesses or slaves, women with childhood recollections of the fruits and fragrances of a succulent vegetation, thick with ferments, though growing from those sun-baked plateaus. (6)

There is an intertextual reference here to the "eight thousand nuns" described by Emilio Cecchi in *Messico*, who comments not only on "the luminous and sumptuous preparation" of their sweets but also on "the clashes in their blood, the pride of their castes, the ambitions, the jealousies, the atavistic and dark fevers."[25] But above all for me, the passage evokes the memory of Sor Juana de la Cruz in the splendid pages written about her by Octavio Paz in *El laberinto de la soledad*.[26] The sacred architecture Cecchi discusses is also pertinent,[27] for in Calvino's story it is "the background to the lives of those religious; it, too, was impelled by the same drive toward the extreme that led to the exacerbation of flavors amplified by the blaze of the most spicy *chiles*," which "opened vistas of a flaming ecstasy" (7). It is the baroque architecture, "a dancing and acrobatic baroque," of the seminary built by the Jesuits during the eighteenth century at Tepotzotlán "to compete with the splendor of the Aztecs" (7), and it provides the necessary historical and anthropological background for Calvino's inquiry:

> There was a challenge in the air, . . . the ancient rivalry between the civilizations of America and Spain in the art of bewitching the senses with dazzling seductions. And from architecture this rivalry extended to cuisine, where the two civilizations had merged, or perhaps where the conquered had triumphed, strong in the condiments born from their very soil. Through the white hands of novices and the brown hands of lay sisters, the cuisine of the new Indo-Hispanic civilization had become also the field of battle between the aggressive ferocity of the ancient gods of the mesa and the sinuous excess of the baroque religion. (7–8)

During a masterfully and tastily described supper of guacamole, *guajolote con mole poblano*, and *quesadillas*,[28] the narrator persistently watches Olivia's lips pause "right in the midst of chewing," while "her face had a special concentration" (8–9). When then the couple, continuing their trip, go on to Monte Albán with its "temples, reliefs, grand stairways, platforms for human sacrifice," the narrator observes that "horror, sacredness, and mystery are consolidated by tourism, which dictates preordained forms of behavior, the modest surrogates of those rites. Contemplating these stairs, we try to imagine the hot blood spurting from the breast split by the stone axe of the priest" (12–13). After visiting these sacred places, Olivia asks the native guide, without getting a satisfactory answer: "But what did they do with the victims' bodies afterward?" (15); and during the return trip on the jolting bus the narrator notices a strange change in his own attitude toward his companion: "I realized my gaze was resting not on her eyes but on her teeth (she kept her lips parted in a pensive expression), which I happened to be seeing for the first time not as the radiant glow of a smile but as the instrument most suited for their purpose: to be dug into flesh, to sever it, tear it" (16). Here the narrator, with a self-reflexive movement, becomes explicitly aware ("I realized") of his own attitude toward Olivia, which he had mentioned a few pages earlier; and his meditation, which superimposes an anthropological dimension on the erotic one, calls to mind the many similar images already noted in Calvino's preceding texts.

The interest in human sacrifices that had always animated Calvino's mentor and friend, Cesare Pavese (in the ethnographic area of a Kerényi or a Frazer), is combined here with a post-Freudian and post-Sadean intellectual curiosity that is similar to, but independent of, that of René Girard.[29] Calvino contemplates the individual and collective unconscious in its most unexplored and disquieting levels in an effort to understand the most obscure sides of desire, eros, and culture.

Not by chance, Salustiano, the couple's Mexican friend, functions in these pages as the illustrator of well-known anthropological notions, such as those Peggy Reeves Sanday discusses in the recent *Divine Hunger: Cannibalism as a Cultural System*. Significantly, the treatise by Sahagún that accompanies Calvino's story in *FMR* serves as the primary historical source and preliminary documentation for her anthropological interpretation: the "ritual meal," the victim considered as "divine food," the participants including priests, princes, and warriors, but not the one person who had captured the victim.[30] Olivia, however, is not satisfied by such accounts. Her desire to know is directed toward what Reeves Sanday calls "a gourmet appreciation of human flesh" and

includes among other possible explanations for cannibalism: psychological ("revenge, masculine bravado"), political ("ambition"), and cosmological and religious ("desire to communicate with and feed the gods")
explanations.[31]

In her desire to know, in her insistent probing, Olivia seems truly to
embody literature as Calvino conceives it: a cognitive instrument that
goes beyond anthropology and postulates an inexhaustible and limitless
inquiry. In "Cibernetica e fantasmi" Calvino asks: "But is the tension in
literature not continually striving to escape from this finite number [of
elements and functions of language]? Does it not continually attempt to
say something it cannot say, something that it does not know, and that
no one could ever know?"[32] Olivia's prodding questions echo Calvino's
rhetorical repetitions: "But this flesh—in order to eat it . . . The way it
was cooked, the sacred cuisine, the seasoning—is anything known about
that?" (19). Salustiano concedes that human flesh had "a strange flavor,
they say" and that "all other flavors had to be brought together, to hide
that flavor" (20). But Olivia objects that "perhaps that flavor emerged,
all the same—even through the other flavors," and Salustiano, enigmat-
ically enough, replies that the sacred cuisine "had to celebrate the harmony of the elements achieved through sacrifice—a terrible harmony,
flaming, incandescent" (20).

Later on, taking up the anxious debate again, Olivia remarks to the
narrator that "perhaps the death of time concerns only us. . . . We who
tear one another apart, pretending not to know it, pretending not to
taste flavors anymore," while the Aztecs dared to look at the horror
in front of them (22). So Olivia proposes her conjecture on the "sacred" taste of human flesh: "Perhaps it couldn't be hidden. *Shouldn't*
be. Otherwise, it was like not eating what they were really eating. Perhaps the other flavors served to enhance that flavor, to give it a worthy
background, to honor it" (22). At these words by Olivia, the narrator feels again "the need to look her in the teeth" (22) as he had done
earlier, and he does so when the two are eating *sopa de camarones* and
cabrito:[33]

> It was the sensation of her teeth in my flesh that I was imagining, and I could
> feel her tongue lift me against the roof of her mouth, enfold me in saliva, then
> thrust me under the tips of the canines. I sat there facing her, but at the same
> time it was as if a part of me, or all of me, were contained in her mouth,
> crunched, torn shred by shred. The situation was not entirely passive, since
> while I was being chewed by her I felt also that I was acting on her, transmit-

ting sensations that spread from the taste buds through her whole body. I was the one who aroused her every vibration—it was a reciprocal and complete relationship, which involved us and overwhelmed us. (23)

What the narrator describes is an entirely inner sensation, an intense and silent act of imagination that makes me remember Rinaldo in Armida's arms in Torquato Tasso's *Gerusalemme liberata* (xvi, 19, 1–2): "e i famelici sguardi avidamente / in lei pascendo si consuma e strugge" (and nurturing the famished gazes avidly / in her he is consumed and yearning). With an entirely modern sensitivity, then, Calvino's text develops and varies an ancient literary topos. This is the point where the anthropological and the erotic components are fused together, but it is also a narrative turn because the narrator's silence prompts a strong reaction from Olivia, who accuses him of being "always sunk into" himself, "depressing, indifferent," and even "insipid!" (24–25).[34] In response to this charge, the narrator muses: "There: I was insipid, I thought, without flavor. And the Mexican cuisine, with all its boldness and imagination, was needed if Olivia was to feed on me with satisfaction. The spiciest flavors were the complement—indeed, the avenue of communication, indispensable as a loudspeaker that amplifies sounds— for Olivia to be nourished by my substance" (25).

Of course, the narrator is wrong; and only the thought of the *chac-mool*, a "half-reclining human figure, in an almost Etruscan pose, with a tray resting on his belly," a tray on which "the victims' hearts were offered to the gods" (25), will be useful in resolving the couple's conflict. In fact, Salustiano explains, the *chac-mool* could have been both the victim and the sacrificer, who "assumes the pose of the victim because he is aware that tomorrow it will be his turn. Without this reciprocity, human sacrifice would be unthinkable . . . the victim accepted his role as victim because he had fought to capture the others as victims" (26). These words find precise confirmation in anthropological studies,[35] but here they have the essential narrative function of provoking a psychological reaction in the narrator: "Meanwhile I understood: my mistake with Olivia was to consider myself eaten by her, whereas I should be myself (I always had been) the one who ate her. The most appetizingly flavored human flesh belongs to the eater of human flesh. It was only by feeding ravenously on Olivia that I would cease being tasteless to her palate" (26).

The small private drama is then solved through a metaphorical attitude patterned after the surrounding anthropological and cultural real-

ity. Hence the following supper confirms the couple's newfound linguistic accord, which is a prelude to a more properly erotic harmony:

> I concentrated on devouring, with every meatball, the whole fragrance of
> Olivia—through voluptuous mastication, a vampire extraction of vital juices.
> But I realized that in a relationship that should have been among three
> terms—me, meatball, Olivia—a fourth term had intruded, assuming a domi-
> nant role: the name of the meatballs. It was the name "*gorditas pellizcadas con
> manteca*" [literally "the small chubby ones (feminine plural) pinched with
> butter"] that I was especially savoring and assimilating and possessing. And,
> in fact, the magic of that name continued affecting me even after the meal,
> when we retired together to our hotel room in the night. And for the first
> time during our Mexican journey the spell whose victims we had been was
> broken, and the inspiration that had blessed the finest moments of our joint
> life came to visit us again. (27)

This ironic, happy ending is prolonged the following morning by "the
chac-mool pose" of the couple in bed, with "the tray with the anonymous
hotel breakfast" in their laps (27). But if the *fabula* is solved, a conclusion
is still lacking—what Manzoni would have called "the juice" of the
whole story.

In fact, the couple's newfound harmony foreshadows the arduous and
uneasy sense of universal harmony that the narrator experiences later on
at Palenque, like a vertigo, when he imagines himself a cut-up victim
falling down the steps of the Mayan Temple of the Inscriptions. He has
just visited the underground crypt "with the highly complicated carved
stone slab" representing "the descent of the body to the subterranean
gods and its rebirth as vegetation," and the high and intense words he
uses to convey what he felt bring out the meaning of the title "Under
the jaguar sun" and could rightly belong among the poetic texts Perella
analyzes in *Midday in Italian Literature*:[36]

> I went down, I climbed back up into the light of the jaguar sun—into the sea
> of the green sap of the leaves. The world spun, I plunged down, my throat cut
> by the knife of the king-priest, down the high steps onto the forest of tourists
> with super-8s and usurped, broad-brimmed sombreros. The solar energy
> coursed along dense networks of blood and chlorophyll; I was living and
> dying in all the fibers of what is chewed and digested and in all the fibers that
> absorb the sun, consuming and digesting. (28–29)

Here the narrator is like his ancestor Qfwfq who yearned to devour and
be devoured by Zylphia under the medusa sun in the depths of the pri-

mordial ocean; and he is like the contemporary thinker Michel Serres, who experiences "the living organism," the "hypercomplex system" that "receives, stores, exchanges, and gives off both energy and information—in all forms, from the light of the sun to the flow of matter which passes through it (food, oxygen, heat, signals)."[37]

Prompted first by Olivia and then by the sun and the environment, the narrator has understood that today, as Serres says, "it is no longer necessary to maintain the distinction between introspective . . . and objective knowledge. There is only one type of knowledge and it is always linked to an observer, an observer submerged in a system or in its proximity. And this observer is structured exactly like what he observes."[38]

Appropriately, such knowledge receives its definitive narrative seal in the couple's final supper:

> Our teeth began to move slowly, with equal rhythm, and our eyes stared into each other's with the intensity of serpents'—serpents concentrated in the ecstasy of swallowing each other in turn, as we were aware, in our turn of being swallowed by the serpent that digests us all, assimilated ceaselessly in the process of ingestion and digestion, in the universal cannibalism that leaves its imprint on every amorous relationship and erases the lines between our bodies and *sopa de frijoles*, *huachinango a la veracruzana*, and *enchiladas* . . . (29)

Here food is at once the object and the instrument of a transgression of a fundamental taboo—a totally mental and imaginary transgression, to be sure, but nevertheless a powerful and significant one, a transgression already present in Olivia's insistent questioning and the narrator's silent glances. Here the narrator abandons the cognitive perplexity that makes Palomar pause, in analogous circumstances, in front of the *chac-mool* and the serpent: for him too it is impossible "not to interpret."[39]

In fact the narrator, who, after all, is a tourist (that is, a potential observer par excellence), uses the figures and the memories of the ancient myths and rites to suggest the most wide-ranging and rational explanation possible, on the threshold of the unspeakable, for the aspects of human nature that are the farthest from reason, to understand the relations of self to others and the world. The "universal cannibalism" is the "geographical divide" inside him and his companion as subjects and observers (it leaves its mark on their love for each other) as well as outside them, in the objects of their observation (it "erases the lines between our bodies and *sopa de frijoles*, *huachinango a la veracruzana*, and *enchiladas*"). It is a cognitive category that should be juxtaposed with the unconscious Panism of a Gurduloo, for whom "All is soup!"; it is also broader than the biological knowledge of Qfwfq in "Priscilla" and "Il sangue, il mare": *natura naturans* both surrounds us and exists within us, but so does civilization, so does culture.[40] Neither culture nor nature is at all idyllic: both are "hypercomplex systems." As Calvino states in *Collezione di sabbia*, in his account of his own visit (as a tourist following Cecchi's lead) precisely to the Temple of the Inscriptions at Palenque: "Perhaps the gods that rule over discourse are no longer those who repeated the terrible but never desperate tale of a sequence of destruction and rebirth in an endless cycle. Other gods speak through us, aware that what is finished does not return."[41]

For this reason we cannot be cannibals; we can only be tourists, perhaps gluttonous and enamored, but always sensitive and aware. Both the ancient Aztec cannibals and the modern Italian tourists are part of human civilization, with the same status and the same rights, in two phases. The first phase included humankind, synecdochically and metaphorically, in a discourse on the cosmos in which the cycle (the species) was more important than linearity (the individual), and the individual sacrifice served to preserve the species by concretizing the metaphor of "feeding" the gods. In contrast, the second phase, with the coming of Christianity, effects a complete reversal: linearity prevails over the cycle, the individual is valorized to the utmost vis-à-vis the species, and it is God himself, Christ, who through the Eucharist ("Take and eat: this is my body") concretizes an opposite metaphor and "nourishes," and hence saves, the individual.[42]

Today, Calvino's tourists are undoubtedly lay Christians, but it is as tourists, not as believers, that they show an interest in religion and come into contact with it. The contamination of the sacred by the profane, typical of symbolist art and particularly of D'Annunzio's aestheticism, appears to be taken for granted—after all, "Eucharist" means "communion" and hence also "conviviality." However, the couple's gustatory and cognitive exploration through modern scientific categories (from biology to psychoanalysis) can only confirm the fundamental change that has taken place in civilization (and the related taboo), at the very moment when a common root is recognized and interiorized. It is worth recalling in this connection the story on the sense of smell, "Il nome, il naso," in *Sotto il sole giaguaro*: in a situation reminiscent of Qfwfq's, the narrator is in turn a prehistoric man, a nineteenth-century casanova, and a contemporary rock musician, all three united by the irresistible sexual attraction of a trace of feminine perfume in their nostrils—and once more there is a fantastic coherence of a parenthetic sentence dealing with Sidonie, a shopgirl in a Parisian *parfumerie*: "between her parted lips I could glimpse her little teeth, whose bites I knew so well" (69).

It is because of this common root, of this fundamental equality, that Calvino's discourse can be related to other discourses, born of opposing but complementary viewpoints, by Octavio Paz in *El laberinto de la soledad* and by Tzvetan Todorov in *La conquête de l'Amérique: La question de l'autre* (published in Paris in 1982, the year that "Sapore sapere" appeared). For Todorov, from Columbus to Sahagún the history of the European discovery of the other passed through terrible and contradictory phases: discovering and knowing, loving and destroying, produced enslavement and colonialism but also communication and understanding. Analogously, Paz refuses "to regard the human sacrifices of the Aztecs as an isolated expression of cruelty without relation to the rest of that civilization," but acknowledges that the conquest and the consequent colonialism, beyond the massacres and the exploitation, created in the New World both art forms and a cosmological and universal order that somehow redeem the atrocities: "History has the cruel reality of a nightmare, and the grandeur of man consists in his making beautiful and lasting works out of the real substance of that nightmare."[43] It is this type of ideological, historical, and moral discourse, this self-awareness that underlies Calvino's literary invention. Therefore one could say that if it is impossible for us to be cannibals (that is, if we cannot accept a society based on human sacrifice), then, being tourists, we cannot and must not ever be *conquistadores* (that is, we cannot accept a society based on massacres).

The whole story of "Sotto il sole giaguaro" is filtered through the narrator's "verbalization" and "conceptualization," his linguistic conscience, which is also his self-awareness in writing. This self-awareness is revealed by the very first words of the text (" 'Oaxaca' is pronounced 'Wahaka'," p. 3) and is confirmed, particularly in the last extended quotations, by the emphasis on "the magic of the name" *gorditas pellizcadas* (almost an echo from Montale: "Buffalo!—e il nome agì," unless we want to go back to D'Annunzio's magic of the word),[44] and by the last sentence of the story, which ends with the *names* of three exotic foods, followed by suspension dots to indicate that the list is not concluded (and, as I have noted, lists play an important part in Calvino's cognitive itinerary, even beyond the combinatorial process).[45]

This linguistic self-awareness is the key element in Calvino's literary construction, the element that allows him to transcend the horror he has explored at the root of civilization. This horror is indicated but absolutely unspeakable at the end of Joseph Conrad's *Heart of Darkness* (Calvino's very first critical interest). But in Conrad, the idealism, the passivity, and the blindness of the unnamed woman betrothed to Kurtz may be interpreted, according to both B. R. Stark and Giuseppe Sertoli, as the meaning that fills the void of a missing signifier (the "name" of the woman is, narratively speaking, in Marlow's answer, "the horror," whereby primitive cannibalism is turned back ironically against "civilized" colonialism).[46] Instead, in Calvino, Olivia's sensorial concreteness, dynamism, and intellectual curiosity are the forces of an inquiry that takes for granted the equality of human beings no longer divided between civilized and primitive, and that wants to face the horror of a common originary condition. Once again, Olivia is literature, she embodies its cognitive tension: "The struggle of literature is in fact a struggle to escape from the confines of language; it stretches out from the utmost limits of what can be said."[47]

This is the reason why cannibalism is metaphorized—in fact, lived as a metaphor: indeed, Calvino's story seems to illustrate the thesis of the ethnologist Jean Pouillon, who, in explaining how the rules of incest and of cannibalism (called "alimentary incest" by Lévi-Strauss) are always at the foundation of social structures, remarks that in societies where "man is not an object of alimentary consumption," the "eating manners" of cannibalistic societies become "manners of speaking about manners of going to bed."[48] Accordingly, as we have seen, cannibalism is uttered—that is, exorcised in the transference of its field of application—by and in the spasmodic gastronomic sensitivity of "Sotto il sole giaguaro," in a prose miraculously balanced between the sublime (myth) and the comic (tourism), the universal (blood and chlorophyll) and the particular (the couple's meals and bed), the subjective (psychoanalysis) and the objective (anthropology).

In applying to "Sotto il sole giaguaro" the literary "values, qualities, or peculiarities" Calvino discusses in *Lezioni americane*, I hope that I have not loaded the story's "lightness" with undue weight, or slowed down the "quickness" of its narrative pace; all the meditations it inspires are due to the "exactitude" of its descriptions of Mexican foods (with the related perceptions and sensations), and to the "visibility" of primary images like the jaguar sun and Olivia's teeth, which are truly unforgettable; above all, these meditations should be the revealing index of the "multiplicity" of the text.[49]

At the end of his journey, of his search, Calvino arrives indeed at a knowledge ("sapere"), in fact a wisdom ("sapienza") similar to that indicated by Roland Barthes in concluding his inaugural lesson at the Collège de France: "*Sapientia*: no power, a bit of knowledge, a bit of wisdom, and the most flavor possible."[50] *Sapienza* derives from the Latin *sapio*, and according to the note by Niccolò Tommaseo[51] that serves as the epigraph of the story (*FMR*, p. 63), it is superior to science: it is, in fact, a wisdom, a human wisdom that, starting with the sense of taste (the sense that Barthes describes as "oral like language, liminal like eros"[52]), has discovered the most remote conditions, of nature and culture, that made possible the birth and the renewal of desire—that is, of life, of writing. And writing, Calvino says elsewhere,[53] is always a "projection of desire," especially when it deals, as it does here, with "another and ultimate eros, fundamental, mythical, and unattainable."

Our Daily Bread—Pane—Brot—Broid —Chleb—Pain—Lechem —Kenyér: Primo Levi, *Se questo è un uomo*

I HOPE THE READER will not consider a chapter on Primo Levi and the experience of the Nazi Lagers as inappropriate or even irrelevant for the subject of this book. On the contrary, as I have briefly said in the introduction, I believe that to examine the themes of hunger and the humanness-civilization of food in exceptional, extreme historical circumstances and settings is absolutely essential and deserves more than superficial attention. In fact, such an examination implies putting aside the pleasure principle, which is so easily connected with alimentary matters, and focusing on the other fundamental principle, need— thereby foregrounding the intrinsic morality of any discourse on human behavior.

The title I have chosen for this chapter is a collage of two quotations: the first part is, obviously, a fragment borrowed from a Christian prayer, a fragment from which the divine has disappeared and which therefore points to a thoroughly human, immanent concern, and to the morality that is inherent in the collective pronoun "our" indicating a community. The second is a quotation from Primo Levi's *Se questo è un uomo* (p. 34),[1] and I have chosen it because it points to two essential features of the book: one is the Babel of languages in the Nazi concentration camps, the other is the obsession with food necessary for survival.

In the Lagers, individual languages indeed mixed and clashed with one another without being understood, adding to the isolation and desperation of the single prisoners—a referential fact that is, at the same time, the indication of a precise linguistic and hence literary interest. In fact, this quotation is also an intertextual echo from *Gargantua et Pantagruel*, a book Levi loved. In *L'altrui mestiere*, he describes the Rabelaisian character Panurge as "an extraordinary hero in reverse" who "appears on the scene [of the text] asking *for bread in all living and dead languages*" (the italics are mine); and furthermore, for Levi, Panurge is more than just a literary character: he "is us, [he is] man. He is not exemplary, he is not 'perfection,' but he is humanity, alive because it seeks, sins, enjoys, and knows."[2]

The other feature of *Se questo e un uomo* is the representation of hunger. The Nazis deliberately used hunger as a weapon, along with cold and fatigue, to destroy their victims slowly before sending them to their deaths—the most atrocious and shameful page in contemporary history, the most bitter flavor of modernity. Hunger, with the consequent search for food, is perhaps the most preeminent and obsessive theme of *Se questo è un uomo*: obsessive because it illustrates the daily struggle for survival as well as the innermost thoughts and dreams of the prisoners, preeminent because through it the truest problem the book addresses comes eloquently to the fore: the survival of the human personality in an inhuman environment, in beastly circumstances.[3]

To talk of a theme might seem futile in the face of the horrible reality portrayed in the book and of the terrible and fundamental moral issues it raises. But the reality of the Lager was complex, and so is the reality of literature. *Se questo è un uomo* is no exception: as a literary work, it is governed by precise rules, supported by definite structures, built with effective devices—of which a theme is only one. Therefore, before examining the central theme of the book, I shall devote some preliminary remarks to the literariness of *Se questo è un uomo*, that is, to all those typically literary qualities that distinguish Levi's style.

Se questo è un uomo is undoubtedly an autobiographical book from the very first sentence, "I was captured by the Fascist Militia on December 13, 1943" (9); yet the narrating "I" tends to efface himself. His "civilized Cartesian phantoms" (9) disappear after the first paragraph, overwhelmed by the tragic experiences to follow. Or do they? Actually they don't because they are the everpresent yardstick Levi uses to measure—and judge—the good and evil of others and self throughout the book; they are the mental structure through which he presents and narrates the historical facts, so that the autobiography is soon turned into a historical documentation and a personal testimony about "the evil tiding of what man's presumption made of man in Auschwitz" (49). But beyond the urgency of the message to be conveyed to the world, "as an interior liberation" (6), the book is also a moral treatise, "a quiet study of certain aspects of the human soul" (5), and as such it rightly belongs in a tradition that goes from Dante's pilgrimage through hell to Pico della Mirandola's humanistic assertion of the dignity of man, from Leopardi's inquiries into the place of humankind in the universe to Manzoni's investigation of the "muddle (*guazzabuglio*) of the human heart" and on the responsibilities of those who inflict evil (because they also provoke a certain "perversion" in the souls of the victims), from Vittorini's search for "the lost humankind" to Calvino's questioning of the boundaries of reason, even in an "infernal city."

But it is important to remember that Levi's moral attitude is an indispensable framework for understanding his account, which is first and foremost a narration, a representation. Perhaps a few examples will suffice. Early on in the story, a former sergeant of the Austro-Hungarian army named Steinlauf tells him about the importance of washing every day, even if the water is dirty and there is no soap: "Precisely because the Lager was a great machine to reduce us to beasts, we must not become beasts; . . . even in this place one can survive, and therefore one must want to survive, to tell the story, to bear witness; and . . . to survive we must force ourselves to save at least the skeleton, the scaffolding, the form of civilization" (36). Isn't this the same reason why Norbert Elias dedicated his treatise on *The Civilizing Process* precisely to those who died at Auschwitz?[4] Cleanliness in this context is indeed the very principle of an inner-directed civilization that the beastly set-up of the camp is aimed at demolishing and destroying inside every individual. Steinlauf's conclusion is clear: "We are slaves, deprived of every right, . . . but we still possess one power, and we must defend it with all our strength for it is the last—the power to refuse our consent" (36). Levi, still "an incredulous man" brought up on this side of the Alps in a "more flexible and blander doctrine," is unable to make a system out of these straight and clear words, but he accepts and relates them for us to understand and accept in our turn.

However, if the refusal to consent is absolutely necessary, it is not sufficient. The book is also a parable on slavery and freedom. It is not by chance that Levi relates the hanging of a prisoner who was somehow connected with the revolt at Birkenau, only toward the end of his account, in a prominent, climactic position:

> I wish I could say that from the midst of us, an abject flock, a voice rose, a murmur, a sign of assent [to the words of the dying man]. But nothing happened. We remained standing, bent and grey, our heads dropped, and we did not uncover our heads until the German ordered us to do so. . . . The Russians can come now: they will only find us, the slaves, the worn-out, worthy of the unarmed death which awaits us. (135)

Obviously, notwithstanding its assertive tone, Levi's conclusion is not so bleak and hopeless as this quotation might suggest: I use it here only for the purpose of showing the amount of damage and suffering the Nazis inflicted on human beings, and will return to it later on, when it is my turn to conclude.

As a writer, Levi controls his narrative material and his moral message with great precision; in fact, the "exactitude" of his style, to use one of Italo Calvino's "qualities or values" of literature to be saved "for the next millenium,"[5] is the one characteristic of *Se questo è un uomo* that stands out as primary. Levi presents the narrative material both thematically (in chapters dealing with the initiation, the work, the nights and dreams of the prisoners, and so on) and chronologically (the climactic final chapter, in diary form, on the last ten days of the camp)—just as Italo Svevo organized his *La coscienza di Zeno*.

Levi writes with a constant and keen attention to the clarity of his lexical choices, to the descriptive power of words, to the essential connotations of an adjective or an adverb: as just one example, let us remember the presentation of Doktor Pannwitz, who "sits formidably behind a complicated writing-table" (96)—where both the adverb and the adjective are designed to convey the abysmal distance separating the German doctor from the Jewish prisoner he is about to examine.

Levi is also perceptive and effective in his characterization, which is the logical literary consequence of his scientific attitude of observation and human curiosity toward "the characters that chance" put in front of him; he explains in *I sommersi e i salvati*, with an extraordinary alimentary metaphor that seems almost a revenge of the spirit against the privations and hunger suffered in the Lager: "The sample book that Auschwitz had placed open before me was rich, varied, and strange, made up of friends, neutrals and enemies, yet in any case food for my curiosity. . . . A food that certainly contributed to keeping a part of me alive and that subsequently supplied me with the material for thinking and making books."[6] In fact, the gallery of human beings he presents us in *Se questo è un uomo* is unforgettable: consider for instance Flesch, the translator of the bad German words (a religious slur), which come out of his mouth "as if he was spitting out a foul taste" and whom Levi respects because "he has begun to suffer before us" (20); Alberto, "with his head high," "unscathed and uncorrupted," "the rare figure of the strong yet peace-loving man against whom the weapons of night are blunted" (51); and especially Lorenzo, the Italian civilian worker at the Buna factory who gave Levi "a piece of bread and the remainder of his ration every day for six months" without asking or accepting "any reward, because he was good and simple and did not think that one did good for a reward" (109). He saved Levi's life, as the author says, indebted "not so much for his material aid, as for having constantly reminded me by his presence, by his natural and plain manner of being good, that there still existed a just world outside our own, something and someone still pure and whole, not corrupt, not savage, extraneous to hatred and terror; something difficult to define, a remote possibility of good, but for which it was worth surviving" (110–11).

Already the example of Lorenzo has brought the reader closer to the alimentary area and its material as well as spiritual significance. But let us consider, on the other side of the characters' gallery, the haughty Alfred L., who deprived himself of the already scarce ration in order to acquire the appearance of a "prominent" (86) and acted with "extreme severity" towards other prisoners; the bestial Elias, who "can ingest ten, fifteen, twenty pints of soup without vomiting and without having diarrhoea, and begin working again immediately after" (87), a kind of Caliban or Gurduloo without any conscience, a survivor because of his insanity; or Henri, who constantly plays on the pity he is able to arouse, in order maybe to get "an authentic hard-boiled egg" (90), and is always "enclosed in armour, the enemy of all, inhumanly cunning and incomprehensible like the Serpent in Genesis" (91).

Or remember, at the opposite point from Lorenzo, the German girls in the chemical laboratory, with their "smooth, rosy skin, beautiful attractive clothes, clean and warm, blond hair," who "smoke in the corners, publicly eat canapés of bread and jam, file their nails, break a lot of glass vessels and then try to put the blame on" the prisoners (129); and above all remember Alex, the Kapo for whom Levi is guilty of being not only a Jew but an Italian, and not only an Italian but an intellectual, and who is fixed forever in our memory for the one single gesture of wiping his hand, dirtied by grease, on Levi's shoulder, both the palm and the back of the hand, to clean it, "without hatred and without sneering": "he would be amazed, the poor brute Alex, if someone told him that today, on the basis of this action, I judge him and Pannwitz and the innumerable others like him, big and small, in Auschwitz and everywhere" (98).

If Levi is effective in characterization (a literary talent that is fully confirmed by *La tregua*, many short stories, and *Se non ora, quando?*), he is equally so in the rhetorical technique he uses in dealing with the awful subject of his experience. His task is to bring home to all of us, spoiled, secure, and safe readers, the reality of an experience that is intrinsically unthinkable, perhaps unspeakable: the destruction of millions of human beings. The sheer magnitude of the numbers involved seems to preclude our understanding of this enormous reality. So Levi has deliberately chosen to adopt a soft tone of voice, "the quiet and sober language of the witness, not the plaintive one of the victim, nor the irate one of the avenger,"[7] as he himself explains in the important "Appendix" to the 1976 school edition of his book. As a witness, he concentrates on the personal experiences he had, which his readers can understand most immediately: the privation of freedom, of privacy, and of identity; hunger, cold, hard work; the fear of being beaten, the terror of being selected for a horrible death.

A linguistic premonition of what will happen is present in the words a German corporal speaks, referring to the prisoners who have just boarded the train as the six hundred and fifty "pieces" (12)—a frightening example, unobtrusively placed at the beginning of the text, of how the Nazis used the German language in their destructive process, one of those "precise, serviceable words" on which George Steiner has remarked that they "were committed to saying things no human mouth should ever have said."[8] This is only the first step in the dehumanizing process set in motion by the Nazis. The next is the complete, total deprivation of the personal identity, carried out in terms that each of us can understand immediately:

> For the first time we become aware that our language lacks words to express this offence, the demolition of a man. . . . Nothing belongs to us anymore; they have taken away our clothes, our shoes, even our hair; if we speak, they will not listen to us, and if they listen, they will not understand. . . . But consider what value, what meaning is enclosed even in the smallest of our daily habits, in the hundred possessions which even the poorest beggar owns: a handkerchief, an old letter, the photo of a cherished person. These things are part of us, almost like limbs of our body. . . . Imagine now a man who is deprived of everyone he loves, and at the same time of his house, his habits, his clothes, in short, of everything he possesses: he will be a hollow man, reduced to suffering and needs, forgetful of dignity and restraint, for he who loses all often easily loses himself. . . . It is in this way that one can understand the double sense of the term "extermination camp" (22–23).

Levi is always extremely attentive to the power of language, a power that resists even the most unspeakable horrors of historical reality. But faced with the total strangeness of his experience, how can he relate it to us effectively, with words that are neither distorted nor inadequate or nonexistent? The way he fulfills his task successfully is to use the reverse process of the defamiliarization technique,[9] and to oblige the readers to distance themselves from, and then to identify with, those horrible experiences.

Let me give a few examples. Defamiliarization normally implies that an author chooses unusual nouns and adjectives to convey a familiar reality, so that the reader is obliged to stop for a moment and take notice, renew that familiar reality. Conversely, an utterly unfamiliar experience can be described effectively precisely by making it not strange but familiar, by bringing it back to parameters that are common and normal. Here is Levi's narration of the arrival of the Italian Jews on the platform at Auschwitz, an arrival that was made to appear "normal" by the Germans themselves in order to facilitate the operation:

> A dozen SS men stood around, legs akimbo, with an indifferent air. At a certain moment they moved among us, and in a subdued tone of voice, with faces of stone, began to interrogate us rapidly, one by one, in bad Italian. They did not interrogate everybody, only a few: "How old? Healthy or ill?" And on the basis of the reply they pointed in two different directions.
>
> Everything was as silent as an aquarium, or as in certain dream sequences. We had expected something more apocalyptic: they seemed simple police agents. It was disconcerting and disarming. Someone dared to ask for his luggage: they replied, "luggage afterwards." Someone else did not want to be separated from their children: they said, "good, good, stay with child."(15)

Of course readers know, and the text reminds them of it only a few lines later, that what took place was the first selection between those destined to die immediately in the gas chambers and those who were judged capable "of working usefully for the Reich"—ninety-six men and twenty-nine women out of six hundred fifty "pieces" making up the convoy. The fear of the scene is conveyed precisely by its "normalcy," and is revealed and underscored only by the comparison with the aquarium (or the dream). The image of the aquarium returns at another crucial moment in the text, when Doktor Pannwitz examines Levi to ascertain his knowledge of chemistry: "When he finished writing, he raised his eyes and looked at me. . . . That look was not between two men; and if I had known how completely to explain the nature of that look, which came as if across the glass window of an aquarium between two beings who live in different worlds, I would also have explained the essence of the great insanity of the third Germany" (96).

Now let us look at Levi's distancing/identification technique. The first example occurs early in the first chapter, on the eve of the departure of the prisoners from the concentration camp at Fossoli for Auschwitz: "The mothers stayed up to prepare the food for the journey with tender care, and washed their children and packed the luggage; and at dawn the barbed wire was full of children's washing hung out in the wind to dry. . . . Would you not do the same? If you and your child were going to be killed tomorrow, would you not give him to eat today?" (11). As you see, nourishment and humanity—humanness—are strictly fused here, as they are throughout the book, and we, you, the readers, are summoned and made to agree and to suffer with Levi and the others.[10]

Also, another important feature of *Se questo è un uomo* should be emphasized. Levi is both a scientist by profession—a chemist—and a humanist by education. The two qualities have undoubtedly helped him survive the harrowing ordeal, physically and spiritually, and they are equally present in the text. The first guides the exactitude with which he describes the organization of the Lager, its economy, its hierarchical system, its maddeningly complicated rules that made of it "a negative utopia"[11]; it also presides over the description of the Buna factory, the laboratory, the chemicals Levi used for hygienic purposes when the Nazis abandoned the sick to their fate before the arrival of the Russians. The second is present in the quality of writing, as noted already, but above all in the numerous intertextual references scattered throughout the book, from the Bible to Homer, from Sophocles to Dante, from Machiavelli to Hobbes.[12] It is also present in the classic literary topos of men as leaves, rendered here through the filter of the grotesque music of the Lager: "When this music plays we know that our comrades, out in the fog, are marching like automatons; their souls are dead and the music drives them, like the wind drives dead leaves, and takes the place of their wills" (45).

These few, brief, and incomplete considerations should be sufficient to give an idea of Levi's power as a writer and to introduce the central theme of *Se questo è un uomo*, the obsessive attention to food as the necessary nourishment of the body for physical survival and as the yardstick of morality and humanness, necessary for spiritual salvation from the hell of the Lager.

Hunger is indeed omnipresent throughout Levi's book, as it is preeminent in other accounts of the Lager experience, notably in the emblematic *Si fa presto a dire fame*, it is easy to say hunger, by the Italian anti-fascist Piero Caleffi, mentioned in the introduction.[13] Hunger is the constant condition of the prisoners deprived of everything, reduced to things, and even worse, to animals being readied for slaughter. It is not by chance that in *Se questo è un uomo* animal images and similes are quite frequent; they are the logical and almost natural consequence of the process of dehumanization and destruction set up by the Nazis. Already on the train to Auschwitz, Levi contemplates the "dark swarming" of "a human matter, extended across the floor" of his carriage (14); at the Buna factory, some of the Kapos beat the prisoners "from pure bestiality and violence," but others beat them when they are exhausted under a load "almost lovingly, accompanying the blows with exhortations, as cart-drivers do with willing horses" (60); later, "everybody's clothes, humid with mud and snow, give out a dense smoke at the heat of the stove, with the smell of a kennel or of a sheepfold" (62), and the prisoners have to face the wind "like worms emptied of souls" (63); or, "We are always happy to wait; we are capable of waiting for hours with the complete obtuse inertia of spiders in old webs" (95), or: "our neck is long and knobbly, like that of plucked chickens" (129). As the situation worsens, similar images and similes intensify: under the air raids at the Buna, "the countless flock of slaves was directed elsewhere," and they "tremble like beasts"—"But the greater number bore the new danger and the new discomforts with unchanged indifference: it was not a conscious resignation, but the opaque torpor of beasts broken by blows, whom the blows no longer hurt" (107–8); and at the end, when the camp is abandoned, "ragged, decrepit, skeleton-like patients at all able to move dragged themselves everywhere on the frozen soil, like an invasion of worms" (144).

But the example that perhaps stands out as the most atrocious and compelling is the scene when the civilian workers at the Buna throw "a piece of bread or a potato" to the prisoners, or give them their bowls "to scrape and give back washed": "They do it to get rid of some importunate starved look, or through a momentary impulse of humanity, or through simple curiosity to see us running from all sides to fight each other for the scrap, bestially and without restraint, until the strongest one gobbles it up, whereupon all the others limp away, frustrated" (111). This quotation is terribly effective in portraying the degradation of human beings through hunger—deliberately, as part of a dehumanizing and destructive policy aimed at making man an *Unmensch*, a non-man. It is also important because it links the animal simile ("bestially") to the theme of hunger and search for food. This link is evident in yet another quotation where bestiality and hunger are inextricably connected even at the linguistic level: "This way of eating on our feet, furiously, burning our mouths and throats, without time to breathe, really is '*fressen*,' the way of eating of animals, and certainly not '*essen*,' the human way of eating, seated in front of a table, religiously. '*Fressen*' is exactly the word, and is used currently among us" (68–69). Animal feed as opposed to human food, certainly: but the attention given to the linguistic expression is already an affirmation of humanity against the imposed bestiality.[14]

The focus on the Babel of languages contained in the very title of this chapter obeys the same concern that sustains Levi—imprisoned, tattooed, and enslaved—in his effort to save his humanity and to bear witness. Indeed, the fact that he chooses to devote so much of his account to the search for food obeys his fundamental rhetorical premise—to be simple, elementary, and communicative at a level at which we, who were spared the horror of the Lager, can understand by relating the atrocity, even from afar and certainly inadequately, to our own everyday experiences such as eating in a civilized manner and not going hungry.

This is the reason why in Levi's account the search for food takes on such importance: through it humanity (even more than survival) will be ultimately reaffirmed. Levi describes all the infinite ruses, tricks, ingenuities, and cares necessary to procure food; the reader is reminded of the picaresque novel, and of Lazarillo de Tormes, who steals bread and then masks his theft as if a mouse had eaten the precious morsel, with an ingenuity that uses a fake, but verisimilar, animal referent.[15] Yet there, in the case of Lazarillo, the problems of eating and survival were individual by definition; here, in the case of Levi, they have to be returned to the individual from an awful, anonymous mass reality of extermination that is carried out not only through the gas chambers but also through a willful policy of starvation and exhaustion. Let us examine some of the most telling pages of *Se questo è un uomo*.

Hunger is the omnipresent, obsessive condition that is recalled, mentioned, and stressed throughout the book, and that is the prerequisite for understanding the equally obsessive search for food. At the very beginning of the book, Levi remarks, "A fortnight after my arrival I already have the prescribed hunger, the chronic hunger unknown to free men, which makes one dream at night, and settles in all the limbs of one's body" (31); and soon afterwards, "I am hungry and when will they distribute the soup tomorrow? And will I be able to eat it without a spoon? And where will I be able to find one?" (33).

The extent and the importance of hunger are particularly evident in peremptory sentences like, "But how could one imagine not being hungry? The Lager *is* hunger; we ourselves are hunger, living hunger" (67),

and this hunger embodied in the prisoners makes them have hallucina-
tions. In the following quotation, the metaphorical use of language is
the faithful and revealing mirror of a physical condition of need that
makes the prisoners see reality literally in alimentary, edible terms—
with a coherently bestial side, as the verb "snaps," albeit related to a
machine, eloquently indicates:

> On the other side of the road a steam-shovel is working. Its mouth, hanging
> from its cables, opens wide its steel jaws, balances a moment as if uncertain in
> its choice, then rushes upon the soft, clayey soil and snaps it up voraciously,
> while a satisfied snort of thick white smoke rises from the control cabin. Then
> it rises, turns half around, vomits backwards its mouthful and begins again.
>
> Leaning on our shovels, we stop to watch, fascinated. At every bite of its
> mouth our mouths also open, our Adam's apples dance up and down, wretch-
> edly visible under the flaccid skin. We are unable to tear ourselves away from
> the sight of the steam-shovel's meal. (67)

As a result, the prisoners begin talking about food, and one remembers
the "third plate of bean soup" he had failed to finish at a wedding dinner, another recalls "his Hungarian countryside and the field of maize
and a recipe to make meat-pies with corncobs and lard and spices and
. . ." (every ingredient seems to be isolated syntactically in order to be
tasted with greater intensity); and even Levi, who is perfectly aware of
the futility of such "fantasies of hunger," sees "dancing" before his eyes
the dish of spaghetti, "so good, yellow, filling," that he and some of his
companions were eating at the sorting-camp when the news of their
sudden departure came (67).

But as if this, or other scenes and episodes it would be too long to
quote here (such as the recurring dream of the interrupted narration
and the dream of Tantalus, 54–56), were not enough to convey the real
meaning of the hunger he is talking about, Levi feels it necessary to
underscore what he wants to convey and the paucity of the language at
his disposal to do so:

> Just as this hunger of ours is not that feeling of missing a meal, so our way
> of being cold has need of a new word. We say "hunger," we say "tiredness,"
> "fear," "pain," we say "winter" and they are different things. They are free
> words, created and used by free men who lived in comfort and suffering
> in their homes. If the Lager had lasted longer a new, harsh language would
> have been born; and only this language could express what it means to toil
> the whole day in the wind, with the temperature below freezing, wear-

ing only a shirt, underpants, cloth jacket and trousers, and in one's body
nothing but weakness, hunger and knowledge of the end drawing nearer.
(112–13)

So we, the readers in the comfort of our homes and our campuses,
have to make a constant effort to remind ourselves of the true meaning
and force of a word like "hunger" (or should we perhaps write it always
in capital letters, HUNGER, or spell it, h-u-n-g-e-r?), and to understand precisely what effects such hunger could have had on the prisoners, could have on us if we were exposed to it. Only if we try to absorb
the harsh language of the Lager can we begin to understand the practical and moral value of the search for food in *Se questo è un uomo*. At the
beginning of the book Levi recounts:

> We have learnt the value of food; now we also diligently scrape the bottom
> of the bowl after the ration and we hold it under our chins when we eat bread
> so as not to lose the crumbs. We, too, know that it is not the same thing to
> be given a ladleful of soup from the top or from the bottom of the vat,
> and we are already able to judge, according to the capacity of the various
> vats, what is the most suitable place to try and reach in the queue when we
> line up. (28)

Such knowledge is only the beginning of a science or political economy
that only a few prisoners could fully develop. Levi describes it minutely,
especially in the chapter entitled "This Side of Good and Evil" (70–78).
The scarce rations of soup and bread, the only possessions of the prisoners, become the exchange money for acquiring a needed spoon, or a
string, a rag, a second shirt; conversely, various objects, tools, utensils,
materials, or products (such as tobacco) stolen from the factory or from
storage are exchanged for a pint of soup or half a portion of bread. Just
one example among the many possible of the dehumanizing economy
is the lack of spoons in the lager, a lack that is explained in *I sommersi
e i salvati* as a calculated, "useless violence" that obliged the prisoners
to "lap" their daily soup "as dogs do"· "a precise intent to humiliate,"
confirmed by the discovery in an Auschwitz warehouse after the liberation of "thousands of brand new transparent plastic spoons, besides tens
of thousands of spoons made of aluminum, steel, or even silver that
came from the luggage of deportees as they arrived."[16] It is an example
worth quoting at length because it gives a precise idea of the detailed
and absurd mechanisms of the Lager, and of Levi's exactitude in de-
scribing them:

The nurses also make huge profits from the trade in spoons. The Lager does not provide the new arrivals with spoons, although the semi-liquid soup cannot be consumed without them. The spoons are manufactured in Buna, secretly and in their spare moments, by Häftlinge who work as specialists [and who] sell them directly to the new arrivals: an ordinary spoon is worth half a ration, a knife-spoon three quarters of a ration of bread. . . . At the moment of release [from the infirmary], the healthy patient's spoon is confiscated by the nurses and placed on sale in the Market. Adding the spoons of the patients about to leave and those of the dead and selected, the nurses receive the gains of the sales of about fifty spoons every day. On the other hand, the dismissed patients are forced to begin work again with the initial disadvantage of half a ration of bread, set aside to acquire a new spoon. (77–78)

The "Market" is indeed the economic center of the Lager, and in it the Jewish Greeks from Salonica distinguish themselves for their commercial ability, for their contribution to the international jargon of the camp (for instance, "*la comedera es buena*" means that the soup is good, and "*klepsiklepsi*" is theft, 72), and for their "Mediterranean" wisdom, but above all, "their aversion to gratuitous brutality, their amazing consciousness of the survival of at least a potential human dignity" made of them "the most coherent national nucleus in the Lager, and in this respect, the most civilized" (72). In other words Levi, while outlining the precise mechanisms of the economic system of the Lager, never forgets for a moment the moral side of it, and his awareness is clearly present in his account of the way he and his friend Alberto "organized" themselves so as to get more food by stealing (I hesitate to use this term—perhaps I should say "appropriating," but Levi does not allow such a distinction) brooms and celluloid labels respectively—that is, objects that are necessary for life in the Lager, and hence extremely useful for exchange with rations of bread and soup (132–34).

An important way in which Levi emphasizes the moral side of his account is the juxtaposition between, on the one hand, the recollection of the Canto of Ulysses from Dante's *Divina Commedia* (with its message that seems directed to the prisoners, "Fatti non foste a viver come bruti, / Ma per seguir virtute e conoscenza"—You were made not to live like brutes, / but to follow after virtue and knowledge) and, on the other hand, the fetching of the daily vat of soup, made of "cabbages and turnips, *Kraut und Rüben, Choux et navets, Kaposzta és répak*" (103–5). This episode takes up an entire chapter, and in it both the spiritual and the material nourishment are equally necessary for salvation. Levi says, "I would give today's soup to know how to connect 'the like of any day' to the last lines" (104), in order to remember and to convey Dante's message properly to Pikolo, his companion who listens patiently. Ulysses's (and Levi's) "virtue and knowledge" are put to a test, the ultimate test, by the encounter with the insurmountable limit of absolute Otherness: "come altrui piacque," as pleased Another; these words are certainly an "anachronism" for the Middle Ages, but, perhaps just because of this, they make "something gigantic" click inside Levi, something, he says, "I myself have only just seen, in a flash of intuition, perhaps the reason for our fate, for our being here today" (105). Here, in this episode, the sublime of the *Divina Commedia* and the grotesque of the Lager, literature and life, the spirit and the flesh, are more complementary than juxtaposed; here, even more than the cabbage and turnip soup, the remembered text is indeed nourishment.[17]

Another, unstated, juxtaposition is tremendously significant: after the hanging of "the last one," and the lack of any reaction by the "abject flock" of the prisoners, Levi reflects: "We lifted the *menaschka* on to the bunk and divided it, we satisfied the daily ragings of hunger, and now we are oppressed by shame" (136). Shame is juxtaposed with hunger just as the Canto of Ulysses was juxtaposed with the cabbage and turnip soup: it is a moral category superimposed on a physical need, and it is vital, if not heroic, that a prisoner be able to feel shame. Emmanuel Lévinas might comment, from the depth of the Jewish philosophical tradition, that freedom is indeed difficult but absolutely central to that tradition;[18] for my part, I would only add that the shame felt by Levi is the sure sign that if he was not a "strong man" or a hero like the hanged one, he was certainly a man, with his weaknesses and flaws, like Panurge perhaps, but with his moral conscience intact, not destroyed and not conquered by the Germans.

In fact, the moral concern dealt with in *Se questo è un uomo* is not heroism (extremely difficult, if not impossible, given the situation) but solidarity. At this level the humanness of the victims is examined, assessed, and stressed to the very end. In the infirmary of the camp abandoned by the Germans, Levi and two Frenchmen, Arthur and Charles, who are less sick and less weak than the others, labor with great abnegation, courage, and intelligence to preserve decent hygienic conditions in their ward, to fetch a stove to protect it from the intense cold, and to find food for all the inmates—including some Italians from the adjacent ward who are too weak to move and who invoke Primo's name. The story of the final ten days is mostly the story of these labors, of this abnegation, and of the food found in and around the abandoned camp. Food is mostly potatoes: boiled potatoes, potato soup, and potato pancakes made "on Arthur's recipe: rub together raw potatoes with boiled, soft ones, and roast the mixture on a red-hot iron-plate. They tasted of soot" (152); then, pounds of cabbages and turnips; and only later on, thanks to the expedition of some workers to the English prisoner-of-war camp, "wonders never seen before: margarine, custard powders, lard, soya-bean flower, whisky" (154). When the inmates of the infirmary want to reward Levi and the two Frenchmen for their labor, each of them spontaneously gives "a slice of bread" to the three: "Only a day before a similar event would have been inconceivable. The law of the Lager said: 'eat your own bread, and if you can, that of your neighbour,' and left no room for gratitude. It really meant that the Lager was dead" (145).

If this gesture of gratitude is the beginning of the resurrection after the Lager, it is significant that it should have as its object some slices of bread, the daily bread of the picaresque effort to survive, the daily bread of the prayer. And it is significant that bread is present again in the final meditation of the book:

> It is man who kills, man who creates or suffers injustice; it is no longer man who, having lost all restraint, shares his bed with a corpse. Whoever waits for his neighbour to die in order to take his piece of bread is, albeit guiltless, further from the model of thinking man than the most primitive pigmy or the most vicious sadist.
>
> Part of our existence lies in the feelings of those near to us. This is why the experience of someone who has lived for days during which man was merely a thing in the eyes of man is non-human. We three were for the most part immune to it, and we owe each other mutual gratitude. This is why my friendship with Charles will prove lasting. (156)

And this is the reason why the story of Primo Levi's survival and salvation in Auschwitz appropriately ends with a bread that is the tangible sign, at the same time a concrete and emblematic sign, of solidarity and humanness; and with the mention of Charles again (a proper name), and with the words, "I hope to see him again one day" (157)—words of friendship and hope and future, words that bring us back from the infernal city to the daily life of the man Primo Levi—and of all human beings.

NOTES

Introduction. The Flavors of Modernity

1. Louis Marin, *Food for Thought*, trans. Mette Hjort (Baltimore: The Johns Hopkins University Press, 1989), p. 125.

2. In this connection see Eric Auerbach, *Mimesis: The Representation of Reality in Western Literature*, trans. Willard Trask (Princeton: Princeton University Press, 1953), and in particular Folco Portinari, *Un'idea di realismo* (Naples: Guida, 1976), and Ezio Raimondi, *Il romanzo senza idillio* (Turin: Einaudi, 1974), especially the chapters "Verso il realismo" (pp. 3–56) and "L'albero romantico" (pp. 57–76). On metanarrativity see Robert Alter, *Partial Magic: The Novel as a Self-Conscious Genre* (Berkeley: University of California Press, 1975), and Linda Hutcheon, *Narcissistic Narrative: The Metafictional Paradox* (Waterloo, Ontario: Wilfrid Laurier University Press, 1980).

3. This saying is quoted in Italian by Pellegrino Artusi in *La scienza in cucina e l'arte di mangiar bene*, intro. and notes by Piero Camporesi (Turin: Einaudi, 1970), p. 38, and in dialect by Camporesi in his "Introduzione," p. xxx: "It is a metaphor derived from the archaic world of the fields, a metaphor which illuminates the definition 'man-the-beast' with the light of the primitive filtered through the mediation of positivism."

4. See the excellent essay by Maria Catricalà, "La lingua in cucina," *L'italiano e oltre*, 2, 1 (Jan.–Feb. 1987), pp. 14–16. An informative and pleasant history of food is Margaret Visser, *Much Depends on Dinner: The Extraordinary History and Mythology, Allure and Obsessions, Perils and Taboos, of an Ordinary Meal* (Toronto: McClelland and Stewart, 1987). Other useful indications are in Emilio Sereni, *Storia del paesaggio agrario italiano* (Bari: Laterza, 1961), and *Terra nuova e buoi rossi* (Turin: Einaudi, 1981), particularly "Note di storia dell'alimentazione nel Mezzogiorno: i Napoletani da 'mangiafoglia' a 'mangiamaccheroni'," as well as in Massimo Montanari, *Alimentazione e cultura nel Medioevo* (Bari: Laterza, 1988).

5. Claude Lévi-Strauss, *The Raw and the Cooked, From Honey to Ashes*, and *The Origin of Table Manners*, trans. John and Doreen Weightman (New York: Harper and Row, 1969 and 1973, and London: Cape, 1978, respectively).

6. Norbert Elias, *The Civilizing Process*, trans. Edmund Jephcott, vol. 1, *The History of Manners* (New York: Urizen Books, 1978), vol. 2, *State Formation and Civilization* (Oxford: Basil Blackwell, 1982).

7. Pierre Bourdieu, *Distinction: A Social Critique of the Judgement of Taste*, trans. Richard Nice (Cambridge, Mass.: Harvard University Press, 1985).

8. Mary Douglas, "Deciphering a Meal," in *Implicit Meanings: Essays in Anthropology* (London: Routledge and Kegan Paul, 1979), pp. 249–75. An impor-

tant and sensible discussion of Mary Douglas is in John O' Neill, *Five Bodies: The Human Shape of Modern Society* (Ithaca, N. Y.: Cornell University Press, 1985), especially chapter 2, "Social Bodies," pp. 48–66. For an example in Italian history see Ariel Toaff, *Il vino e la carne: Una comunità ebraica nel Medioevo* (Bologna: Il Mulino, 1989).

9. Jean-François Revel, *Un festin en paroles: Histoire littéraire de la sensibilité gastronomique* (Paris: Pauvert, 1979).

10. Emilio Faccioli, "La cucina," in *Storia d'Italia*, vol. 5, *I documenti* (Turin: Einaudi, 1975), pp. 981–1030, and edited by Faccioli, *L'arte della cucina in Italia: Libri di ricette e trattati sulla civiltà della tavola dal xiv al xix secolo* (Turin: Einaudi, 1987).

11. Folco Portinari, *Il piacere della gola: Il romanzo della gastronomia* (Milan: Camunia, 1986).

12. Revel, *Un festin en paroles*, p. 271. Noëlle Chatelet also deals with gastronomical dichotomies in her *Le corps à corps culinaire* (Paris: Seuil, 1977), pp.169–76.

13. See T. S. Eliot, "Tradition and the Individual Talent," in *Selected Essays 1917–1932* (New York: Harcourt Brace Jovanovich, 1950), and Harold Bloom, *The Anxiety of Influence* (New York: Oxford University Press, 1973).

14. Piero Camporesi, *La terra e la luna: Alimentazione folclore società* (Milan: Il Saggiatore, 1989), pp. 64–65 and 61.

15. See for example Giuliano Procacci, *Storia degli italiani* (Bari: Laterza, 1969), vol. 2, chapters 1, 5, and 6.

16. Giuseppe Cocchiara, *Il paese di Cuccagna* (Turin: Einaudi, 1956); see also his *Popolo e letteratura in Italia* (Turin: Einaudi, 1959).

17. Piero Camporesi, *Il paese della fame* (Bologna: Il Mulino, 1984), as well as his *Il pane selvaggio* (Bologna: Il Mulino, 1980).

18. The subject is quite broad. I shall only quote a volume that is still fundamental today: Pasquale Villari, *Le lettere meridionali ed altri scritti sulla questione sociale in Italia* (Turin: Bocca, 1885).

19. See Giovanni Rajberti, *Tutte le opere del medico-poeta*, ed. Cesare Cossali (Milan: Gastaldi, 1964). All references will be to this edition.

20. All references will be to the 1970 Einaudi edition. The English version of Artusi's book is *Italianissimo: Italian Cooking at Its Best*, trans. Elizabeth Abbott (New York: Liveright, 1975), in which "every effort has been made to modernize and Americanize the quantities and preparation of the recipes" ("Publisher's Foreword," p. 7).

21. Camporesi, *La terra e la luna*, p. 76.

22. Giorgio Manganelli, *Laboriose inezie* (Milan: Garzanti, 1986), pp. 256–59.

23. Primo Levi, *Other People's Trades*, trans. Raymond Rosenthal (New York: Summit, 1989), p. 76. On Artusi's language see also Catricalà, pp. 15–16.

24. The references are to Ada Boni, *Italian Regional Cooking* (New York: Bonanza Books, 1969); Alessandro Falassi, "Mangiare e bere del Chianti," in Alessandro Falassi, Riccardo di Corato, and Pierluigi Staccini, *Pan che canti vin che salti* (Castellina: I Torchi Chiantigiani, 1979), pp. 9–44; and Ulderico Bernardi, "La cucina delle generazioni," *Supplemento a L'Accademia Italiana della Cucina*, 1 (Jan.–Feb. 1988), on the 10th "Convegno Internazionale sulla Civiltà

della Tavola" held at Castelfranco Veneto, Oct. 24, 1987. Another particularly meaningful example of the renewed interest for and revival of local traditions is Antonino Uccello, *Del mangiar siracusano* (Siracusa: Ente Provinciale per il Turismo, 1979).

25. Federico De Roberto, *L'imperio* (Milan: Oscar Mondadori, 1981), p. 123.

26. Giorgio Bassani, *The Garden of the Finzi-Contini*, trans. William Weaver (New York: Harcourt Brace Jovanovich, 1977), p. 72.

27. Ibid., pp. 115–16. Elsewhere in the novel Bassani gives some meager indications of Jewish alimentary habits; for instance, on p. 124, in the center of the table set for Passover, there is "the basket that, along with the ritual 'morsels,' contained the bowls of *haròset*, the clumps of bitter herbs, the unleavened bread, and the special hard-boiled egg for me, the first-born." An interesting analysis of the relationship between Italian and Jewish cuisine, between assimilation and original contributions (as for instance in the case of the well-known "carciofi alla Giudìa"—artichokes à la Jewish) is in Edda Servi Machlin, *The Classic Cuisine of Italian Jews* (New York: Dodd, Mead and Co., 1981).

28. Clara Sereni, *Casalinghitudine* (Turin: Einaudi, 1987). The author carries to the extreme the Artusian technique of "narrating" recipes: she never writes "take such and such an ingredient" and "put it in the oven" but always "I take" and "I put." Susan J. Leonardi underscores the juxtaposition between the normative and the narrative, between text and frame of *The Joy of Cooking*, in "Recipes for Reading: Summer Pasta, Lobster à la Riseholme, and Key Lime Pie," *PMLA*, 104, 3 (May 1989), pp. 340–47: but in her case, as well as in Artusi's, it is not a question of recipes conceived in and written exclusively for a feminine community.

29. On the relationship between author and text see Mikhail Bakhtin, *L'esthétique de la création verbale* (Paris: Gallimard, 1964); see also the semiotic analysis of James Brown, *Fictional Meals and their Function in the French Novel, 1789–1848* (Toronto: Toronto University Press, 1984).

30. Camporesi, *La terra e la luna*, pp. 212, 251, 217, 254.

31. Daniele Del Giudice, *Atlante occidentale* (Turin: Einaudi, 1985). All references will be to this edition. Some writers are not happy with the linguistic novelties caused by contemporary alimentary changes; for instance Leonardo Sciascia says of the new term *paninoteca*: "it makes me shiver, it seems it corrupts both bakeries and libraries": in *Il cavaliere e la morte* (Milan: Adelphi, 1988), p. 72.

32. This subject has inspired a notable critical interest in America: see for example Rudolph M. Bell, *Holy Anorexia* (Chicago: The University of Chicago Press, 1985), and Joan Jacobs Brumberg, *Fasting Girls: The Emergence of Anorexia Nervosa as a Modern Disease* (Cambridge, Mass.: Harvard University Press, 1989).

33. Nicolas J. Perella, "An Essay on *Pinocchio*" in Carlo Collodi, *Le Avventure di Pinocchio / The Adventures of Pinocchio*, trans. with intro. and notes by Nicolas J. Perella (Berkeley: University of California Press, 1986), p. 33.

34. Collodi, *Le avventure di Pinocchio*, p. 167.

35. "Lightness" is one of the sixty-three words (and one of the five most important abstract terms) that make up the "small personal dictionary" of Milan

Kundera in *The Art of the Novel*, trans. Linda Asher (New York: Grove Press, 1988), beside obviously being the key word in his novel *The Unbearable Lightness of Being*. As for Italo Calvino, see his "Lightness" in *Six Memos for the Next Millennium*, trans. Patrick Creagh (Cambridge, Mass.: Harvard University Press, 1988), pp. 3–29.

36. On this subject see Sergio M. Gilardino, "Emilio Salgàri (1862–1911): Considerazioni sugli sviluppi del genere romanzesco in Italia nel xix secolo" in *Perspectives on Nineteenth-Century Italian Novels*, ed. Guido Pugliese, University of Toronto Italian Studies 5 (Ottawa: Dovehouse, 1989), pp. 163–78; on p. 174, a "Chinese dinner" in an inn in Sarawak includes live prawns, roasted dog, stewed cat, and mice fried in butter. A "ragout and a roast" of cat meat were also in Ippolito Nievo's *Le confessioni d'un italiano* (see *The Castle of Fratta*, trans. Lovett F. Edwards [Westport, Conn.: Greenwood Press, 1974], p. 44), and more recently, Giuseppe Pederiali's *Il drago nella fiumana* (Milan: Rusconi, 1984) describes a huge dinner that includes an *antipasto* with various salamis and pickled vegetables, broth with *tortellini*, salmis of cat and cat à la *cacciatora*, Parmesan cheese, *bensone* cake, and Lambrusco wine (pp. 6–8).

37. Respectively in Giovanni Verga, *Mastro-don Gesualdo*, trans. and intro. by Giovanni Cecchetti (Berkeley: University of California Press, 1984), pp. 60–61, and in Gina Lagorio, *Golfo del paradiso* (Milan: Garzanti, 1987), p. 16.

38. On this subject there are important considerations by Mary McCarthy concerning the disappearance of landscape descriptions in the modern novel and the concept of "Nature" juxtaposed with history, society, technology, and the individual: "One Touch of Nature" in *The Writing on the Wall* (New York: Harcourt Brace and World, 1970), pp. 189–213. More generally, Clifford Geertz's remarks on the relationship between nature and culture are illuminating: *The Interpretation of Culture* (New York: Basic Books, 1973).

39. Respectively Mikhail Bakhtin, *Rabelais and His World*, trans. Hélène Iswolsky (Cambridge, Mass.: The MIT Press, 1968); Piero Camporesi, *La carne impassibile* (Milan: Il Saggiatore, 1985); and Carlo Ginzburg, *The Cheese and the Worms: The Cosmos of a Sixteenth-Century Miller*, trans. John and Anne Tedeschi (Baltimore: The Johns Hopkins University Press, 1980).

40. Raimondi, *Il romanzo senza idillio*, p. 7. The references are to Lucien Febvre's *Le problème de l'incroyance au xvi siècle: La religion de Rabelais* and to Gaston Bachelard's *La formation de l'esprit scientifique*.

41. The quotation is from Alexandre Kojève, *Introduction to the Reading of Hegel*, trans. James H. Nichols, Jr. (New York: Basic Books, 1969), p. 4; the reference is to René Girard, *Deceit, Desire, and the Novel*, trans. Yvonne Freccero (Baltimore: The Johns Hopkins University Press, 1965).

42. Sigmund Freud, *New Introductory Lectures on Psychoanalysis*, trans. James Strachey (New York: Norton, 1964), p. 100.

43. Italo Svevo, *Confessions of Zeno*, trans. Beryl de Zoete (New York: Vintage Books, 1958), p. 174.

44. Ibid., pp. 372–73.

45. Italo Svevo, *Diario per la fidanzata* (Triest: Edizioni dello Zibaldone, 1962), p. 60.

46. Elio Vittorini, *Conversation in Sicily*, trans. Wilfrid David (Harmondsworth: Penguin, 1961). All references will be to this edition.

47. See the rich and appetizing anthology ed. by M.F.K. Fisher, *Here Let Us Feast: A Book of Banquets* (San Francisco: North Point Press, 1986).

48. The bibliography on this subject is huge. I shall quote only some contributions that deal most directly with my topic: John Freccero, "Bestial Sign and Bread of Angels (*Inferno* 32–33)," *Yale Italian Studies*, 1, 1 (Winter 1977), pp. 53–66; Ronald B. Herman, "Cannibalism and Communion in *Inferno* xxxiii," *Dante Studies*, 98 (1980), pp. 53–78; Robert Hollander, "*Inferno* xxxiii, 37–74: Ugolino's Importunity," *Speculum*, 59, 3 (July 1984), pp. 549–55; Donna Yowell, "Ugolino's 'bestial segno': The *De Vulgari Eloquentia* in *Inferno* xxxii–xxxiii," *Dante Studies*, 104 (1986), pp. 121–43. More generally, see also Robert Durling, "Deceit and Digestion in the Belly of Hell," in *Allegory and Representation*, ed. Stephen Greenblatt (Baltimore: The Johns Hopkins University Press, 1981), pp. 61–93; and Gino Moliterno, "Mouth to Mandible, Man to *Lupa*: The Moral and Political Lesson of Cocytus," *Dante Studies*, 104, (1986), pp. 145–61.

49. On a subject closely related to the one under examination, see Laura Sanguineti White, *La scena conviviale e la sua funzione nel mondo del Boccaccio* (Florence: Olschki, 1983).

50. On the theme of hunger in the picaresque novel see Pedro Salinas, *Ensayos de literatura hispanica* (Madrid: Aguilar, 1961); on hunger in Malerba there is an illuminating essay by Guido Almansi, "Il silenzio rumoroso" in his *La ragion comica* (Milan: Feltrinelli, 1986), pp. 65–110.

51. Mikhail Bakhtin, *The Dialogic Imagination*, trans. Caryl Emerson and Michael Holquist (Austin: University of Texas Press, 1981).

52. Marin, *Food for Thought*, p. 117.

53. All references will be to Ippolito Nievo, *The Castle of Fratta*, trans. Lovett F. Edwards (Westport, Conn.: Greenwood Press, 1974).

54. I am reminded of the "homely illustration" used by Virginia Woolf as an ironic explanation of the change in human character that occurred "on or about December, 1910": "The Victorian cook lived like a leviathan in the lower depths, formidable, silent, obscure, inscrutable," while "the Georgian cook is a creature of sunshine and fresh air": in "Mr. Bennett and Mrs. Brown" in *The Captain's Death Bed and Other Essays* (New York: Harcourt Brace Jovanovich, 1950), p. 96.

55. Federico De Roberto, *The Viceroys*, trans. Archibald Colquhoun (New York: Harcourt Brace and World, 1962), p. 187.

56. Italo Calvino, *If on a winter's night a traveler*, trans. William Weaver (New York: Harcourt Brace Jovanovich, 1981), pp. 142–43.

57. Hans Blumenberg, *Die Lesbarkeit der Welt* (Frankfurt: Suhrkamp, 1981).

58. On this subject see Ivan Illich, *Tools for Conviviality* (New York: Harper, 1973), and Massimo Montanari, *Convivio: Storia e cultura dei piaceri della tavola* (Bari: Laterza, 1989).

CHAPTER ONE. THE JUICE OF THE STORY

1. Quoted by Giovanni Getto, *Letture manzoniane* (Florence: Sansoni, 1964), p. 582. A preliminary exploration of the subject under examination is in Gino Raya, "*Homo edens* nei *Promessi sposi*" in *Nuovi Annali della Facoltà di Magistero dell'Università di Messina* (Rome: Herder, 1985), pp. 125–29.

2. Alessandro Manzoni, *The Betrothed (I Promessi Sposi)*, trans. Archibald Colquhoun (New York: Dutton, 1961), p. xi. All subsequent references will be to this edition, with a few touch-ups. When necessary I shall also refer to the Italian edition, *I promessi sposi*, ed. Luigi Russo (Florence: La Nuova Italia, 1964).

3. References are to Lucien Febvre, *Combats pour l'histoire* (Paris: Colin, 1953) and Fernand Braudel, *Ecrits sur l'histoire* (Paris: Flammarion, 1969). Ezio Raimondi emphasized the importance (even the methodological importance) of the anti-idealistic materiality of Febvre's *Combats* in his "L'invito di Lucien Febvre," *Convivium*, 12, 1 (Jan.–Feb. 1954), pp. 108–13.

4. Carlo Ginzburg, *The Cheese and the Worms: The Cosmos of a Sixteenth-Century Miller*.

5. Getto, *Letture manzoniane*, pp. 204–5.

6. In Alessandro Manzoni, *I promessi sposi*, ed. Ezio Raimondi and Luciano Bottoni (Milan: Principato, 1987), p. 105. Their comments are extremely valuable because they utilize Giovanni Cherubini's *Vocabolario milanese-italiano*, which allows them to trace the dialectal calques of Manzoni's language. As for the grey polenta, Raimondi and Bottoni note that "buckwheat, a less nutritious cereal than maize, was imported to Italy only in 1630; in *Fermo e Lucia* it was 'a grey polenta of *fraina* (or if you wish of *poligonum fagopyrum*).' " Folco Portinari remarks that it is a "polenta *taragna*, typical of Valtellina": in *Il piacere della gola*, p. 307.

7. At other moments the famine remains in the background, but its presence is felt nevertheless: at the village inn Renzo and Tonio eat "what meagre fare there was" (85); similarly, during their flight to Milan Renzo, Lucia and Agnese stop at a country inn in Monza, where they "made a frugal breakfast, as was dictated by the poverty of the times, their small appetite, and the little money which they dared spend in view of the uncertain future" (127). Even Gertrude has a moment of hesitation before accepting Lucia in her convent: "really, times are so bad that we had decided not to replace that girl" (133). And Cardinal Federigo, who "takes the bread from his own mouth to give to the hungry," with his behavior reinforces the words of his preaching, "even if there is a famine, we ought to thank the Lord and be content" (368).

8. Giuseppe Cocchiara, *Il paese di Cuccagna*, and Piero Camporesi, *Il paese della fame*; in this connection see the second paragraph of the introduction.

9. On the social classes of seventeenth-century Spain see José Antonio Maragall, *Poder, honor y elites en el siglo xvii* (Madrid: Siglo Veintiuno de España, 1979); a useful book for understanding Manzoni's concerns is Alexis de Tocqueville, *L'ancient régime et la révolution* (Paris: Gallimard, 1952); and on the relationship between the seventeenth and the nineteenth centuries see Robert S. Dombroski, "The Seicento as Strategy: 'Providence' and the 'Bourgeois' in *I promessi sposi*," *Modern Language Notes*, 91, 1 (Jan. 1976), pp. 80–100.

10. On *raveggioli*, Raimondi and Bottoni gloss: "It is *robioeula*, that is, as Cherubini explains, a cheese made with sheep, goat, and sometimes also cow milk, alone or mixed" (p. 666).

11. I am referring to the two main elements of the "Gothic novel" (centered on Lucia) and the "adventure novel" (with Renzo as protagonist), which Fredric Jameson suggested in his analysis of *I promessi sposi* in "Magical Narratives: Ro-

mance as Genre," *New Literary History*, 7, 1 (1975), pp. 135–63, on p. 151. But Franco Fido's remarks on Renzo Tramaglino and Fermo Spolino should also be kept in mind: "Per una descrizione dei *Promessi sposi*: il sistema dei personaggi," *Strumenti critici* 25 (Oct. 1974), pp. 345–51, especially on p. 351: "Renzo, who goes back and forth between city and country, between Spanish Lombardy and the Venetian Bergamasco, but who from a narrative viewpoint does not proceed one step and is in fact always still, seems to me the last paradox of the book. . . . Perhaps also because of this reason the name Fermo Spolino [Still Spool], with which the character had presented himself to Manzoni's imagination at first, seemed too obvious." Actually, far from remaining "still," Renzo does have experiences, learns how to speak (and to keep silent), and above all is part of an active, dynamic system of interpersonal relationships: see Gregory L. Lucente, *Beautiful Fables: Self-consciousness in Italian Narrative from Manzoni to Calvino* (Baltimore: The Johns Hopkins University Press, 1986), pp. 56–57, and Ezio Raimondi, "L'osteria della retorica" in his *La dissimulazione romanzesca* (Bologna: Il Mulino, 1990).

12. Louis Marin, *Food for Thought*, pp. 24–25. On the history and the canonical interpretation of the sacrament of Eucharist see the homonymous entry in *New Catholic Encyclopedia* (New York: McGraw-Hill, 1967), 5, pp. 594–615.

13. Marin, *Food for Thought*, p. 25. In this connection see also the essay by Eric Heller, "The Hazard of Modern Poetry" in *The Disinherited Mind* (London: Bowes and Bowes, 1975), pp. 261–300: starting from the theologic controversy between Luther and Zwingli on the nature of Eucharist, the author singles out the separation between symbol and reality (which originated in that controversy) as the crucial element for understanding modern sensitivity.

14. Portinari, *Il piacere della gola*, p. 162, points out that "the chocolate becomes the bitter sign" of Gertrude's defeat, and he comments that Manzoni must have somewhat moved up the times, since chocolate was imported in the Milanese area during the second half of the seventeenth century. Raimondi and Bottoni explain such anachronism as "the literary whimsicality of combining together chocolate and *toga virilis*" (pp. 183–84).

15. Ezio Raimondi, *Il romanzo senza idillio*, pp. 306–7. In this connection Italo Calvino's pages on *I promessi sposi* as "the novel of ratios of power" should also be kept in mind: in *The Uses of Literature: Essays*, trans. Patrick Creagh (San Diego: Harcourt Brace Jovanovich, 1986), pp. 196–212.

16. Mirto Stone, " 'He Was Tall, Dark and Bald': Aristocratic Desire and Fantasies of Authority in *I promessi sposi*," *Forum Italicum*, 25, 1 (Spring 1991), pp. 3–16. She recalls the relevant remarks on the Austrian and the Milanese nobility by Marco Meriggi, *Amministrazione e classi sociali nel Lombardo-Veneto (1814–1848)* (Bologna: Il Mulino, 1983). See also Kent Robert Greenfield, *Economics and Liberalism in the Risorgimento: A Study of Nationalism in Lombardy, 1814–1848* (Baltimore: The Johns Hopkins University Press, 1934) and Marino Berengo, *Intellettuali e librai nella Milano della Restaurazione* (Turin: Einaudi, 1980).

17. Raimondi, *Il romanzo senza idillio*, p. 78.

18. Marin, *Food for Thought*, pp. 124–25; the third element of the culinary sign, eros, remains secondary in Manzoni's text, as if it were implicit, perhaps, in the "reasons" of the speaker.

19. See Nicolas J. Perella, *The Kiss Sacred and Profane* (Berkeley: University of California Press, 1969), p. 39. Perella made me note that "suavis" is found in the text of the *Vulgata*, commonly used by Christian writers, while the Psalms *juxta Hebraeos* have "bonus."

20. Alessandro Manzoni, *Fermo e Lucia*, in *Tutte le opere*, ed. Alberto Chiari and Fausto Ghisalberti (Milan: Mondadori, 1964), vol. 2, III, p. 669.

21. Norbert Jonard, "L'Epilogue des *Promessi sposi*," *Italianistica*, 9 (1980), 130–40, on p. 132. See also S. B. Chandler, "Rassegna sul 'lieto fine' ne *I promessi sposi*," *Critica letteraria* 8 (1980), pp. 581–97; and Raimondi, *Il romanzo senza idillio*, pp. 219–22.

22. Cf. the comment by Raimondi and Bottoni, p. 778: "The 'juice of the whole story' reestablishes the lexical color of the spoken language, since it echoes the Milanese *sugh d'on discors, d'on liber*, which likens the very concrete *sugh* both to 'juice' and to 'précis, summary, substance'; so that the narrative voice identifies itself, so to speak, twice with the dialogic voices of the narrated universe."

CHAPTER TWO. HOW TO MAKE A STEW

1. Sergio Campailla, *Anatomie verghiane* (Bologna: Pàtron, 1978), especially the chapter "Il corpo e i suoi simboli," pp. 17–105; quotations are on pp. 54, 37, 66–73. A first approach to this subject is in Gino Raya, *La lingua del Verga* (Florence: Le Monnier, 1962), pp. 43–50 ("Metafore e logica della fame").

2. Giovanni Verga, *The House by the Medlar Tree*, trans. Raymond Rosenthal, new intro. by Giovanni Cecchetti (Berkeley: University of California Press, 1983). All references will be to this edition. I have modified the text in a few instances to make it consistent with the original.

3. In this connection, the tax on salt and its economic importance should also be noted (as, for example, on p. 44).

4. See also Master 'Ntoni who hires La Locca's son, "who came to their door blubbering that his mother was dying of hunger and that Uncle Crocifisso didn't want to give him anything" (179). On this subject see Vittorio Spinazzola, "Legge del lavoro e legge dell'onore nei *Malavoglia*" in *Verismo e positivismo* (Milan: Garzanti, 1977), and Vitilio Masiello, "I 'Malavoglia' e la letteratura europea della rivoluzione industriale" in *I miti e la storia* (Naples: Liguori, 1984) and "Introduzione" in *Il punto su Verga* (Bari: Laterza, 1985), pp. 47–48.

5. Campailla, *Anatomie verghiane*, pp. 59–60, with a useful reference to Giuseppe Pitrè, in whose *Usi e costumi: Credenze e pregiudizi del popolo siciliano* (Florence: Barbera, no date, vol. 2, p. 229) there are recorded many of the same popular expressions, like "ben di Dio," God's good things or God's bounty, used in *I Malavoglia*.

6. In this connection see Matilde Serao's appropriately titled *Il paese di Cuccagna*, where, unlike Verga's few indications, pizzas and calzoni, as well as various kinds of Neapolitan pastries, take up entire pages of the novel, giving it a documentary flavor.

7. See the realistic connotations of food in the presentation of Donna Rosolina, who is constantly looking for a husband by showing off her culinary

abilities: first she brags with Don Silvestro "about all the big chores she had on her hands, ten bobbins of warp on the loom, beans to be dried for the winter, tomato paste to be made, for she had her little secret and so had fresh tomato paste all through the winter" (42–43); then she goes after Don Michele, and "she was always there with her tomato paste or her jars of peppers, to show what she could do as a housewife" (210). For her part, La Santuzza, when she has a crush on 'Ntoni, "saved all the leftovers from the dishes of her customers, putting them under the counter for him; and by taking a drop here and a drop there, she also filled his glass" (200). Comare Venera is seen "with her hair all prinkled and set—but with hands coated with flour, for she'd started to prepare the dough for the bread just to show that she no longer cared about going to the Malavoglia party" (113). And Cinghialenta and his companions smuggle "sugar and coffee" (101).

8. See Juri Tynyanov's contributions in *The Problem of Verse Language*, trans. Michael Sosa and Brent Harvey (Ann Arbor: Ardis, 1981).

9. Roman Jakobson, *Essais de linguistique générale* (Paris: Minuit, 1964), and more particularly "Linguistics and Poetics," in Thomas Sebeok, ed., *Style in Language* (Cambridge, Mass.: The MIT Press, 1960), p. 370.

10. Other sentences belonging in this area are: "another bit of rain would have been as welcome as bread" (44); "he had taken that money right out of his mouth, and he didn't have a crust of bread to eat, as true as there is a God above!" (121); "You're so rich, you could easily give some bread to poor Master 'Ntoni" (182); or consider Don Michele's words to Lia: "Open the door quick, because if they see me here I'll lose my daily bread" (225), and conversely, Don Michele "at least would give some bread" to Lia (238).

11. See Campailla, *Anatomie verghiane*, pp. 45–58, on the verbs to dine, to eat, to suck, to taste, to swallow, and other similar ones.

12. Analogously, according to the physician, Master 'Ntoni, sick at home, "was uselessly eating up his own flesh and that of his family" (243), and the old man himself says, "Here I eat up your weekly earnings" (245). One should also remember the examples of "mangiare con gli occhi," to eat with or through one's eyes, used to express erotic desire (pp. 50, 183, 199). See Campailla, *Anatomie verghiane*, pp. 69–73, 90, and 101.

13. I am referring to the two critical contributions by Guido Baldi, *L'artificio della regressione* (Naples: Liguori, 1980) and by Giancarlo Mazzacurati, "Parallele e meridiane: l'autore e il coro all'ombra del nespolo" in *I Malavoglia* [a critical anthology by various authors] (Catania: Fondazione Verga, 1982), pp. 163–73.

14. On this subject see my "Note sulla stremata poesia de *I Malavoglia*," *Forum Italicum*, 6, 1 (1972), pp. 3–18, especially pp. 14–15.

15. Giacomo Debenedetti, *Il romanzo del Novecento* (Milan: Garzanti, 1971), p. 699.

16. Ibid., p. 701; and Debenedetti, *Verga e il naturalismo* (Milan: Garzanti, 1976), pp. 381–426.

17. For instance, Romano Luperini emphasizes the decadent, suggestive musicality of certain passages of *I Malavoglia* in his *Pessimismo e verismo in Giovanni Verga* (Padua: Liviana, 1968), p. 81; Mazzacurati notes the symbolic function of "the author's view" in Verga ("Parallele e meridiane," p. 164); and

Spinazzola deals with the relationship between *verismo* and symbolism, particularly in "Rosso Malpelo" (*Verismo e positivismo*, pp. 51–66).

18. Nino Borsellino, *Storia di Verga* (Bari: Laterza, 1982), pp. 126–40.

19. Italo Calvino, *Una pietra sopra* (Turin: Einaudi, 1980), p. 26.

20. Borsellino, *Storia di Verga*, pp. 69–70. Already in 1914 Renato Serra had written about Verga: "Years pass by, and his figure is not diminished: the master of *verismo* is lost, but the writer is great": in *Scritti*, ed. Giuseppe De Robertis and A. Grilli (Florence: Le Monnier, 1958), 1, p. 321.

21. J. Hillis Miller, "Mr. Carmichael and Lily Briscoe: The Rhythm of Creativity in *To the Lighthouse*," in *Modernism Reconsidered*, ed. Robert Kiely (Cambridge, Mass.: Harvard University Press, 1983), pp. 167–90. All references will be in the text.

22. See Walter Benjamin, *Illuminations*, trans. Harry Zohn, ed. Hannah Arendt (New York: Schocken, 1969), pp. 83–110.

23. Borsellino, *Storia di Verga*, p. 71.

24. Giovanni Verga, *Lettere a Luigi Capuana*, ed. Gino Raya (Florence: Le Monnier, 1975), p. 117.

25. Ibid., p. 168.

CHAPTER THREE. TEA FOR TWO

1. Gabriele D'Annunzio, *Il piacere* in *Prose di romanzi* (Milan: Mondadori, 1964), vol. 1, p. 3. This passage, and many others, are missing from the English edition, *The Child of Pleasure*, trans. Georgina Harding (Boston: Page, 1906): although it is inadequate, I shall quote from this edition, and provide my translation from the original whenever necessary. Page numbers in parentheses preceded by "It." refer to the Mondadori 1964 text. A new edition with introduction by Ezio Raimondi was published in 1988–89.

2. Ezio Raimondi, *Il silenzio della Gorgone* (Bologna: Zanichelli, 1980), p. 124.

3. Bourdieu, *Distinction*, chapter 1 and passim. On this subject it might be useful to compare some remarks by Piero Camporesi in *La terra e la luna*, p. 209: "If they are examined in a different light, the years of D'Annunzio were also the years of leftovers like rabbit and broth made with beef muzzle, which 'costs little and is quite nutritious.' The waste of 'the inimitable living' necessarily had to fascinate readers accustomed to living with constant parsimony." We should also recall Roland Barthes's analysis of the "ornamental cookery" offered by the weekly *Elle* to its petit bourgeois readers, in marked contrast with the solid, "realistic" gastronomy of *L'Express*: in *Mythologies*, trans. Annette Lavers (New York: Hill & Wang, 1972), pp. 78–80.

4. Raimondi, *Il silenzio della Gorgone*, p. 83. See also Luigi Barzini, *Memories of Mistresses* (New York: Macmillan, 1986), pp. 28–33, on the Italian fin de siècle aristocracy and D'Annunzio.

5. Niva Lorenzini, *Il segno del corpo: Saggio su D'Annunzio* (Rome: Bulzoni, 1984): see the chapter "Nel segno della liquidità: La metafora del bere" (pp. 81–136) and in particular p. 108 on *Il piacere*.

6. Nicolas J. Perella, *The Kiss Sacred and Profane* (Berkeley: University of California Press, 1969), p. 39 and passim.

7. In Ugo Ojetti, *Alla scoperta dei letterati* (Florence: Le Monnier, 1967), p. 83.

8. This is a point on which there is wide agreement in Dannunzian criticism. See Ezio Raimondi, "Gabriele D'Annunzio" in *Storia della letteratura italiana*, ed. Emilio Cecchi and Natalino Sapegno (Milan: Garzanti, 1969), vol. 9, *Il Novecento*, new 1987 edition ed. Natalino Sapegno, 1, pp. 375–456, with an extensive bibliography. An iconographic documentation is in the catalogue *The Sacred and Profane in Symbolist Art*, ed. Luigi Carlucci (Toronto: Art Gallery of Ontario,1969): the exhibition originated at the Museo Civico d'Arte Moderna at Turin.

9. Lorenzini defines the synesthesia in *Il piacere* as having connotations of mannerism and preciosity (p. 63).

10. On D'Annunzio's ideology there are important points in Carlo Salinari, *Miti e coscienza del decadentismo italiano* (Milan: Feltrinelli, 1960), pp. 29–105; and in Paolo Valesio, "The Lion and the Ass: The Case for D'Annunzio's Novels," *Yale Italian Studies*, 1, 1 (Winter 1977), pp. 67–82, now in his *Gabriele D'Annunzio: The Dark Flame*, trans. Marilyn Migiel (New Haven: Yale University Press, 1992). As for Rabelais, the obvious reference is to Bakhtin, *Rabelais and His World*.

11. In Ojetti, *Alla scopereta dei letterati*, pp. 351–52. This is the well-known interview that appeared in 1895. But Giorgio Fabre has shown that "this interview actually is a well-balanced collage of two earlier articles by D'Annunzio" from 1892 and 1893, which in turn were reworked from even earlier writings: see Giorgio Fabre, *D'Annunzio esteta per l'informazione (1880–1900)* (Naples: Liguori, 1981), p. 63, n. 29.

12. Ojetti, *Alla scoperta dei letterati*, pp. 352–53.

13. Raimondi, *Il silenzio della Gorgone*, pp. 80–81.

14. See the notions of "The Credenda and Miranda of Power," "The Poverty of Power," and "The Shame of Power" in Charles E. Merriam, "Political Power," in *A Study of Power* (Glencoe, Ill.: Free Press, 1950).

15. E. M. Forster, "A Whiff of D'Annunzio" (1938), in *Two Cheers for Democracy* (New York: Harcourt Brace, 1951), pp. 236–41, on p. 240. See Gabriele D'Annunzio, *La città morta* (Milan: Treves, 1900), p. 38; the same oranges bitten like bread are evoked again on p. 215.

16. Forster, "A Whiff of D'Annunzio," p. 240.

17. On this subject see the remarks developed in the introduction.

18. Forster, "A Whiff of D'Annunzio," p. 240.

19. Gabriele D'Annunzio, *Il fuoco* in *Prose di romanzi*, vol. 2, pp. 679–81.

20. Juri Lotman, *The Structure of the Artistic Text*, trans. Ronald Vroon (Ann Arbor: The University of Michigan Press, 1977).

CHAPTER FOUR. A WISE GOURMET

1. All the quotations are from Giuseppe Tomasi di Lampedusa, *The Leopard*, trans. Archibald Colquhoun (New York: Pantheon, 1960); an occasional reference to the original is to *Il Gattopardo* (Milan: Feltrinelli, 1975).

2. Other meals in the novel should not be forgotten, such as the rustic picnic during the hunt: Don Fabrizio and Don Ciccio drink "tepid wine from the

wooden bottles" and eat a "roast chicken" and "little cakes called muffoletti dusted with raw flour" (124).

3. It is also possible to interpret the meaning of this jelly as a "symbolic destruction" of the Prince's estate, a consequence of his decision to support Tancredi's revolutionary choice: "By the time the dish reaches Francesco Paolo, it is entirely demolished. Little, we can easily imagine, will be left of the family estate when the boy is old enough to inherit": Richard Lansing, "The Structure of Meaning in Lampedusa's *Il Gattopardo*," *PMLA*, 93, 3 (May 1978), pp. 409–22, on p. 415. I am not entirely convinced by this interpretation because it excessively anticipates the developments of the novel (after all, the Prince supports Tancredi precisely in order to prolong the status quo) and because it endows the text with a meaning that does not seem consonant with the tone, which is fundamentally serene; even the final toast alludes to the disappearance of the Bourbons, not the squandering of the family estate.

4. Here I take up and confirm in its essential lines the interpretation of Tomasi di Lampedusa's novel I proposed several years ago in "The Prince and the Siren," *Modern Language Notes*, 78, 1 (Jan. 1963), pp. 31–50. I would only correct those points based on the 1958 edition, which was made obsolete by the subsequent edition conforming to the manuscript; for instance, the commentary on the "Glorious and Sorrowful Mysteries" of the original first paragraph should now consider the more correct liturgy of "Sorrowful Mysteries."

5. See Giuseppe Tomasi di Lampedusa, "Lezioni su Stendhal," *Paragone*, 112 (Jan. 1959), pp. 3–49, especially pp. 6 and 16, where he points out that Stendhal's epicurean-type morality implies, in a romantic manner, waiting for pleasures more than satisfying them.

6. On the social function of meals see James Brown, *Fictional Meals and Their Function in the French Novel*.

7. See Jean-François Revel, *Un festin en paroles*.

8. See Pellegrino Artusi, *La scienza in cucina e l'arte di mangiar bene*, pp. 305–7. His intention of unifying Italian cuisine is evident even in this recipe "according to the usage of Romagna," as, for example, in the advice he gives of using "long *maccheroni*, Neapolitan style, made with superfine dough, thick and with a narrow hole, so that they keep well and absorb more sauce" (p. 306). Camporesi comments: "The triumphal *pasticcio di maccheroni* (which in Romagna also has a more complex variation, with *cappelletti*)" is "a dish clearly derived from the Renaissance [in fact, "born perhaps in the refined Estense courts," p. 34, n.1], and inexplicably spread throughout the social sectors, of which Artusi proposes only the most reduced, sober, and elementary version, perhaps in order not to frighten the readers from other regions" (pp. xxx–xxxi). See also the pages on the aristocratic cuisine in Mary Taylor Simeti, *Pomp and Sustenance: Twenty-Five Centuries of Sicilian Food* (New York: Knopf, 1989).

9. On the study of plot and the search for meaning see Peter Brooks, *Reading for the Plot: Design and Intention in Narrative* (New York: Vintage, 1985), particularly chapter 3 on *Le Rouge et le noir*, pp. 62–89.

10. See Claude Lévi-Strauss, *The Origin of Table Manners*, trans. John and Doreen Weightman (London: Cape, 1978) and Norbert Elias, *The Civilizing*

Process, vol. 1, *The History of Manners*, trans. Edmund Jephcott (New York: Urizen, 1978).

11. On this subject see Pierre Bourdieu, *Distinction*, especially the first chapter on aristocracy and culture.

12. Often the disgust of the Prince is tied to the materiality of existence, and in particular to sensuality: Mariannina is compared to "a kind of Bendicò in a silk petticoat" (37), or the Paul Neyron roses have turned into "things like flesh-colored cabbages, obscene," so much so that the Prince in smelling them "seemed to be sniffing the thigh of a dancer from the Opera," and even Bendicò "drew back in disgust" (20–21). See also Giovanna Jackson, "Of Cabbages and Roses: Some Considerations on the Food Images of Lampedusa's *Il Gattopardo*," *Italian Culture*, 6 (1985), pp. 125–41.

13. Such examples are numerous. Here I would add only the ankle of Don Calogero's wife swollen "like an eggplant" (163), the efforts of the northern Cardinal of Palermo to "leaven . . . the inert and heavy dough of the island's spiritual life" (315), and the heraldic pretense of Don Calogero, who thinks he has a right to the Baronial title of "Sedàra del Biscotto [the Biscuit]; a title granted by his Majesty Ferdinand IV for work on the port of Mazzara" (154–55). In this connection see the important considerations by Gregory L. Lucente: in examining the narrator's assertion that the "wild rabbit" shot by Don Ciccio was "*ipso facto* promoted to the rank of hare," he shows that the metaphorical relationship at the core of Lampedusa's language "is purposefully dissected by the knowledgeable narrator," but in the novel as a whole the literal and the figurative discourses coexist, making possible the "allegorical-realistic presentations": in *Beautiful Fables: Self-consciousness in Italian Narrative from Manzoni to Calvino*, p. 207.

14. Giuseppe Paolo Samonà rightly notices a "lowering of tone" in these presentations of Angelica because the flavor of fresh cream and that of strawberries "are commonplaces, fit for a mediocre fable": in *Il Gattopardo, i Racconti, Lampedusa* (Florence: La Nuova Italia, 1974), pp. 72–73.

15. Giuseppe Tomasi di Lampedusa, "The Professor and the Mermaid," in *Two Stories and a Memory*, trans. Archibald Colquhoun (New York: Grosset and Dunlap, 1968), p. 151.

Chapter Five. The Cornucopia of the World

1. Carlo Emilio Gadda, "La casa," in *Novella seconda* (Milan: Garzanti, 1971), pp. 125 56. All references will be to this edition.

2. For further technical explanations about the "throne" see also Carlo Emilio Gadda, *Le bizze del capitano in congedo e altri racconti*, ed. Dante Isella (Milan: Garzanti, 1981), pp. 40–42.

3. James Joyce, *Ulysses* (New York: Random House, 1946), p. 68.

4. Ibid., p. 756.

5. Pellegrino Artusi, *La scienza in cucina e l'arte di mangiar bene*, pp. 688–705. Dinner menus are arranged and suggested by months and feasts; the sequence in a dinner often includes also *principii*, fried dishes, *tramesso*, and cheeses.

6. See p. 156: "My companions at table were the beautiful Signora Isalinda, whose praises we wove, the Pitagorean Dr. Pappo, the epicurean lawyer Stappo, the canon Scialappo, who, however, does not take a pheasant's behind jokingly and is a very good storyteller when he is well-Barooed up to both his ears. . . . We were also made merry by the Marquis Fava-Leccaris," who told the story of a certain person who maintained that "in Italian one should say 'faceva' and not 'fava.' " The three names Pappo, Stappo, and Scialappo (in rhyme) are alimentary referents to eating eagerly, uncorking a bottle, and tasting wine in one's mouth. Fava-Leccaris refers to General Bava Beccaris, who put down the Milanese riots in 1898; the distorted name has erotic as well as gastronomic overtones.

7. Carlo Emilio Gadda, *Acquainted with Grief*, trans. William Weaver (New York: Braziller, 1969). All references will be to this edition. For the complex network of repetitions and variations of the same motifs throughout Gadda's oeuvre see Dante Isella, "Saggio di una bibliografia gaddiana," in Gadda, *Le bizze del capitano in congedo*, pp. 193–223.

8. See Mikhail Bakhtin, *The Dialogic Imagination*.

9. In *Rabelais and His World*, Bakhtin considers the ways in which popular culture was juxtaposed with cultivated and predominant culture during the Middle Ages and the Renaissance by privileging laughter, carnival, and festivities, and by celebrating explicitly the "lower" bodily functions through the grotesque and the comic.

10. Critics have dealt with these problems in texts that have become classic by now—from Gianfranco Contini to Gian Carlo Roscioni, from Arnaldo Ceccaroni to Jacqueline Risset. On the last point I wish to mention the particularly significant contribution by Albert Sbragia, "The Comic and the Sublime: An Approach to Carlo Emilio Gadda's Narrative," Ph.D. Dissertation, University of California at Berkeley, 1988.

11. Gorgonzola is also an occasion of anger and jealousy when Gonzalo's mother receives a violinist dwarf (103) and a peon's "eighty-three-year-old mother" (200). Lots of semi-illiterate boys come down from "the stinking cheeses of Monte Viejo" (159), while Gonzalo thinks of the "buttery mush" pears make "on the croconsuelo-tongue of the old crows" (209–10). Even in the poem "Autunno," the people's Sunday picnics spread "egg-shells and gorgonzoloid papers" all around: in *La cognizione del dolore* (Turin: Einaudi, 1970), p. 221.

12. Joyce, *Ulysses*, pp. 169 and 171.

13. The narrator specifies that Poronga excluded "infallibly from his harvest the Boletus Atrox Linnaei, which resembles the Boletus Edulis the way a crook resembles his own identity card" (197).

14. Compare Gianfranco Contini, "Saggio introduttivo" in *La cognizione del dolore*, p. 11: "Precisely when the reader should fall into abysses of darkness and anguish, I don't know what incongruous and beneficent genius raises both author and reader to the fruition of extraordinary virtuoso performances or *pezzi di bravura* (where being a piece is equally important as the *bravura*), such as the Triumph of the satisfied bourgeois at the restaurant."

15. The scene is seen from the mother's viewpoint. She thinks that Gonzalo "would have hurled away the knife . . . against a portrait, maybe the most visible

... his uncle's—against the portrait of his father!" (153). It is a clear prelude to the actual "parricide," when Gonzalo tramples his father's portrait under his feet "as if he were pressing grapes in a vat" (181). All these images connect food and eros unequivocally in what one might call, in Freud's terms, Gonzalo's oral phase, later developed into his Oedipal complex and neurosis. On this subject see in particular Elio Gioanola, *L'uomo dei topazi* (Genoa: Il Melangolo, 1977) and my "The Pen, the Mother," in *Literary Diseases: Theme and Metaphor in the Italian Novel* (Austin: University of Texas Press, 1975).

16. In this connection it is helpful to recall the "Prince of Analysis and Duke of Good Cognizance" in "La casa."

17. See Contini, "Saggio introduttivo," p. 12: "Gadda's only good is the present, the exalting peel of things"; and "the real offers itself as richly, voraciously appetizing to him, an optimist *malgré lui*."

18. Carlo Emilio Gadda, *L'Adalgisa: Disegni milanesi* in *I sogni e la folgore* (Turin: Einaudi, 1955). All references will be to this volume, which also includes *La Madonna dei filosofi* and *Il castello di Udine*. Many short stories by Gadda are quite relevant for alimentary customs and the connected literary techniques: for example "La fidanzata di Elio" in *Il castello di Udine* (233–40), and "San Giorgio in casa Brocchi," "Una buona nutrizione," "Socer generque," and "Accoppiamenti giudiziosi" in *Racconti* (Milan: Garzanti, 1963).

19. See pp. 427–28, note 16: in 1943 in the north of Italy "the ordinary intakes of food" were called: *caffelatte* or *caffè e latte* in the morning, *colazione* the midday meal, *pranzo* the evening meal, while in central Italy, "more appropriately, they call *pranzo* the above-mentioned *colazione, cena* or *desinare* the *pranzo*, and *colazione* the *caffelatte* of the following day."

20. See p. 427, note 13: " 'Beignet,' French; in Rabelais *beuignet* . . . is the diminutive of a noun similar to the Lombard *bügna* (architectural term) = ashlar."

21. Carlo Emilio Gadda, *Le meraviglie d'Italia: Gli anni* (Turin: Einaudi, 1964), p. 155. The two pieces are on pp. 143–57 and 188–204, respectively.

22. Ibid., pp. 205–8.

23. Artusi, who was from Romagna and was "Tuscanized," does not have "the pretense of imposing upon the Milanese cooks, who are learned and clever in this matter" (p. 104), therefore he gives three recipes for the risotto *alla milanese* (pp. 103–4); the second is the closest to Gadda's, except for the use of white instead of red wine. For a vigorous defense of other, non-Milanese recipes see Alessandro Falassi, "I percorsi del risotto," in *Cucina, cultura e società*, ed. Luciano Bonanni and Giancarlo Ricci (Milan: Shakespeare & Co., 1982), pp. 119–22.

24. Carlo Emilio Gadda, *That Awful Mess on Via Merulana*, trans. William Weaver (New York: Braziller, 1965). All references will be to this edition. I shall also refer to the original, *Quer pasticciaccio brutto de via Merulana* (Milan: Garzanti, 1962) for questions involving dialectal words.

25. In this connection see Gadda's pertinent essays collected in *I viaggi la morte* (Milan: Garzanti, 1958) and *Il tempo e le opere* (Milan: Adelphi, 1982).

26. Cf. Joyce, *Ulysses*, p. 55: "Mr. Leopold Bloom ate with relish the inner organs of beasts and fowls. He liked thick giblet soup, nutty gizzards, a stuffed roast heart, liver slices fried with crustcrumbs, fried hencod's roes. Most of all he liked grilled mouton kidneys which gave to his palate a fine tang of faintly scented urine."

27. For example, see the telephone conversation from the Marino Carabinieri station, with such interferences as "thirty-six quintals of Parmesan shipped from Reggio Emilia" (189); Ingravallo's breakfast, with "toasted crusts and curls of butter" he hastily devours—"crunch crunch" (365); or again the police car, smelling with "Lambroesk" wine and mortadella (367); or the comparison between Zamira and "certain witch doctors-priests of Tanganyika" who offer a "Mennonite missionary" their spit "whipped up with coconut milk in a coconut shell, a sign of subtropical honor" (296). The last passage recalls Gadda's essay "Come lavoro" in *I viaggi la morte*, pp. 19–20, where the Tanganyika reverential drink is used as an apt quotation from Emilio Salgari to illustrate the assertion that "our words are . . . everyone's words, very much made public, quite published"—that is, chewed up and spit out.

28. This is Gadda's own definition of Angeloni in *I viaggi la morte*, p. 115, in a comic self-defense of his own status as a single man (against the special tax imposed on singles by fascism) and of his own gluttony (as a revenge against the deprivations and scarcity of the Second World War).

29. Camporesi, *La terra e la luna*, p. 222; of course these words refer to the market as an institution.

30. Cf. Marcel Mauss, *The Gift: Form and Function of Exchange in Archaic Societies*, trans. Ian Cunnison (New York: Norton, 1967).

31. Gadda, "L'Editore chiede venia del recupero chiamando in causa l'Autore," in *La cognizione del dolore*, p. 32. In this connection it is useful to keep in mind Heinrich Wölfflin's considerations on the multiplicity and fullness of the baroque in his *Renaissance and Baroque*, trans. Kathrin Simon (Ithaca: Cornell University Press, 1966), as well as Eugenio D'Ors's ideas on the baroque as a "style of culture" juxtaposed with "historical styles" and hence capable of innumerable variations and extensions in time and space: in *Lo Barroco* (Madrid: Aguilar, 1964), pp. 89–90. It is also interesting that Severo Sarduy proposes a comparison between Gadda and the Cuban writer José Lezama Lima, who is remarkable for the opulent abundance of foods, the cornucopia, the baroque of his images, the techniques of accumulation and collage, with references to Gongora, Flaubert and Archimbold: in *Escrito sobre un cuerpo* (Buenos Aires: Editorial Sudamericana, 1969), pp. 74–77.

32. It is useless to say that those who want to know how *Quer pasticciaccio* ends should read Gadda's *Il palazzo degli ori* (Turin: Einaudi, 1983). But the non-finished seems to be a characteristic of Gadda's writing in general.

CHAPTER SIX. UNDER OLIVIA'S TEETH

1. Italo Calvino, "Sapore sapere," *FMR*, 4 (Jun. 1982), pp. 63–77. The reproductions are between pp. 61 and 86, and a note by Pietro Corsi, "Il Codice Fiorentino: Nota storica," pp. 80–86 and 134, gives important information on the vicissitudes of Sahagún's text.

2. Italo Calvino, *Sotto il sole giaguaro* (Milan: Garzanti, 1986). All references will be to the English edition, *Under the Jaguar Sun*, trans. William Weaver (San Diego: Harcourt Brace Jovanovich, 1988).

3. See Michel Serres, *Les cinq sens: Philosophie des corps melés* (Paris: Grasset, 1985). Antonio Tabucchi mentions a book written by five Portuguese writers, *Poètica dos cinco sentidos* (Lisbon: Bertrand, 1979), in order "to point out a possible line of inspiration and perhaps of belonging" for Calvino: in "Calvino, in che senso?" *L'Espresso* (Aug. 17, 1986), p. 103. The international success of Patrick Süskind's *Parfume* is also worth mentioning. The contemporary revival of the senses should be related to the history of scientific thought, with the preeminence of smell and touch between the sixteenth and seventeenth centuries, and of sight in the eighteenth century: pertinent remarks (and comments on Lucien Febvre and Gaston Bachelard) are in Ezio Raimondi, *Il romanzo senza idillio*, pp. 3–7.

4. Paul Fussell, *Abroad: British Literary Traveling Between the Wars* (Oxford: Oxford University Press, 1980).

5. Respectively, Turin: Einaudi, 1976, and Milan: Adelphi, 1985. In 1976 Calvino traveled to Mexico as a tourist.

6. Roberto Antonelli, "Storia e geografia, tempo e spazio nell'indagine letteraria," in *Letteratura italiana: Storia e geografia*, vol. 1, *L'età medievale* (Turin: Einaudi, 1987), p. 25.

7. It is useful to quote also the clarification that follows in parentheses: "And you mustn't rebut that the same result can be achieved by visiting the exotic restaurants of our big cities; they so counterfeit the reality of the cuisine they claim to follow that, as far as our deriving real knowledge is concerned, they are the equivalent not of an actual locality but of a scene reconstructed and shot in a studio" (p. 12).

8. Italo Calvino, *Difficult Loves*, trans. William Weaver, Archibald Colquhoun, and Peggy Wright (San Diego: Harcourt Brace Jovanovich, 1984), p. 46. All subsequent references dealing with short stories will be to this edition.

9. Italo Calvino, *Marcovaldo: The Seasons in the City*, trans. William Weaver (San Diego: Harcourt Brace Jovanovich, 1983). Subsequent references are to this edition. On p. 67 there is the disquieting list of "threats, traps, and frauds" presented by "the simplest foods" and taken from contemporary newspaper reports, so that the sight of the shopping bag fills Marcovaldo not with joy but with fear, "as if hostile presences had infiltrated the walls of his house."

10. See Piero Camporesi, *La terra e la luna*, pp. 224–26: in the supermarket, unlike the traditional market, "everyone remains alone with one's own temptations." See also the chapter on "Consumer Bodies" in John O'Neill, *Five Bodies: The Human Shape of Modern Society*, pp. 91–117.

11. All references are to Italo Calvino, *The Path to the Nest of Spiders*, trans. Archibald Colquhoun (New York: Ecco Press, 1976). Lucia Re examines this novel thoroughly from multiple critical approaches in *Calvino and the Age of Neorealism* (Stanford: Stanford University Press, 1990).

12. Chestnuts are a traditional but by now no longer used food among the peasants and mountain population of the Apennines: see Emilio Faccioli, "La cucina" in *Storia d'Italia*, vol. 5, *I documenti* (Turin: Einaudi, 1975), 1, pp. 981–1030.

13. Italo Calvino, "Smog," in *Difficult Loves; Smog; A Plunge into Real Estate*,

trans. William Weaver and D. S. Carne-Ross (London: Secker and Warburg, 1983), pp. 109–160.

14. All references will be, respectively, to Italo Calvino, *The Nonexistent Knight and The Cloven Viscount*, trans. Archibald Colquhoun (New York: Harcourt Brace Jovanovich, 1962), and *The Baron in the Trees*, trans. Archibald Colquhoun (New York: Random House, 1959).

15. As the title suggests, *Cosmicomiche vecchie e nuove* (Milan: Garzanti, 1984) combines (and regroups) all the preceding old and new cosmicomic stories contained in *Cosmicomiche, Ti con zero*, and *La memoria dei mondi*. All references will be to Italo Calvino, *Cosmicomics* and *t zero*, trans. William Weaver (San Diego: Harcourt Brace Jovanovich, 1968 and 1969, respectively). The latter will be identified by a "T" before the page number.

16. John Barth, "The Literature of Replenishment: Postmodernist Fiction," in *The Friday Book: Essays and Other Nonfiction* (New York: Putnam, 1984), pp. 193–206, on p. 204.

17. Michel Serres, *Hermes: Literature, Science, Philosophy*, trans. Josué V. Harari and David F. Bell (Baltimore: The Johns Hopkins University Press, 1982), p. 83.

18. Raymond Queneau, *Petite cosmogonie portative* (Paris: Gallimard, 1950), pp. 84–85. Another author of the Oulipo group who should be remembered is Georges Perec, whose work (particularly *La vie, mode d'emploi*) is congenial to Calvino's.

19. Italo Calvino, *The Castle of Crossed Destinies*, trans. William Weaver (New York: Harcourt Brace Jovanovich, 1977), p. 5; the repetition-variation of the tavern (p. 51) is also worth mentioning.

20. All references will be to Italo Calvino, *Invisible Cities*, trans. William Weaver (New York: Harcourt Brace Jovanovich, 1974).

21. All references will be to Italo Calvino, *If on a winter night a traveler*, trans. William Weaver (San Diego: Harcourt Brace Jovanovich, 1981).

22. All references will be to Italo Calvino, *Mr. Palomar*, trans. William Weaver (San Diego: Harcourt Brace Jovanovich, 1985).

23. See Georges Duthuit, *Le musée inimaginable* (Paris: Corti, 1956), a book that was conceived as a reaction against André Malraux's conception of the museum.

24. See Mary Douglas, "Deciphering a Meal," in *Meanings: Essays in Anthropology* (London: Routledge and Kegan Paul, 1979), pp. 249–75; the pages on Jewish dietary norms are exemplary. And see O'Neill's own discussion not only of Douglas (pp. 48–61) but also of the American preference for beef (from steaks to hamburgers and barbecue) and its implications for world food (*Five Bodies*, pp. 62–66).

25. Emilio Cecchi, *Messico*, preface by Italo Calvino (Milan: Adelphi, 1985), pp. 163 and 165.

26. Octavio Paz, *The Labyrinth of Solitude*, trans. Lysander Kemp, Yara Milos, and Rachel Phillips Belash (New York: Grove Press, 1985), in the chapter on the conquest and colonialism, pp. 89–116.

27. Compare Cecchi, *Messico*, pp. 148–56. The adjectives used by Calvino call to mind the conception of the baroque Eugenio D'Ors proposes: baroque

style is "all music and passion" and in it "the flying forms dance their dance"; it is juxtaposed with classical style, "all economy and reason, the style of the 'heavy forms' ": in *Lo Barroco*, p. 82. One understands, then, why "lightness" is such an important stylistic quality for Calvino.

28. Guacamole: "the fat softness of the *aguacate*—the Mexican national fruit, known to the rest of the world under the distorted name of 'avocado'—is accompanied and underlined by the angular dryness of the tortilla, which, for its part, can have many flavors, pretending to have none"; *guajolote con mole poblano*: "turkey with Puebla-style *mole* sauce, one of the noblest among the many *moles*, and most laborious (the preparation never takes less than two days), and most complicated, because it requires several different varieties of *chile*, as well as garlic, onion, cinnamon, cloves, pepper, cumin, coriander, and sesame, almonds, raisins, and peanuts, with a touch of chocolate"; and quesadillas: "another kind of tortilla, really, for which cheese is incorporated in the dough, garnished with ground meat and refried beans": the whole is served on p. 8.

29. One should remember at least Cesare Pavese's essays and diary, as well as *Dialoghi con Leucò* and *La luna e i falò* (Turin: Einaudi, 1947 and 1950). The most intriguing texts on the ritual of sacrifice that is at the foundation of society and civilization are René Girard's *Violence and the Sacred*, trans. Patrick Gregory, and *The Scapegoat*, trans. Yvonne Freccero (Baltimore: The Johns Hopkins University Press, 1977 and 1986).

30. Peggy Reeves Sanday, *Divine Hunger: Cannibalism as a Cultural System* (Cambridge: Cambridge University Press, 1986), in particular chapter 8, "Precious Eagle-Cactus Fruit: Aztec Human Sacrifice," pp. 169–95. The most important references to Sahagún are on pp. 16 and 169–72.

31. Ibid., p. 194. In this connection see also the brief remark by Margaret Visser, "Most of the remainder of the body [of the victim] may have been eaten in the form of a 'man-stew'—with maize": in *Much Depends on Dinner*, p. 34.

32. Italo Calvino, *The Uses of Literature: Essays*, trans. Patrick Creagh (San Diego: Harcourt Brace Jovanovich, 1986), p. 18.

33. "Shrimp soup, that is, immeasurably hot, thanks to some variety of *chiles* we had never come upon previously, perhaps the famous *chiles jalapeños*," and "roast kid—every morsel of which provoked surprise, because the teeth would encounter first a crisp bit, then one that melted in the mouth" (p. 23).

34. Indulging for a moment, and with due irony, the "biographical fallacy," I would like to recall that Calvino had "a very long intestine that for many years gave him serious troubles," as Cesare Cases reveals: "He hinted with his hands at the gesture of unwinding it to show how complicated and interminable it was, with a certain resigned disgust as if he were dealing with a very bad novel. One can understand that Calvino did not belong in the category of 'visceral' writers": in *Patrie lettere* (Turin: Einaudi, 1987), pp. 174–75.

35. Beside Girard's contributions, already mentioned, see also the chapters on the Aztecs and on "The Faces of the Soul's Desires: Iroquoian Torture and Cannibalism in the Seventeenth Century," in Reeves Sanday's *Divine Hunger*, pp. 125–50.

36. Nicolas J. Perella, *Midday in Italian Literature: Variations on an Archetypal Theme* (Princeton: Princeton University Press, 1979).

37. Serres, *Hermes*, p. 74.
38. Ibid., p. 83.
39. See *Mr. Palomar*, pp. 95–98.
40. In this connection see Lévi-Strauss's analyses of primitive societies' attitudes toward raw and cooked foods, with the related notion of "cannibalism" extended to the vegetable and animal realms (in *The Raw and the Cooked*); see also his assertion that the nature-culture juxtaposition is itself cultural, an artificial creation of culture (in the preface to the second edition of *Les Structures élémentaires de la parenté* [The Hague: Mouton, 1967]); and Geertz's *The Interpretation of Culture*, already quoted.
41. Italo Calvino, "La foresta e gli dèi" (1976) in *Collezione di sabbia* (Milan: Garzanti, 1984), pp. 201–3. It is significant that at the beginning of the piece there are the same images of the sun and the vertigo later conflated in one narrative situation in "Sotto il sole giaguaro": "The vegetable tangle thickens even in my head, dazzled by the sun and the vertigo in climbing and descending those grand steep stairways, and among the ramifications of arguments I seem to glimpse a decisive reason, which after an instant disappears" (p. 201).
42. One should remember the pages Louis Marin devotes to the formula of the Eucharist: "The Body of the Divinity Captured by Signs" in *Food for Thought*, pp. 3–25. On the alleged "cannibalism" of Christianity and its psychoanalytic sides, see André Green, "Cannibalisme: Réalité ou fantasme agi?" in *Nouvelle Revue de Psychanalyse*, 6 (Autumn 1972), *Destins du cannibalisme*, pp. 27–52, on pp. 34–35. On this subject see also Maggie Kilgour, *From Communion to Cannibalism: An Anatomy of Metaphors of Incorporation* (Princeton: Princeton University Press, 1989).
43. See Tzvetan Todorov, *The Conquest of America: The Question of the Other*, trans. Richard Howard (New York: Harper, 1984), and Paz, *The Labyrinth of Solitude*, especially chapter 5, "The Conquest and Colonialism," pp. 89–116 (quotations on pp. 103–4).
44. Eugenio Montale, *Le occasioni* (Milan: Mondadori, 1963), p. 23.
45. On this point see also Andrea Battistini, "Ménage à trois: Scienza, arte combinatoria e mosaico della scrittura" in *Nuova civiltà delle macchine*, 5, 1 (17) (1987), pp. 11–24, on pp. 19–20, and JoAnn Cannon, *Postmodern Italian Fiction: The Crisis of Reason in Calvino, Eco, Sciascia, Malerba* (London and Toronto: Associated University Presses, 1989), especially pp. 103–4 on *enumeración caótica*.
46. See B. R. Stark, "Kurtz's Intended: The Heart of 'Heart of Darkness', " *Texas Studies in Literature and Language*, 17, 1974, pp. 535–55, and Giuseppe Sertoli, "Conoscenza e potere: Su 'Heart of Darkness' di Joseph Conrad," *Altri termini*, 4–5 (1974), pp. 115–99, especially pp. 141–42.
47. Calvino, "Cybernetics and Ghosts," in *The Uses of Literature*, p. 18.
48. Jean Pouillon, "Manières de table, manières de lit, manières de langage," in *Nouvelle Revue de Psychanalyse*, 6 (Autumn 1972), *Destins du cannibalisme*, pp. 9–26, on pp. 21–22.
49. Italo Calvino, *Six Memos for the Next Millennium*, trans. Patrick Creagh (Cambridge, Mass.: Harvard University Press, 1988). In particular, as far as lightness is concerned, an obvious reference should be made to Milan Kundera's *The Unbearable Lightness of Being* and to Eugenio D'Ors's "dancing" ba-

roque; Camporesi makes some interesting considerations in the alimentary and cultural area: "Lightness, one of the idols of our times, . . . has singular correspondences with the lively and light spirit of the *philosophes*"; in fact, "if in the eighteenth century the project of renewal was aimed against the heavy, sumptuous, expensive, and aromatic cuisine of the baroque age, [today] in the age of robotics, electronics, and computer science, the new program of postmodern, reformist culinary lightening is juxtaposed with the nineteenth-century-style cuisine of the age of factories and heavy works, tied to a proletariat who has by now disappeared": in *La terra e la luna*, pp. 272 and 271.

50. Roland Barthes, *Leçon* (Paris: Seuil, 1798), p. 46.

51. Niccolò Tommaseo? Precisely he, who at the beginning of *Fede e bellezza* inflicts upon the protagonist a "desinarino," a small dinner that is not appetizing at all ([Milan: Bompiani, 1942], p. 4).

52. Roland Barthes, "Reading Brillat-Savarin," in *On Signs*, ed. Marshall Blonsky (Baltimore: The Johns Hopkins University Press, 1987), pp. 61–75, on p. 67.

53. Italo Calvino, "Literature as Projection of Desire: On Northrop Frye's *Anatomy of Criticism*," and "Definition of Territories: Sex and Laughter," in *The Uses of Literature*, pp. 50–61 and 65–73, on p. 50 and p. 66, respectively. In outlining the archetypal myth of the "quest-romance," Frye defines it as the victory of fertility over the waste land, and "fertility means food and drink, bread and wine, body and blood, the union of male and female": in *Anatomy of Criticism* (New York: Atheneum, 1970), p. 193.

CHAPTER SEVEN. OUR DAILY BREAD-PANE-BROT-BROID
-CHLEB-PAIN-LECHEM-KENYÉR

1. All references to *Se questo è un uomo* (Turin: De Silva, 1947, then Einaudi, 1958) will be to the English translation by Stuart Woolf, *Survival in Auschwitz* (New York: Collier Books, 1961), which I have modified when necessary to make it agree with the original.

2. Primo Levi, *Other People's Trades*, p. 135.

3. I am reminded of the study that Leo Spitzer made of the metaphors used by Italian prisoners of war to elude Austrian censure during World War One: *Die Umschreibungen des Begriffes "Hunger" im Italienischen* (Halle: Druck von Kanas, Kröber and Nietschmann, 1920); but the hunger of those prisoners was not, certainly, a "Grenzsituation" (as Jaspers might say) like the one described by Levi.

4. Norbert Elias, *The Civilizing Process*, vol. 1, *The History of Manners* (New York: Urizen Books, 1978), and vol. 2, *State Formation and Civilization* (Oxford: Basil Blackwell, 1982), both trans. Edmund Jephcott.

5. Italo Calvino, *Six Memos for the Next Millenium*, pp. 55–80. On Levi's clarity of style and effective use of parataxis see Pietro Frassica, "Aspetti della narrativa italiana postbellica (Beppe Fenoglio e Primo Levi)," *Forum Italicum*, 7, 3 (September 1974), pp. 365–80. For a general historical-literary framework encompassing "The Silver Age of Italian Jews 1924–1974" (from Svevo and

Alberto Moravia to Carlo and Primo Levi, from Natalia Ginzburg to Giorgio Bassani), see H. Stuart Hughes, *Prisoners of Hope* (Cambridge, Mass.: Harvard University Press, 1983).

6. Primo Levi, *The Drowned and the Saved*, trans. Raymond Rosenthal (New York: Summit Books, 1988), p. 141.

7. Primo Levi, "Appendice" in *Opere*, vol. 1 (Turin: Einaudi, 1987), pp. 183–212, on p. 187. Fiora Vincenti perceptively remarks that Levi's indignation never becomes hatred: "In fact, unlike hatred, which belongs to the realm of instincts, indignation implies a moral judgment, or better still, it is itself a moral judgment, and hence it pertains to the sphere of reason": in *Invito alla lettura di Primo Levi* (Milan: Mursia, 1987), p. 150. Precisely the soft-voiced tone without hatred of Levi's testimony may make one recall the analogous tone of another famous testimony, Silvio Pellico's *Le mie prigioni*.

8. George Steiner, *Language and Silence: Essays on Language, Literature and the Inhuman* (New York, Atheneum, 1982), p. 199. The whole section on "Language out of Darkness" is relevant to the present topic.

9. In different form, this concept goes back to Aristotle's rhetorics and to baroque poetics; it was reintroduced especially by the Russian formalist critics at the beginning of this century (*ostranenje*: estrangement).

10. It is also useful to consider the alternation of the personal pronouns I, we, and they throughout the narration, and the use of past and present tenses in various episodes, as, for example, when the prisoners are ordered to undress and to watch out that their shoes are not stolen: "Stolen by whom? . . . We all look at the interpreter, and the interpreter asked the German, and the German was smoking and looked him through and through as if he were transparent, as if no one had spoken" (19). The urgency of the feelings in the present tense is made tremendously immediate by the contrast with the cold indifference of the German in the past, and there is no doubt that the readers are made to feel in the present while reading the past-tense narration. Another particularly effective use of the present tense is self-reflexive or metanarrative: the author shares with his readers the genesis and the shaping of his book. *Se questo è un uomo* was born in the Lager, and was made materially possible by the fact that Levi was assigned to a chemical laboratory where there was no hard work and no cold, and where he had a pencil and a notebook: there he was assailed by "the pain of remembering, the old ferocious longing to feel myself a man. . . . Then I take my pencil and notebook and write what I would never dare to tell anyone" (128). In a different manner, Gabriel Motola distinguishes between Levi's present tense, which has to do with an "actual reliving of a particular experience," and the past tense, which deals with "a more general though no less terrifying communal experience" and involves "objectification" and "historicity": in "Primo Levi: The Auschwitz Experience," *The Southwest Review*, 72 (1987), pp. 258–69, on pp. 260–61.

11. Cesare Cases, "Levi racconta l'assurdo," in *Patrie lettere*, p. 137. See also his introduction, "L'ordine delle cose e l'ordine delle parole," in Levi, *Opere*, vol. 1, pp. ix–xxxi.

12. Such references can be quite explicit, as is the case with most of the Biblical ones (pp. 59, 66, 91, 143) or with Dante's Canto of Ulysses (99–105); or

they can be implicit, part of a vastly accepted classical and humanistic background: for instance, the comparisons with Polyphemus (133) and with Oedipus in front of the Sphinx (96) do not need to recall Homer and Sophocles explicitly, nor does the "struggle of each against all" (84) need to hark back to Hobbes. These are all true cultural clichés. Other references to Dante are equally obvious, such as the mention of Charon (17), the devils of Malebolge (98), and the "bolgia" of the block (108); on the contrary, the memory of Machiavelli's *The Prince* is subtly interwoven in the analysis of the character of Alfred L. and the considerations on the relationship between being strong and being feared (80) and on the importance of the appearance of power (86).

13. See Piero Caleffi, *Si fa presto a dire fame*, 6th ed. (Milan: Edizioni Avanti, 1958).

14. Forty years after the experience of the Lager Levi meditates upon it in *The Drowned and the Saved*, and hunger is again preeminent, to the point that in discussing his situation as a nonbeliever in comparison with the believers in a religious or political faith, he says that the latter "lived better" because they had some explanation for their suffering, and even "their hunger was different from ours. It was a divine punishment or expiation, or votive offering, or the fruit of capitalist putrefaction" (p. 147).

15. See *El Lazarillo de Tormes* (Barcelona: Editorial M & S, 1966), pp. 25–26, where Lazarillo's ruse is called "un pequeño remedio."

16. *The Drowned and the Saved*, p. 114.

17. In fact, see the confirmation after so many years in *The Drowned and the Saved*, p. 139: "I had neither lied nor exaggerated. I would really have given bread and soup, that is, blood, to save from nothingness those memories which today with the sure support of printed paper I can refresh whenever I wish and gratis, and which therefore seem of little value. Then and there they had great value. They made it possible for me to reestablish a link with the past, saving it from oblivion and reinforcing my identity."

18. Emmanuel Lévinas, *Difficile liberté: Essais sur le Judaïsme* (Paris: Albin Michel, 1976). In an interview reported by Fiora Vincenti (*Invito alla lettura*, p. 159), Levi mentions his own "recovery of the Jewish tradition: Judaism juxtaposed with fascism, as freedom is juxtaposed with terror, because I also discovered that many principles of freedom are well inside the substance of the purest Jewish tradition."